200 Open Games

DAVID BRONSTEIN
TRANSLATED BY PHILIP J. BOOTH

Macmillan Publishing Co., Inc.
New York

Macmillan Publishing Co., Inc.
866 Third Avenue, New York, N.Y. 10022

First published in 1970 in the USSR under the title *200 Otkritikh Partii*
First American edition 1974.

Library of Congress Catalog Card Number: 73–22018

Printed in Great Britain

Contents

Contents vii

Foreword

This book lays no claims to being either encyclopaedic or to being an openings manual. My aim is quite a different one: it is to show that quite a large number of similar games are in fact different in the way they have been created in the minds of the players. And although they are different, all these games, with their identical first move, still retain for a considerable time traces of one and the same inherited pattern.

I shall not be relating what I have said to the whole of chess (although the notion of common basic and characteristic strategical ideas can be extended, with certain corrections and qualifications, to apply to any opening without exception); this book will be concerned only with that very popular opening 1 P–K4 P–K4.

During the last century books on the opening used to be divided up into 80 per cent open games and the remainder, 'irregular' openings. Nowadays there has been a sharp turnabout. The greater part of any book is devoted to openings previously considered irregular, and only out of historical interest are the main variations of open games given.

Such an approach to the introductory moves 1 P–K4 P–K4 is unjust. In the first place, many readers of chess books commonly use open games in practical play, and they are offended because no one thinks about them. In the second place, there is no agreement even among grandmasters as to which first move is the strongest. Grandmaster Petrosian plays almost exclusively 1 P–Q4, whilst Grandmaster Fischer chooses with amazing consistency the spurned 1 P–K4.

Which of the two moves is the better, the first or the second? We cannot expect an answer to this problem: there simply isn't one.

Meanwhile, for those who like to play 1 P–K4 for White, and in answer 1 ... P–K4 for Black, and would not begrudge a few evenings for a cursory analysis of a couple of hundred of the author's games . . . in short, this book is for you, the reader!

BEFORE THE FIRST MOVE

The position you see in the diagram is like an empty canvas standing on an easel. If you have any aptitude, talent or, no less important, desire, then boldly take up your brush and paints, decide upon the necessary colour and embark upon your creative work.

But how should one begin?

I cannot say what feelings artists experience at that moment, but, whenever I have to start a game with an 'empty' chess board in front of me, I cannot stop thinking that today, right now, I have the very fortunate possibility of playing the most beautiful, the most fighting, and the most profound game since the time of my birth and since long before it.

The idea is not as abstract as all that, when one remembers that people have been playing chess on this earth for a good thousand, or even two thousand, years. And if I can take advantage of the experience of even only the last five centuries. . . .

Yes, but how should one begin?

It is now over thirty years that I have been coming regularly to the Sacred Hall of Chess Creativeness and have reverently been taking up the White King's Pawn, sending it forward with a prayer to heroic feats.

And as soon as the Enemy's Forces' King sends out his Herald to meet mine, invariably, to the great pleasure of the spectators, gapers, newspaper correspondents and even onlooking masters, candidate grandmasters or grandmasters, I become engrossed in deep reflection, as if lethargically day-dreaming.

And it is all for one reason, which is well-known to the reader himself. Well, of course, I am tormented, given no rest, and am cut to pieces by that eternal sword of Damocles known to generations of chess-players: the question of how to begin the attack.

But before condemning or justifying the author's creative sufferings, the reader should go through this book carefully, from beginning to end. And I believe that nobody will be too lazy to do that.

But meanwhile let us have a dress rehearsal together and decide which of White's second moves is really worthy of playing the lead role!

THE FOLLOWING ARE CHARACTERISTIC AIMS FOR ALL POSITIONS OF AN OPEN TYPE

White

1 the attack on KB7
2 to control the QB4–KB7 diagonal
3 to control the KR5–KB7 diagonal

4 to control the KB–file

5 the knight march –KB3–KN5 –KB7
6 an attack on the K5 square

7 the pawn move P–Q4
8 the pawn move P–KB4
9 a strong pawn centre

10 open K– and KB–files

11 to obtain the maximum control of Q5, as a springboard for an attack on KB7 with the queen and bishop and on QB7 with the QN via QB3 and Q5
12 by means of any subterfuge or material concessions to try and gain time to bring the dormant Q-side pieces into the attack on the obvious targets (KB7 and K5)

13 not to be distracted by material gains, where these allow either Black's queen, QR, QB or QN to noticeably increase its radius of activity and be included in the attack on the vulnerable points in your camp.

Black

1 the defence of KB2
2 to challenge control of the K3–QB5 diagonal
3 to control the white queen's movements when it is on its KR5
4 to control the route the white KR takes from KR1 to KB1
5 to control the white KN's movements
6 judicious defence of the pawn on K4
7 to try and get . . . P–Q4 in
8 not to move the KBP
9 to demolish White's KP and QP pair
10 to avoid opening the K– and KB–files
11 to fight for the control of Q4

12 not to yield to the fatal temptation to take one white pawn or piece too many. To stop at one piece is an extremely good rule. Don't get greedier; and best would be to give up your spoils at the right moment and get the initiative back
13 to observe carefully the number of active Q-side pieces White has by comparison with Black. Take every measure to ensure that the numerical difference in White's favour never exceeds one. Return your gains in time, and if this is not adequate, make sacrifices yourself without self-pity or tears.

1 The Queen's Attack

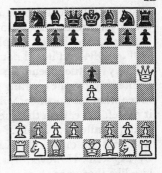

The attack with the queen alone – 2 Q–R5 – is well-known to everyone. When we have only just learnt how to move the pieces, we are not yet able to direct a co-ordinated attack; on the other hand, we are immediately aware of the grandiose power of the queen! Our eyes light up, we start believing in our own strength, and 2 Q–R5 is the expression of this blind faith: if only we can get a little closer to the black king, then our imagination and life experience will suggest the right move!

Alas, we have all of us trodden the same path. The difference lies in how soon we have each turned away from it. And here everything depends on the personal qualities of the player.

There are in every chess club a number of stubborn people who even in these days try to win with this hasty Queen's Attack. But for the person who wishes to make a deeper study of the art of chess such attacks should serve only as a starting point for a genuinely scientific examination of the normal laws of chess and exceptions to them.

It is illogical to bring the queen into the game early on: the opponent's pawns and minor pieces immediately begin pursuing her, and whilst she is running from square to square, the opponent is bringing a large number of small fighting units into play quite unnoticed. A single queen is stronger than each of these units, but together they inevitably force the queen to flee, and she will be happy if she can escape alive and unharmed.

Will you not be in such a rush now to play your queen out?

The most pleasant variation of the Queen's Attack for White is as follows: 2 Q–R5 K–K2 3 Q × KP mate.

In other words, because of the carelessness of his king, Black has lost on the third move.

If one leaves the king where it is, there is nothing to fear. One can defend the KP by . . . N–QB3 and then drive the queen away with . . . N–KB3. But Black must not, after 3 B–B4, move his KB, his QN or his QR. There is no need either, of course, to hurry with . . . N–KB3.

After 2 Q–R5, 2 . . . P–KN3 would be bad because of 3 Q × KP + and 4 Q × R; but now, after 2 . . . N–QB3, one can play it boldly.

2 The Bishop's Attack

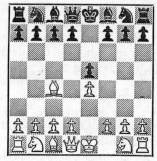

The bishop move is a great improvement on the adventuresome 2 Q–R5 or 2 Q–B3.

Firstly, the bishop is placed extremely well on QB4 and it will not be easy to drive it away in the opening stages; secondly, White employs the cunning tactic of waiting to see what his opponent will do. Sometimes it is useful to call on the queen for help. For example, after 2 ... B–K2? 3 Q–R5! White threatens not only 4 Q ×KP, but also mate by 4 Q ×BP. However, it is only possible to lose like that once ...

In the last century, or even in the one before that, many hotheads used to play 2 ... P–KB4, but against an experienced opponent such an early thrust can lead to a quick death. One can recommend the symmetrical bishop move, whilst it is also not bad to seize the initiative immediately and bring the white pawn in the centre under fire by 2 ... N–KB3.

The main thing is not to lose a single tempo and not to allow White to peacefully build up his forces for an attack on Black's KB2 – the ancestral home of the black king. Of course, one has to reckon with this danger in nearly all openings of the open, and even more, the gambit, type. My advice to you is, play the bishop boldly to QB4 and let your opponent find the best defence.

And that is not an easy task. It goes without saying that, if he has acquired certain skills, your adversary will be able to repel the first attack, and possibly the second, the third. . . . But do not lose heart, with every move create new complicated situations for him to resolve. Somewhere, at some time, he will destroy the necessary equilibrium between attack and defence and will make a hasty move. Then your bishop on QB4 will be at its most useful.

Having hidden itself in some quiet corner, such as QN3 or QR2, your bishop, as if sensing the approach of spring weather, will slowly shake off its mantle and, gathering up its full strength, will leap to KB7!

There are other advantages to 2 B–QB4: the white KBP is not shut in and is always ready to advance; White's queen does not disclose its intentions – perhaps it will go to KR5; but possibly to KB3.

I should like, in confidence, to pass on to the most inquisitive readers my own method of defence: 2 B–B4 B–B4! 3 Q–N4 P–Q4! 4 Q ×P Q–R5! 5 Q ×R Q ×BP+ 6 K–Q1 Q ×NP with hectic play.

ONE BETWEEN TWO

White: P. Keres – Amsterdam 1956, Candidates Tournament

4B

If Black was hoping to draw, then why didn't he play 9 . . . Q–B7 + ? After 10 N–K2 Q–K6 + 11 K–K1 Q–B7 + a draw would be forced. It would be good to get half a point in the first round, but it would have been a pity to part with the game. All the same I should have made the check, and then played not 10 . . . Q–K6 +, but 10 . . . N–QB3. I spent a long time calculating variations with 10 N–K2 N–QB3 11 K–Q3 N × RP 12 B–K3 N–KN5, but just could not find an advantageous way of continuing the attack. Probably, I should not take the KRP, but play . . . N–KB3.

Sometimes people ask: what are grandmasters exactly?

I should very much like the reply to be: grandmasters are those fanatics amongst the fanatics of the art of chess who will never prefer a quick draw if a hard fight is still possible.

And if they sometimes, very, very rarely, transgress this law and agree to a draw then, believe me, it is only in order to throw themselves with redoubled zeal into a fresh skirmish with an invisible opponent the next day.

Why invisible? Because all chess combinations take place, as a rule, behind the scenes. Even if we see several of them, these form such a small part of the total!

1 P–K4 P–K4	13 Q–B4 B–R3 +	25 P–QN3 P–R4	36 R–K4 R–Q4
2 B–B4 N–KB3	14 K–Q2 Q × Q	26 BP × P	37 B–B5 R–Q6 +
3 N–QB3 N–B3	15 B × Q N × QP	26 . . . B × QNP	38 K–B2 R–Q4
4 P–B4 B–B4	16 B × QBP	27 R–QR1	39 B–Q4 P–Q3
5 P × P QN × P	16 . . . N × B +	27 . . . P–QR5	40 R–B4 P–B4
6 B–N3 B × N	17 RP × N B–N2	28 NP × P R × P	41 K–B3 K–N3
7 R × B N3–N5	18 P–K5 N–K5 +	29 R × R B × R	42 R–B3 B–R3
8 P–Q4 Q–R5 +	19 N × N B × N	30 K–B3 R–N3	43 R–K3 K–B2
9 K–Q2 (4)	20 B–Q6 P–KR4	31 P–N3 R–N5	44 R–K1 B–N4
9 . . . N–QB3	21 R–R4 B–B3	32 R–B5 R–N4	45 R–QR1 K–K3
10 Q–B3 N–B3	22 R–KB4 R–R3	33 R–B2 K–B2	46 R–R8 K–Q2
11 K–Q3 P–QN3	23 P–B4 P–B3	34 P × P P × P	47 R–R7 + K–B3
12 B–K3 B–N2	24 P–QN4 P–QN4	35 R–K2 B–N4	Draw agreed.

EASTERN WISDOM

White: V. Mukhin – Moscow 1959, USSR Team Championship

'If it had not been for the wolves, our sheep would have got to Mecca', goes the Eastern proverb. In chess terms this truth would read: if my opponent had not made a move, it would have been easy to checkmate him right at the beginning of the game.

But just as a sheep fails to recognize its own defencelessness and will hope to manage the longest of treks, so human beings, having barely learnt to distinguish the queen from the king, think that they know everything: 1 P–K4, 2 B–B4, 3 Q–R5, 4 Q×BP mate. Admittedly, this condition quickly passes.

In the game we shall be looking at now White played both B–B4 and Q–R5.

I recollected that every single chess manual for beginners recommended only 7 . . . P–B4, and it struck me: but why weaken my KP?

The resolute . . . P–B3 did not, to put it mildly, have its desired effect.

To my good fortune, however, my opponent committed three errors:

1) he was too hasty in capturing my KR (stronger was 10 N–B3);
2) he took something of a risk in castling K-side;
3) he was careless in allowing me to open up the KR-file by 19 . . . B×NP!

But could White have won with 10 N–B3, or not? To be honest, I don't know. For example: 10 N–B3 B–QR3 11 N×P N×N 12 Q×N+ K–Q1 13 Q×R Q–B3 14 Q×B+ K–B2 15 Q–B3 Q×Q 16 P×Q R–K1+ 17 K–Q1 B–K7+ 18 K–K1 B–Q6+ 19 K–Q1 B–K7+ etc. *ad infinitum*.

1 P–K4 P–K4	9 Q×P P–N3	17 Q–R3 B–Q3	25 Q–B4 Q–R1
2 B–B4 N–KB3	10 Q×R B–QN2	18 Q–N4 R–R1	26 B–B1 Q–R4
3 N–QB3 N×P	11 Q×RP 0–0–0	19 P–N3 B×NP	27 P–N4 Q–R5+
4 Q–R5 N–Q3	12 N–K2 N–B4	20 P×B R–R4 (5)	28 K–K2 P–KN4
5 B–N3 N–B3	13 P–Q3 N/3–Q5	21 R–B2 Q–R1	29 Q×NP
6 N–N5 P–KN3	14 N×N P×N	22 R–N2 R–R8+	29 . . . N–N6+
7 Q–B3 P–B3	15 0–0 Q–B3	23 K–B2 Q–K1	30 R×N Q×R
8 N×BP+Q×N	16 P–KB3 Q–B3	24 B–Q2 R×R	White resigns.

3 The QP Attack

The QP Attack, 2 P–Q4, is a most dangerous opening. There are various ways of conducting the attack.

One can retake the pawn with the queen and then aim for very speedy development of the Q-side pieces and Q-side castling.

Some people like to throw a pawn into the fire, or even two: they play 3 P–QB3, inviting those who enjoy winning material to gorge themselves. Whilst the one is picking up dead pawns, the other gradually sneaks up on his complacent opponent's king.

The best defence is to return the accepted sacrifices as quickly as possible at the slightest signs of a mating attack and establish approximate equality in the number of pieces developed into active positions and the number of open lines. Other tactics are almost always fatal.

But those players that have grown the most wise from experience refuse the sacrifices in the first place.

It remains to be added that the attack 2 P–Q4 is in complete accordance with all the requirements of the positional school of chess: lines are opened up for a great number of White's pieces and his whole position becomes straight away far more refractory.

It is also worth remembering that the QP advance forms an organic part of almost any opening variation beginning with 1 P–K4 P–K4, since without P–Q4 it is very difficult to create any initiative. Thus, it matters little on what move White plays his QP to Q4; the move makes its way imperceptibly into every opening of an open type, and we are fully justified in considering the QP Attack a most dangerous fighting weapon, dangerous, that is, of course, for Black, not White.

HOBBLED HORSES

Black: A. N. Other – Sochi 1950, Simultaneous Display

A rather droll final position! Black has his pieces ideally developed, but one of his knights has got fatally pinned and, however much it may want to, it cannot take the rook on Q1.

On the other hand, if the king were to take the rook the greedy move, Q ×Q, would be possible, for then Black's second knight is tied down.

All Black's misadventures began when he played his queen to K5, pinning the white knight on K5. In revenge White thought up a little trick, the combination 8 0–0–0! Q ×N 9 R–Q8+.

I do not know how you like this miniature, but it pleases me a lot! Why? As I have already admitted, because of Black's ludicrous hobbled horses!

What is this game remarkable for? Probably for the move 4 Q–R4. In text-books only one move is recommended, 4 Q–Q1, but who can believe that such a powerful piece as the queen has such a limited range of movement?

As soon as I have a convenient opportunity I will try to work out a harmonious plan of attack even, say, with a move so illogical at first sight as 4 Q–Q2. One needs only to be aware of all the pluses and minuses of this idea and everything will be fine.

Above all one should not hurry with P–QN3 and B–QN2. These moves must be held in reserve; it is better to develop the K-side pieces first: B–Q3, P–KB4, N–KB3, 0–0, and only then, according to how things stand, find work for the QR, QB and QN.

I can further recommend one move already known to us, 3 B–QB4, but now it is perhaps even more dangerous than before! Because of the trap 3 B–QB4! B–N5+? 4 P–QB3 P ×P 5B ×P+! K ×B 6 Q–N3+, and White wins back the sacrificed bishop.

1 P–K4 P–K4	4 Q–R4 N–B3	7 N ×P Q–K2	9 R–Q8 + (7)
2 P–Q4 P ×P	5 N–QB3 P–Q4	8 0–0–0 Q ×N	Black resigns.
3 Q ×P N–QB3	6 B–KN5 P ×P		

4 The King's Gambit

There is not a single true chess-player in the world whose heart does not beat faster at the mere sound of such long beloved and familiar words as 'gambit games'.

In the first instance our delight is for the ancient weapon of the Romantics, Neo-Romantics and other chess d'Artagnans – the legendary King's Gambit.

Why such delight, such worship, so much love? No other single opening offers such wide possibilities for the emergence of creative initiative; in no other opening are so many difficult and confusing problems created in the very first moves; no other opening moves allow the players to confront each other straight away, without preparatory reconnaissance, in open fighting, and to unfold the most fascinating battle over the whole of the board. If one was to pick out at random only one variation from the multifarious King's Gambit: 1 P–K4 P–K4 2 P–KB4 (8) P×P 3 N–KB3 P–KN4 4 B–B4 P–N5 5 0–0 P×N 6 Q×P Q–B3 7 P–K5 Q×P 8 B×P+ K×B 9 P–Q4!, that in itself would be sufficient to earn for the opening the eternal gratitude of chess-players.

Since in many branches of the King's Gambit both kings often, right in the opening, find themselves in the very thick of a seething skirmish, both players feel the desire (and there is foundation for it) to try and win not by collecting a material tax from the physically weakened enemy, but by using the strength of their own imagination.

It is no secret that any talented player must in his soul be an artist, and what could be dearer to his heart and soul than the victory of the subtle forces of reason over crude material strength! Probably everyone has his own reason for liking the King's Gambit, but my love for it can be seen in precisely those terms.

THE SCOURGE OF CHAMPIONS

White: F. Duz-Khotimirsky – Moscow 1954, match 'Lokomotiv' v. 'Dinamo'

9B

It is commonly thought that chess is a game for silent people.

As soon as my opponent had played P–KB4 I suddenly heard an angry:

'And I'm having no refusal! Accept the sacrifice! If you don't take the pawn I won't continue the game!'

There was nothing I could do. I accepted the old maestro's gambit.

Several moves later Duz-Khotimirsky played a hurried move and, whilst I was considering my reply, decided . . . to change his move.

The spectators gasped, the judges wanted to stop the clocks, but Fedor Ivanovich suddenly shouted at everyone:

'What on earth is this? Look, I made a bad move and now I'm changing it for a good one. Rules, you say? To hell with your rules, this is chess. Besides, you don't object?' said my opponent, turning to me.

'Please, it's my pleasure!'

And the game went on as if nothing had happened.

F. I. Duz-Khotimirsky defeated at the international Chigorin Memorial Tournament in St. Petersburg in 1909 both first prize-winners – the world champion and the champion of Russia, Lasker and Rubinstein.

In his game with Em. Lasker he conducted a K-side attack with exceptional accuracy, and in his game with A. Rubinstein he took over the initiative with a cunning pawn move and forced his opponent to make an unfavourable combination.

These successes earned the veteran fame with the chess public for many years, and he was called none other than 'the scourge of champions'.

1 P–K4 P–K4	6 P×P P–KR3	11 B×P N×P	16 Q–Q2 Q×P
2 P–KB4 P×P	7 Q–K2+ B–K2	12 Q–Q2 N×B	17 R–Q1 P–B5
3 N–KB3 P–KN4	8 N–K4 P–KB4	13 Q×N K–N2	18 N–B3 P–B6
4 P–KR4 P–N5	9 N–B2 N–KB3	14 B–K2 R–K1	19 P×P Q–R7+!
5 N–N5 (9)	10 P–Q4 0–0	15 0–0 B–Q3	White resigns.
5 . . . P–Q4			

CATASTROPHE FOR BLACK ON KB2 AND KB5

Black: P. Dubinin – Leningrad 1947, USSR Championship

In that year the King's Gambit was not being used at all in big competitions and the effect of using it was almost always the same: Black, as a rule, would burn with the desire to punish his opponent and, instead of quickly returning the pawn, he tried to hang on to his material advantage at any price. Exactly as in the last century!

That is what happened this time too.

Play through just the first seven moves on your board and you will see completely diverse approaches to the problem of development. Whilst White seized the centre, Black was primarily playing his K-side pawns on. Whilst White actively developed his minor pieces, establishing them in ideal attacking positions (B–QB4, N–KB3–K5) Black spent two valuable tempi on . . . R–R2 and . . . B–R3 – with a more modest aim: to defend his pawns on KB2 and KB5.

In itself Black's plan has a healthy foundation: as long as Black's KBPs are alive, the black king is too; but that is precisely where the trouble lay for Black, both pawns fell!

You should look without fail at the old handbooks on the King's Gambit. There you will find all the moves of my game with Dubinin. True, instead of 8 . . . P–Q3 Black strengthened the defence by 8 . . . N–QB3, but this small detail did not alter the general assessment of the variation.

Not all old moves are by any means old.

1 P–K4 P–K4	9 N×BP R×N	16 N–Q5 B–Q2	22 Q–B3+ N–B3
2 P–KB4 P×P	10 B×R+ K×B	17 P–K5 P×P	23 R×N Q×R
3 N–KB3 P–KN4	11 B×P B×B	18 P×P B–B3	24 Q×Q+ K–R2
4 P–KR4 P–N5	12 0–0 Q×P	19 P–K6 B×N	25 Q–B5+ K–R3
5 N–K5 P–KR4	13 R×B+ K–N2	20 R–B7+ (10)	26 Q×B K–N3
6 B–B4 R–R2	14 Q–Q2 P–Q3	20 . . . N×R	27 Q–Q7
7 P–Q4 B–R3	15 R1–KB1 N–Q1	21 R×N+ K–R1	Black resigns.
8 N–QB3 N–QB3			

THE BATON OF GENERATIONS

White: A. N. Other – Kiev 1941, simultaneous display

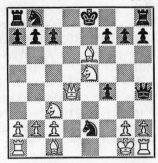

Amongst the rich legacy of the famous P. Morphy there is one combination which has always pleased me, I think, more than any other. And then success: I was able in a simultaneous display to use Morphy's idea in an original, and at the same time surprisingly similar, mating combination.

The start to Black's combination was 6 ...P×P! The correct reply for White was the quiet 7 B×P+ K×B 8 N×P+ K–N1 9 Q×N P–KN3 10 Q–K2, but surely it was hard to decline the tempting 7 N×P? It created two terrible threats: N×KBP! and Q×N!, and at the same time the bishop on QB4 still remained intact.

When Black had luckily passed this dangerous point, the contours of the envisaged sacrifice became clearer: the move ...Q–R5+, which White did not fear, since the variation 8 K–B1 N–N6+ 9 K–N1 N×R 10 B×P+! K–K2 11 B–R5 N–B7 12 Q–K2! is not good for Black. In fact this move was the prelude to a completely different plan: it was not the black knight that was trying to get to White's KR1, but the black queen that was simply bursting with the desire to penetrate ...to K8!

How is that, to K8? White has his queen and king there, surely, and even if one was to suppose that the king went to KN1 and the queen disappeared, ...Q–K8 would still be a weak threat: with the cool B–KB1 White would be able to avoid any trouble.

So in order that the bishop should not save its king, Black played 8 ...B–K3 – this is the move that I had seen in one of Morphy's games.

And so it is that from century to century, from the oldest of us to the youngest, the most beautiful moves are passed on. The baton of generations.

1 P–K4 P–K4	5 N–B3 P–Q3	9 B×B N–N6+	(11)
2 P–KB4 P×P	6 B–B4 P×P	10 K–N1 B–B4+	13 N×N Q–K8
3 N–KB3 N–KB3	7 N×P Q–R5+	11 P–Q4 B×P+	mate!
4 P–K5 N–R4	8 K–B1 B–K3	12 Q×B N–K7+	

THE WORLD OF ADVENTURES

Black: I. Kan – Moscow 1945, USSR Championship

One can easily detect the traces of past battles in the diagrammed position: the knight on KR8, the queen on KN2, the brave pawn on K6 and White's active queen on KB4.

The battle was so swift that not all the pieces have managed to enter the game – Black's rooks still lie dormant, as does White's QR. The time was just ripe for White's Q-side pieces to take up the struggle.

Why, in answer to N–QB3, did Black not castle Q-side?

Black's king had long before made the choice to move just one square at a time. Chess diagrams are incomplete: they do not show the movements of the pieces. You will have to glance at the text of the game and find Black's 10th and 18th moves.

Could Kan have won this game?

Undoubtedly. For example, by not hurrying with 12 ... N×R and choosing the more cunning 12 ... P–KR3. However, after 13 ... P–KR3 White would have been in a position to play more strongly: 14 Q–B5+ K–K1 15 Q–N6+ K–B1 16 Q–B5+ with a draw. But after I had been lucky enough to win this game, and later two more King's Gambits, everyone noticed my 'insolence'. Even my friend Boleslavsky.

And this is what was said about it in three different numbers of 'Chess in the USSR' in 1945:

'... the master Bronstein raised a storm on the board by using the King's Gambit, but was frequently unable himself to find the correct combinations. But, fortunately for him, his opponents failed to capitalize on the rich possibilities the positions offered them ...' – this was an article by Boleslavsky in issue No. 8.

'... Bronstein was bold enough to play the King's Gambit three times. This, of course, was risky, but all the same his opponents, Alatortsev, Kan and Koblencs, suffered unpleasant defeats. Unpleasant for them because a master should not lose a game in an opening which is considered incorrect ...' – this was from S. Flohr's account in Nos. 4 and 5.

And, finally, the particularly sober voice of A. Kotov in No. 3: '... the young master should remember that the praises of certain chess experts to the effect that he has "breathed new life" into the King's Gambit are not worth a brass farthing. In the first place, in two of the three games begun with the King's Gambit he had hopeless positions right in the opening. Secondly, Bronstein must know that if these games had ended in his defeat the same "authors" would have burst out with attacks on "light-hearted" play in such a serious tournament . . .'

And yet I do not regret venturing the insolent, for those days, experiment of P–KB4.

It is really a pity, – not a great one, but all the same a pity – that Kan played 16 . . . Q–N2! and successfully avoided the variation 16 . . . N–Q5? 17 QN–B3 N×BP+ 18 K–Q2 N×R 19 B×B P×B 20 N–Q5! after which White has an easy and enjoyable game.

Complex opening problems deprived both players of almost all of their allowed time, and by the 20th move we were both already in the most awful time-trouble. In these conditions one of my traps at last came off: 25 N/6–N5! P–R3? 26 R×R R×R 27 N–B7 transposing to a won knight ending.

As one might expect, I drew the necessary lessons from this puzzling game, and when the Moscow team played a friendly match in Bratislava a year later, I played the opening more solidly in my encounter with the master Khukl: 1 P–K4 P–K4 2 P–KB4 P×P 3 N–KB3 N–KB3 4 P–K5 N–R4 5 P–Q4 P–Q4 6 P–B4 B–K2 7 B–K2 B–R5+ 8 K–B1 B–K2 9 P×P Q×P 10 N–B3 Q–Q1 11 P–Q5, secured strong points with my pawns and won, though not without difficulty.

1 P–K4 P–K4	11 B–K6 Q–K2	20 Q–K3 Q–Q5	29 P–B3 R–K5
2 P–KB4 P×P	12 P–Q5 N×R	21 Q×Q N×Q	30 P–K7 N–N5
3 N–KB3 N–KB3	13 Q×P P–KR3	22 0–0–0 N–B7	31 P–K8=Q
4 P–K5 N–R4	14 N–K4 B×B	23 N×P+ K–K2	31 . . . R×Q
5 P–Q4 P–KN4	15 P×B N–B3	24 R×N QR–Q1	32 N×R+ K×N
6 P–KR4 P–N5	16 B×P Q–N2	25 N/6–N5 P–R3	33 K–Q2 K–K4
7 N–N5 P–Q4	17 B×B+ P×B	26 R×R R×R	34 N–N7 N–B3
8 P×P e.p. B×P	18 Q–B4+ K–K1	27 N–B7 R–Q5	35 K–K3 N–Q4+
9 B–B4 N–N6	(12)	28 N/3–Q5+	36 K–B3
10 B×P+ K–B1	19 QN–B3 R–KB1	28 . . . K–Q3	Black resigns.

A WONDER OF THE TWENTIETH CENTURY

Black: EVM 'M-20' – USSR 1963, training match

There were reports not so long ago in the press about a match between electronic grandmasters of the USSR and the USA. The result was a victory, 3–1, in our favour.

The sensation was before our eyes, and at literally every lecture we gave we, the live grandmasters, were attacked with the question: how strongly does the robot play?

We replied as best we could: it plays quite well, it is said, but it is still a long way off world champion level; science cannot be expected to perform miracles of that order.

And then on one occasion. . . .

– Grandmaster, I am speaking on behalf of your old fans. We have a very serious request: could you possibly come and spend an hour or two with us?

– Thank you for your attention, but I can't, I'm terribly busy.

– That's a pity, a very great pity. We are so counting on you. We really need to check one variation with you, and with you alone. That's a pity.

– So you're not inviting me to give a simultaneous display? It's simply to help you check a variation? And who are 'you' exactly?

– We're computer programmers. We have trained our robot to play chess and he has already beaten everyone, but they won't allow us to enter him in a tournament with people. And our head of department only said: 'All this is complete nonsense! On the other hand, if it were to outplay a grandmaster, then I would believe it.'

– You've talked me into it. I'll play your robot. Only not on equal terms, of course. Tell him he can have my queen – as odds.

And so I met the robot. I was satisfied at first with my position, but, when he began impudently exchanging off one piece after the other, I realised my foolishness and regretted offering the queen as a sacrifice.

Meanwhile the young programmers were busy mocking me: your efforts are in vain, they said. He won't blunder anything away to you, he never blunders; there's nothing human about him! Look out, you're in check . . .

Applause, a din, congratulations. The programmers were about to turn out the lights and go off home, but I voiced a protest:

– A return match. I demand a return match. And give me my white queen back!

And it was then that I played my immortal game, culminating in a forced ten-move mating combination on the electronic black king.

The opening was played according to the very latest recommendations of theory and those of the young programmers. The high point of the game was 13 Q–B4 P–N4.

Black did not much like the white queen's move and thought so long over his reply that he unwittingly ended up in time-trouble, using all the time for the game (not only his, but his opponent's as well). The chief referee (who was also the chief programmer) wanted to adjourn the game but I protested repeatedly: I was afraid of home analysis.

– Just give me one minute, please, only one minute. Yes? Look, you are mated in ten moves! I am playing 14 N×NP+.

– Don't be in such a hurry, grandmaster, write down your move and seal it in an envelope. Everything must be according to FIDE rules, said the 'specialists'.

Next morning my telephone rang at 7.30 exactly.

– Congratulations on your victory, said a squeaking electronic voice. It hesitated slightly and added: 'But I'll still always beat you when you're without a queen. You can go back to your live chess! And don't forget we are drawing at the moment, 1–1.'

I wanted to say 'thank you' but wasn't quick enough; there was a click and I realised that my EVM M-20 robot considered our conversation was over.

Seven long years have gone by since that memorable day, and I still cannot forgive myself for my foolishness: to play against such a monster without my queen! And the beautiful mate in the second game does not even give me consolation. But nothing can be done about that.

But whatever you might say and whatever I might say, a machine which can play chess with people is one of the most marvellous wonders of our 20th century!

1 P–K4 P–K4	8 N–K4 N–K6	14 N×NP+	18 N–Q5+ K–K1
2 P–KB4 P×P	9 N–B6+ K–K2	14 ... Q×N	19 Q×QB+
3 N–KB3 N–KB3	10 B–Q2 N×BP+	15 N×QBP++	19 ... Q–Q1
4 P–K5 N–N5	11 K–B2 N×R	15 ... K–K2	20 N–B7+ K–K2
5 P–Q4 P–KN4	12 N–Q5+ K–K3	16 N–Q5+ K–K3	21 B–N4+ P–Q3
6 N–QB3 N–K6	13 Q–B4 P–N4	17 N×P++	22 B×P+ Q×B
7 Q–K2 N×B	(13)	17 ... K–K2	23 Q–K8 mate!

LIVE CHESS

Black: T. Petrosian – Tiflis 1963, theatricalized game

14W

For as exactly as many years as chess has existed in the world people have been including chess subjects in theatre productions and in books, and chess terms in their everyday vocabulary.

But for a long time it has also been the custom for chess games themselves to be the centre-piece of a programme: spectators observe the movements of the pieces, not on a diminutive board, but on a big town square where pieces and spectators alike are life-size.

One such theatricalized presentation took place in Tiflis, in the Dinamo stadium.

As commander of the attacking army I chose as our subject one of the variations I had analysed in the well-known Keres attack and which I had once tested out on Alekhine himself.

Probably Keres knew the variation 8 P×P N×P 9 Q–R2 N×R 10 B–Q3 P–KB4 11 P×Pep P–KN3, and therefore played 8 Q–N2.

But even in the variation above White does not have such a bad game: He has only to play 11 N–B3 instead of 11 P×Pep, and then B–Q2, 0–0–0 and R×N, and Black is immediately subjected to strong pressure along the KN- and KR-files.

15 ... Q–K2 was not obligatory; 15 ... RP×B 16 Q×P+ K–R1 17 Q–R6 + etc. would easily force the draw, but Black declined the idea of perpetual check. Incensed by this, White sacrificed his queen (17 B×BP) and was chagrined that Black did not want to play for the 'self-mate': 17 ... Q×Q 18 N–K7 mate.

1 P–K4 P–K4	8 P×P N×P	14 B×B P–KB3	19 Q×Q+ K×Q
2 P–KB4 P×P	9 Q–R2 N×R	15 B×NP Q–K2	20 P×R+ K×B
3 N–KB3 N–KB3	10 B–Q3 P–KN3	16 N×P Q–N2	21 N×P N–B3
4 P–K5 N–R4	11 Q–R6 P–Q4	*(14)*	22 N×R N×P
5 Q–K2 B–K2	12 N–B3 N–N6	17 B×BP R×B	23 0–0–0 B–B4
6 P–Q4 0–0	13 N–KN5 B×N	18 B×P+ K–R1	Draw agreed.
7 P–KN4 P×Pep			

WASTED ENERGY

Black: C. Lemoine – Munich Olympiad 1958

With every day, every month, every move an even greater number of chess secrets cease to be the coveted weapons of individuals and gradually become common property.

No, today any player, even one who only learnt the game yesterday, will, in answer to the question 'Which is the weakest square in the opening position?', reply with confidence: Black's KB2. And this is true.

But now do you know which are the strongest squares? Let me help you. They are White's K2 and Black's K2.

If the French master Lemoine had been able to read these lines before our game, he would not for anything have allowed my rook to penetrate to K7.

The popular opening variation led to an early exchange of queens, but Black needlessly consented to the endless manoeuvres ... B–K2–Q3–K2 –Q3 ...

When the queens did disappear from the board it would have been better to take the queen with the king.

The bishop, having worked so hard to no end, was lost all the same and after its exit there was nobody left to defend the weak squares.

However, lest it should seem to the reader that I am concerned only with reproving Black, I will say a word too about White.

Deserving praise are both the subtle tactics of the light-squared bishop, which, by its manoeuvre from Q3–QN5–QB6, looked as if it was gunning for Black's QR, whereas in fact its sights were set on Black's QP, and the elegant leap of the white knight from KB3–K5 and then to KB7.

If Black had captured on KB2 with his rook, after 26 B × P N × B 27 R–K8 + ! he would have been mated.

1 P–K4 P–K4	8 Q–K2 + Q–K2	15 0–0 0–0	22 B–R6 B–B1
2 P–KB4 P × P	9 Q × Q + B × Q	16 P–QN3 N–B3	23 B–N5 P–QR3
3 N–KB3 B–K2	10 P–Q4 B–Q3	17 QR–K1 B–N5	24 B–B6 R–N1
4 B–B4 N–KB3	11 N–K4 N–Q2	18 R–K7 QN–Q2	25 N × P (15)
5 P–K5 N–N5	12 N × B+ P × N	19 B–K5 P–QN3	25 ... B–N5
6 N–B3 P–Q3	13 QB × P N–N3	20 B × N N × B	26 R × N
7 P × P B × P	14 B–Q3 P–Q4	21 N–K5 B–K3	Black resigns.

QUEEN SACRIFICE

Black: A. Koblencs – Moscow 1945, USSR Championship

On a cursory examination of this game the most curious feature seems to be the finale: White's last move.

However, this is not the case, or not quite. Here, as in any game, a whole variety of subtleties are hidden behind each move.

For example, instead of the quiet 11 Q–Q3 White's pieces could have immediately thrown themselves into a K-side attack.

11 N–K5 would have set Black the interesting problem of whether to strike back straight away by advancing his pawn on K6 to K7, or whether to think first about the unpleasant threats to his king.

If he were to go 11 ... B–B3, then after 12 N–K4 Q–N3 13 N×B + P×N 14 Q–R5 Q×QP 15 K–R1 P×N 16 R×P the black king would be in a mating net.

It might look as if he could play the natural 11 ... B–K3, but how would he answer 12 N–N5?

The queen must retreat to QN3, when White will capture Black's bishop on K3 and after 13 B×B P×B 14 R×R + B×R 15 Q–R5 the attack is irresistible.

And if the queen were not to retreat to QN3 but to Q1, then again 13 B×B P×B 14 R×R + B×R, and now not 15 Q–R5, but 15 Q–N4! so as to answer 15 ... Q–B1 by boldly taking Black's QBP with the knight.

And then very bad for Black would be 16 ... Q×N?, because of 17 Q×KP + K–R1 18 N–B7 + K–N1 19 N–R6 + + K–R1 20 Q–N8 mate!

Does this extensive commentary mean that N–K5 would have given White a swift and simultaneously beautiful victory? Not at all. Any player is capable of embellishing his wins in such a way that even the plainest of moves begins to throw up combinations, where each is more brilliant than the last. But if one were to analyse such a production of chess thought seriously and in a business-like manner, what in fact would be left of the combinations would not be worth talking about.

This very thing might happen here to the author of this book were some lover of microscopic analysis not to verify the set of variations (what is the sense in mere bare variations?) and cast doubt upon Black's very first reply, B–K3.

On the other hand, if you have read this page carefully, you cannot have helped noticing the phrase 'the queen must retreat'.

But the queen must not retreat anywhere. One can reflect upon what terrible threats N×Q holds, but surely it is a move which does not give check! Since that is so, is it not possible to use the time and . . . let us say, take the bishop? – let us try 12 . . . B ×B!.

Whatever sceptics might say, over the last 12 moves White has been pretty successful in weakening his K2. How? As follows: his KP has left K2, his king has moved away, the KN has lost control over K2, and the QN has forgotten about the square too. Only the lone queen is left, as well as the bishop on QB4 – but we have just eaten that up.

To sum up: the variation 11 N–K5 B–K3 12 N–N5 B ×B 13 N ×Q P–K7 14 N/6 ×B P ×Q =Q! would reduce a very sharp position to . . . the most boring endgame.

And now, on your honour, what would you yourself have played, 11 N–K5 or 11 Q–Q3?

I will also say a few words about the game as a whole. Black played well, but, firstly, he was wrong to retreat his bishop to QN3 – better was B–K2; and secondly, he should have taken White's bishop with the pawn, not the rook. Having conceded his KB4 to White's knight, Black crowned his sorrows by blundering away the QNP, and this was already the beginning of the end.

And if you have already managed to work critically through my commentary, then probably a gross mistake will not have escaped you – there is no need to play 11 N–K5?, just as there was no need to play 11 Q–Q3?.

The solution to the position is the energetic move 11 N–QN5!, which was pointed out immediately after the game by Boleslavsky.

Now the black queen must retreat, and only then 12 N–K5, and Black is in a bad way: 11 . . . Q–Q1 12 N–K5 B–B3 13 Q–R5 Q–K2 14 N ×KBP R ×N 15 B ×R + Q ×B 16 Q ×Q + K ×Q 17 N ×BP and 18 N ×R.

1 P–K4 P–K4	9 N–B3 N–K6	16 P ×N B–QB4+	24 N–B5 Q–N4
2 P–KB4 P ×P	10 B ×N P ×B	17 K–R1 B–K3	25 Q ×P R–Q7
3 N–KB3 B–K2	(16)	18 N–K4 B–N3	26 Q–B3 B–B4
4 B–B4 N–KB3	11 Q–Q3 N–B3	19 P–B3 QR–Q1	27 P–QN4 B–B1
5 P–K5 N–N5	12 QR–K1 B–N5	20 Q–K2 KR–K1	28 N–Q4 K–R1
6 0–0 P–Q3	13 R ×P Q–R3	21 B ×B R ×B	29 N–K6
7 P ×P Q ×P	14 R/3–K1 B–Q3	22 Q–B3 R–K2	Black resigns.
8 P–Q4 0–0	15 N–K5 N ×N	23 N–N3 R/2–Q2	

STALEMATE! BUT IN WHOSE FAVOUR?

Black: R. Kholmov – Moscow 1961, Training Game

17W

The title poses a strange question, don't you think?

Everyone knows nowadays that stalemate means a draw, half a point to me, half a point to you.

But here I have asked the question 'In whose favour?'.

In the draw's favour!

According to the modern rules of play this is the case; but in olden days stalemate was considered a win for the side which lost the right to move.

In the diagram position I would in those days have had either to force a draw by perpetual check: 52 R–B2 + K–N6 53 R–B3 + K–N7 54 R–B2 +, or quickly sweep the whole board clean: 52 R–QN7 P–R7 53 R × P+ K–R8 54 R–QR5 K–N7 55 R × P +.

It is very probable that I could have won the rook in a more favourable situation, but I mistakenly supposed that my king would get to QR1 before his black colleague could reach its QN7. I failed. Kholmov found a brilliant route for his king. I am referring to the king flight on moves 42–45. A fair draw, then.

1 P–K4 P–K4	17 R × R+ R × R	32 P–R3 P–N4	47 R × P+K–Q6
2 P–KB4 P × P	18 K–K2 B–B5	33 K–B5 R–KB7+	48 R–Q7 + K–B7
3 N–KB3 B–K2	19 N–N4 N–K2	34 K–K6 R–KN7	49 K–K3 P–R5
4 B–B4 N–KB3	20 R–Q1 R–N1	35 K–B6 R–KB7+	50 R–QB7+K–N7
5 P–K5 N–N5	21 N–Q4 P–KR4	36 K–N7 R–B6	51 K–Q2 P–R6
6 N–B3 P–Q3	22 N × P P × N	37 P–N6 R × P	*(17)*
7 P–Q4 P × P	23 N × B R–K1	38 K–B8 R × P	52 R–B2 + K–N6
8 P × P Q × Q+	24 P × P N–B3	39 P–N7 R–KN6	53 R–B5 P–N5
9 N × Q B–K3	25 P–K6 N–Q1	40 P–N8 = Q	54 K–B1 K–R7
10 B × B P × B	26 P–N5 N × P	40 ... R × Q+	55 R–B2 + K–R8
11 P–KR3	27 N × N R × N+	41 K × R P–R4	56 R–B4 P–N6
11 ... N–KR3	28 K–B3 R–K4	42 K–B7 K–Q2	57 R–QN4
12 B × P N–B3	29 K–B4 R–K7	43 K–B6+ K–Q3	57 ... P–N7 +
13 N–K3 0–0–0	30 R–KR1	44 K–B5 K–Q4	58 K–B2 P–R7
14 P–B3 KR–B1	30 ... R × QNP	45 K–B4 K–Q5	59 R × P
15 B × N P × B	31 R × P R × NP	46 R–Q7 + K–B6	Stalemate!
16 R–Q1 B–N4			

SAVELY TARTAKOVER'S GAMBIT

Black: B. Ivkov – Vienna 1957, European Team Championship

It is pointless looking in the books for this gambit – you will not find anything like it there. The move 4 B–K2 was invented by the master Muchnik, and the name by myself.

What would you have called this variation if you had known that in the great international tournament that took place in New York in 1924, Savely Grigorevich Tartakover allowed himself the luxury of playing the openings of his games against the world champion, Capablanca, and the claimant to the chess throne, Alekhine, as follows: 1 P–K4 P–K4 2 P–KB4 P×P 3 B–K2?

Does this historical reference have any bearing on the present game?

Of course. Here the moves N–KB3 and ... B–K2 have been added, but the essence of the matter has not changed: the white bishop comes out to K2 so as not to be attacked by the black QP when the latter deems it judicious to make its journey to the central Q4 square.

And whilst with the bishop on QB4 White has a limited choice, either to take the pawn or retreat, with the bishop on K2 he has the new possibility of going round the side of the pawn.

I managed to realize this plan, but any further attack was checked by the precise action Ivkov took.

The reader has a chance here to study the Yugoslav grandmaster's highly professional manner of play and adopt the best of it for himself.

And when you have a free moment, you most certainly should find Alekhine's book on the 1924 New York Tournament and play through the Tartakover–Capablanca and Tartakover–Alekhine games. You can acquaint yourselves at the same time with many other games from that great tournament, annotated in masterly fashion.

1 P–K4 P–K4	4 ... N–KB3	8 P–Q4 0–0	12 B×R N–B3
2 P–KB4 P×P	5 P–Q3 P–Q4	9 0–0 P×P	Draw.
3 N–KB3 B–K2	6 P–K5 N–N5	10 N×P N×N	
4 B–K2 (*18*)	7 B×P P–KB3	11 B×N R×R+	

THE TEARS OF THE KNIGHT OF THE ATTACK

Black: A. Matanovic – Vienna 1957, European Team Championship

How often the whimperers and the failures love to repeat: 'Now if I'd done it earlier!' or 'If only I had . . .!' As if in different circumstances they would not also have found reasons for justifying their mistakes.

But there is one failure – a native of Venice, the famous knight of the attack, Rudolf Spielmann – whom I can sympathise with: his article 'At the bedside of the ailing King's Gambit' brought tears to my eyes.

And if it was difficult in the 20's to win with the sharp King's Gambit (for chess knowledge had rendered its most poisonous arrows harmless), then what can we say thirty, forty or even fifty years later?

Nevertheless, remember the immortal chess masterpieces of Venice's favourite, Spielmann, and play the King's Gambit in his honour.

And if you are not well enough prepared find some old collections of gambit tournaments and play each game through. It is an extremely pleasant occupation. Whilst doing it one should be thinking not about who is winning or losing, but only about the immortality of real beauty, Whatever form it presents itself in.

If the reader shares my views on this topic, he would do better not to play through my game with Matanovic: there are no sacrifices in it. Black conducted the defence so energetically that White had to sound a hasty retreat. And all I could achieve was the opportune recapture of the KBP I had once rashly sacrificed. This sacrifice was the sharpest moment in the game. There was also a trap: 14 . . . R × B? 15 Q–Q8 +!, but Black safely avoided that.

1 P–K4 P–K4	6 0–0 0–0	11 B × B P × B	15 K–R1 N–B3
2 P–KB4 P × P	7 N–QB3 P–QB3	12 N–K5 B × N	16 P–B3 Q–B5
3 N–KB3 P–Q4	8 P–Q4 P × P	13 P × B Q × P	17 B–K3
4 P × P N–KB3	9 N × P B–K3	14 B × P (*19*)	Draw.
5 B–B4 B–Q3	10 N × N + Q × N	14 . . . Q–QB4 +	

ANALYSIS OR IMPROVISATION?

Black: M. Botvinnik – Moscow 1952, USSR Championship

Whilst preparing for my match for the world championship in 1951 I just could not discover for myself the secret of Botvinnik's continuous run of successes. On the other hand I was lucky enough to find out something more important: the plan for my own play in the forthcoming duel. After studying more than a hundred of the world champion's games, I took an important decision: at all costs, and notwithstanding the obvious risk, to improvise tirelessly at the board.

It was perfectly obvious why. Botvinnik himself is always right at the front in chess theory; what becomes known to us today, was known to him yesterday. And that means that what will only be understandable to us tomorrow, Botvinnik already knows today.

By following this simple rule, I successfully kept the score balanced around the 50 per cent mark throughout the whole match and finished with the honourable result of 12–12.

But only a year later I forgot my golden rule and extremely naively played a King's Gambit against the world champion. Needless to say, he was ready for this opening.

There was a fleeting moment in the game, however, when Black was on the verge of a catastrophe: 13 ... P×P? 14 N–N5 P×P+ 15 K–R1 P–N3 16 R×P K–R1 17 R×P mate; but with 13 ... N–N3 he eliminated the threats of the main enemy, White's bishop on QB4, and completely put out the smouldering spark of the attack.

I should have reconciled myself to the inevitable and chosen the variation 14 B×P/4 B×B 15 P×B N×B 16 Q×N Q–Q4 17 Q×Q P×Q 18 N–K5 B–B4, but that day my mind was only on winning.

1 P–K4 P–K4	8 P–Q4 B–Q3	14 B–N3 P–QB4	20 P–QR4 B–K7
2 P–KB4 P×P	9 0–0 0–0	15 P–B4 Q–B3	21 Q–QB3 N–Q2
3 N–KB3 P–Q4	10 N–B3 N×N	16 N–K5 B×N	22 P–R5 N–B3
4 P×P N–KB3	11 P×N B–KN5	17 P×B Q×P	23 B–R4 R–K3
5 B–N5+ P–B3	12 Q–Q3 N–Q2	18 B×P Q–R4	24 K–N2 N–K5
6 P×P P×P	13 P–N3 (20)	19 KR–K1	25 Q–R3 P–N4
7 B–B4 N–Q4	13 ... N–N3	19 ... KR–K1	White resigns.

GENEROUS-HEARTED LILIENTAL

Black: A. Liliental – Moscow 1953, Moscow Championship

Our magazines are filled with various kinds of chess material: articles, problems, studies and so on. There are few just simple tales about the chess-players themselves. But surely people are the most important thing.

I have no doubt that many people are acquainted with the creative hand of André Arnoldovich Liliental, and of course you know of his famous victory over Capablanca, when the Cuban was beaten with a queen sacrifice!

But does everyone know that Liliental has the kindest chess heart in the world? His gentle, sympathetic nature often prevents him from playing tournaments with the necessary competitive malice. He pities older colleagues, as well as those of his own age, and is afraid of offending younger ones.

Liliental and I are old friends and he does not pity me in the slightest when he meets me at the chess-board!

If you want proof of this, play through our game from the Moscow championship.

And if Black's bold, uncompromising play appeals to you, run to a bookshop and get a collection of the best games of A. Liliental for your favourite shelf. You will find beautiful moves, subtle combinations and elegant endgames in it.

1 P–K4 P–K4	11 P×N N–Q2	19 QR–K1 N–K6	28 R–KB2 R–K3
2 P–KB4 P×P	12 B–Q3 P–QB4	20 R×N P×R	29 P–Q5 R×N
3 N–KB3 P–Q4	13 N–Q2 P×P	21 Q×P Q–R5	30 B×R B×B
4 P×P N–KB3	14 P×P N–B3	22 P–R3 B–KR4	31 Q×B B–N3
5 B–N5+ P–B3	15 N–K4 B–KN5	23 P–N4 B–KN3	32 P–Q6 B×R+
6 P×P P×P	(21)	24 Q–B3 P–KR4	33 K×B Q–Q7+
7 B–B4 N–Q4	16 Q–Q2 B–B2	25 R–B2 QR–Q1	34 Q–K2 Q×BP
8 0–0 B–Q3	17 P–B3 N–Q4	26 R–K2 P×P	35 P–Q7 Q×B
9 P–Q4 0–0	18 B–R3 R–K1	27 Q×NP Q–R3	White resigns.
10 N–B3 N×N			

MUCHAS GRACIAS, SEÑOR CAPABLANCA!

Black: V. Ragozin – Stockholm 1948, Interzonal Tournament

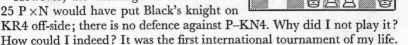

22W

The ex-world champion, José-Raoul Capablanca, has explained in his book in amazingly clear and simple terms the winning method when one has a material advantage: transpose to an endgame and then promote a passed pawn.

White succeeded in winning this difficult ending by using this key idea of the Cuban champion's.

However, the exchange 24 N–K5 N×N 25 P×N would have put Black's knight on KR4 off-side; there is no defence against P–KN4. Why did I not play it? How could I indeed? It was the first international tournament of my life.

Out of our whole delegation (Flohr, Boleslavsky, Ragozin, Kotov, Bondarevsky, Liliental and myself) only I had the 'ordinary master title'; all the rest were grandmasters of world renown. And for the youngest to suddenly start playing such reckless moves as the dashing P–KN4!...

1 P–K4 P–K4	19 N–B3 N–R4	35 N×N N×N	52 K–Q4 K–Q3
2 P–KB4 P–Q4	20 B–K3 Q–B2	36 R–K1 R×R+	53 N–B4+ K–B2
3 KP×P P×P	21 Q–Q1 Q–R4	37 N×R K–B1	54 K–B5 B–Q2
4 N–KB3 N–KB3	22 B–Q2 Q–R2	38 K–B2 K–K2	55 N–Q6 P–R5
5 B–N5+ QN–Q2	23 P–B5 P–N3	39 K–K3 K–Q3	56 B–K2 P–B4
6 0–0 N×P	(22)	40 P–QN4 N–R3	57 P–N3 P×P
7 P–B4 N–B3	24 B–N5 B×B	41 B–K2 N–B2	58 P×P N–B1
8 P–Q4 B–K2	25 N×B N/4–B3	42 N–B3 N–Q4+	59 N×N B×N
9 B×P 0–0	26 R×R+ R×R	43 K–Q4 N–B5	60 B–B3 B–N2
10 B–R4 N–N3	27 Q×P Q×Q	44 B–B1 P–B3	61 P–R5 P–N4
11 B–QN3 B–KN5	28 N×Q P×P	45 N–Q2 N–K3+	62 B–N2 P–B5
12 N–B3 P–B3	29 P×P R–K7	46 K–B3 N–B2	63 P×P P×P
13 Q–Q2 P–QR4	30 B–B4 R–QB7	47 N–B4+ K–K2	64 B–B3 B–R3
14 P–QR3 P–R5	31 B–N3 R–K7	48 N–N6 N–N4+	65 B×P B–K7
15 B–R2 QN–Q2	32 N–KB3 N–K5	49 K–N2 B–B4	66 P–N5 P–B6
16 QR–K1 R–K1	33 B–Q1 R–K6	50 P–QR4 N–R2	67 P–R6
17 N–KN5 B–R4	34 K–N1 N/2×P	51 K–B3 P–R4	Black resigns.
18 K–R1 B–N3			

THE BLUE BIRD

White: B. Spassky – Leningrad 1960, USSR Championship

23W

It was the devil who prompted me to reply 1 ... P–K4??.

The fact that Spassky, like Spielmann in the last century, very much likes to play the King's Gambit had gone completely out of my head.

And when it was too late to take my first move back, I remembered that about 100 years ago Anderssen, playing Neumann, had tried to construct a defence around ... B–Q3 and ... N–K2. This idea appealed to me, but I overdid things and spent a pointless tempo on the mysterious ... P–KR3.

Spassky's strong reply, 9 N–K4 (this is why Black's knight should be on KB3), immediately gave White a decisive advantage.

There was nothing to be done, but with 14 ... P–K7 Black set White the tricky question: 15 R–B2 or 15 N–Q6? I had no doubt at all that the clear 15 R–B2 would follow, since the more elegant choice, 15 N–Q6, allowed the Black king in certain variations to escape the impending troubles.

When Spassky still in fact plunged into the whirlpool of complications I committed my final error: I trusted, in spite of my preliminary calculations, that my opponent had found a clear-cut mating finish after 15 ... B×N 16 Q–R7+ K–B1 17 P×B P×R=Q+ 18 R×Q P×P 19 Q–R8+ K–K2 20 R–K1+ N–K4 21 Q×NP, and I avoided it in favour of something worse, which I still regret today.

However, to everyone his due. The blue bird soaring in the clouds, that is, the beauty prize, was won in this way by the future world champion.

1 P–K4 P–K4	8 0–0 P–KR3	15 N–Q6 N–B1	19 Q–B4 B–B3
2 P–KB4 P×P	9 N–K4 N×P	16 N×BP	20 N/3–K5 Q–K2
3 N–KB3 P–Q4	10 P–B4 N–K6	16...P×R=Q+	21 B–N3 B×N
4 P×P B–Q3	11 B×N P×B	(*23*)	22 N×B+ K–R2
5 N–B3 N–K2	12 P–B5 B–K2	17 R×Q B–B4	23 Q–K4+
6 P–Q4 0–0	13 B–B2 R–K1	18 Q×B Q–Q2	Black resigns.
7 B–Q3 N–Q2	14 Q–Q3 P–K7		

A THIRST FOR ADVENTURE

Black: R. Gorenstein – Kiev 1940, Championship of the Palace of Pioneers

24B

If your library is crammed with weighty tournament bulletins and if millions of chess combinations are preserved in these yellowing volumes, then, willingly or unwillingly, your heart too cannot remain indifferent to them; you too are afflicted with an unquenchable thirst for exploration and chess adventures.

In the year when this game was played I had neither any yellowing volumes nor any tournament bulletins, but I was already striving whole-heartedly for complicated, unknown positions, even, one might say, for positions where one might hear the harsh 'Checkmate!' at any move.

I liked to experience the sensation of impending chess death and ... then find a hidden path to salvation.

Of course, in my more mature years I would have been wary of playing 3 N–QB3, since by the energetic advance of his QP, Black could have seized the key white Q3 square.

Here is a commendable model of possible play: 3 ... P–Q5 4 QN–K2 P–Q6 5 P×P N–QB3 6 N–KB3 N–N5 7 N×P Q×P 8 N×Q N×N mate!

Swift, simple and beautiful.

You do not believe me?

And yet I am always afraid of precisely such improbable variations.

Chess is infinite, and one has to make only one ill-considered move, and one's opponent's wildest dreams will become reality.

1 P–K4 P–K4	5 BP×P N–N5	9 B–QB4 B–K2	12 ... Q×P+
2 P–KB4 P–Q4	6 N×P N×KP	10 N/3–N5 0–0	13 Q×Q N×Q
3 N–QB3 N–KB3	7 P–Q4 N/4–B3	11 0–0 N–B3	14 P–B3 N–B7
4 P–Q3 QP×P	8 N–KB3 N–Q2	12 N×BP (*24*)	15 R–N1 N×N

Draw because of 16 N–R6+ K–R1 17 R×R+ B×R 18 N–B7+ etc.

CHESS-PLAYERS OF A COMPETITIVE DISPOSITION

Black: A. Bykhovsky – Tallinn 1966, USSR Championship

The national championship of 1966 was neither an eliminator nor a trial – a good tournament for all those who missed normal chess competitions.

But whilst in a normal tournament each participant has free rest time, in Tallinn I had practically none: very often heated discussions about chess developed amongst the players, and the leaders of these discussions were generally the international master Bykhovsky and myself.

And whatever the subject was – the insatiable chase after points, the unceremonious copying of old masters' combinations, the crippling amount of chess material of various kinds – every time, Bykhovsky, after exhausting all other arguments, would angrily say:

'But look here! Now you, David Ionovich, are a player of a creative disposition, whilst I am a player of a competitive disposition. My disposition gives me different aims from yours. Can we not each have our own views?'

And I would invariably reply:

'You can have what views you like, but there is no such thing as a competitive player – that's plain fiction. There are simply strong, medium and weak players, as well as knowledgeable amateurs, but "competitive" players do not exist.'

And then after this prelude our turn came to resolve our dispute in deeds, not in words.

It was clear to me that if I failed in the opening stages to draw my opponent onto the untrodden path of the chess combination, I could say farewell to any dream of winning: Bykhovsky is in his element and as firm as a rock in well studied schemas.

After a long search I arrested my attention on the move 3 N–QB3, for the reasons that follow.

Whilst studying my opponent's games, I came to the conclusion that his favourite move as White was P–Q4, and as Black . . . P–Q4, too. What if I were not to allow him this move?

Certainly Black could still have gone 3 . . . P–Q4, but this would have been a pawn sacrifice and Bykhovsky will not sacrifice unless there is an arithmetically clear variation.

If it was that simple, why was it that I got no sleep for two days? Alas, my opponent on his own would not think of sacrificing, but what if he were suddenly to come across this idea in an openings book?

As a result I spent a lot of time and mental energy trying to find winning chances in the sharp variation 3 N–QB3 P–Q4 4 N×P Q–R5+ 5 K–K2 B–KN5+ 6 N–KB3 N–QB3 7 N×QBP+ K–Q1. It would be senseless to take the rook now because of 8 ... N–K4! (9 P–Q4? N×N 10 P×N B×P+ 11 K×B Q–R4+ 12 K–B2 Q×Q). I studied the cunning manoeuvre 8 N–Q5! N–K4! 9 N–B3 for a long time, but here as well things are not too pleasant for White. He could, of course, force a draw: 8 N×R N–K4 9 P–KR3 B×N+ 10 P×B Q–N6 11 P–Q3 Q×BP+ 12 K–Q2 Q–K6+ 13 K–B3 Q–B4+ 14 K–Q2 Q–K6+ etc., but this would be equivalent to capitulation. All the more so since my sober-minded opponent would not be likely to test fate here in the variation 9 ... B–R4 10 P–Q4 N×N 11 P×N B×P+ 12 K×B Q–R4+ 13 K–N2 Q×Q 14 B–Q3 Q–R4 15 B×P with wild play.

There remained one glimmer of hope: that Bykhovsky himself would reject the check on KR5; but this straw was burnt by Simagin just before we took our seats for the game: 'What will he play here? He'll check on KR5, of course ...'

I should also tell the reader that at lunch-time, when the participants were gathering as usual in the restaurant for their meal, Bykhovsky came up to me and said:

'I've already studied the whole of the Evans Gambit!'

'That means he's been swotting up the King's Gambit,' I thought.

When the game was over and we were analysing it together my opponent had this to say to some masters around us who were criticizing him:

'Yes, I saw Q–R5+; of course I saw it. But the white king goes to K2, and what then, eh, what then?'

1 P–K4 P–K4	12 B–B4 N–Q2	23 P–B4 B–B1	34 N–K7+ K×R
2 P–KB4 P×P	13 KR–K1	24 B–Q2 R×R	35 N×R N–Q2
3 N–QB3 P–QB3	13 ... KR–K1	25 B×R K–B2	36 K–Q3 B–Q3
(25)	14 P–Q5 N–N3	26 B–R5 R–B3	37 P–KR3 K–N2
4 N–B3 P–Q4	15 P×P P×P	27 R–Q8 B–K2	38 B–B3+ K–B2
5 P–Q4 P×P	16 B–QR6 B–QB1	28 R–KR8 P–R4	39 K–K4 K–K3
6 N×P N–B3	17 B×B QR×B	29 R–R7+ K–K1	40 N–Q8+ K–K2
7 Q–K2 N×N	18 N–Q4 P–N3	30 R–R6 K–B2	41 N–N7 K–K3
8 Q×N+ Q–K2	19 P–B3 K– N2	31 N–R4 P–B4	42 N–Q8+ K–K2
9 Q×Q+ B×Q	20 K–B2 P–QR3	32 N×BP B–B1	43 K–Q5
10 B×P B–KB4	21 P–QN3 P–QB4	33 R–R7+ K–N1	Black resigns.
11 0–0–0 0–0	22 N–B3 P–B3		

THE GUEST FROM OVERSEAS

Black: V. Alatortsev – Moscow 1945, USSR Championship

It was reported not so long ago, either on the radio or in the newspapers, that in Mexico Carlos Torre had given a thirty board simultaneous display.

Torre. A familiar name. Is it really the same person?

Yes, the same Torre who at 20 had come to Moscow wearing a summer suit, without an overcoat or a hat, naively supposing that if the sun shines constantly in his native Mexico, the same will be true of the other end of the planet.

The story is told that when on that frosty January day of 1925 Muscovites saw this youth in his summer clothes step lightly out of the train, they themselves began to feel cold, although they were very well wrapped up.

That year the frosts were very hard, but Torre managed to thaw the Moscow cold and perform brilliantly in the tournament. He not only finished in an honourable position (5th), but he also beat the great Lasker in their personal encounter, whilst also producing a masterly draw against the world champion Capablanca from a seemingly hopeless position.

Why am I talking about Torre when my game was against Alatortsev? Because a long time before my counter with Alatortsev one of the chess journals published an interesting article by Torre in which the Mexican tried to salvage White's reputation in the impudent variation 5 K–K2 B–KN5+ 6 N–KB3 N–QB3 7 N×QBP+ K–Q1 8 N×R N–K4. It seemed to him that after 9 Q–K1 N×N 10 Q×Q N×Q+ 11 K–K1 White's pawn phalanx promised him quite a good attack, in addition to which his knight on QR8 was still alive! I, to be honest, would prefer to play Black's position – but what do the readers think about this?

Alatortsev, true to his style, was unwilling to enter blindly into a maze of intricate variations and found a simple way of refuting White's opening strategy. Though it was only after White had voluntarily reverted to rigid defence (perhaps the extra pawn would tell!) and had refused a draw on move 14 by rejecting the manoeuvre Q–Q2–K1–Q2 etc.

But the white king's life hung on a thread. All depended on the staunchness of his bishop on Q2. There was a moment when, with the graceful move 23 ... B–N6, Black could have forced an immediate capitulation: 24 Q–K3 B–B5 25 Q×B Q×B, and there is no good defence to the threats of ... R×B or ... N–Q6+. Or 25 Q–B5 Q×B 26 B×B Q×R(B1) 27 Q×R+ R×Q 28 R×Q N–Q6+.

Alatortsev played the weak: 23 ... B–N3 24 KR–K1 Q–B7? (it was still not too late to play 24 . . . B–B7 25 R–KB1 B–N6!) and dissipated all his advantage.

The logical conclusion to the battle would have been a draw after 27 R–R1! B×P 28 K–B2, but here White erred and Black again had a won position – the passed KRP was extremely dangerous. In answer to 29 B–K3 Black should have exchanged off all four rooks and promoted his passed pawn, but he chose the mysterious move 29 . . . N–B3.

How can one explain the abundance of mistakes by White and Black? Time-trouble, of course. And what time-trouble: we had spent two hours each on moves 5–15! We had thirty minutes each for the remaining moves, but we found use for those on moves 16–21. Which left us pitifully little time for the rest of the moves up to 40.

Players of the older generation know that Alatortsev had a firmly established reputation as the king of time-trouble. Twenty moves in two minutes was child's play to him; but nineteen moves in as many seconds was beyond even him.

If, however, Black had had time to make just one or two more moves who could have guaranteed that White's flag would not have fallen first? I had no time to spare myself. If I had had as much as a minute on my clock I would not have chosen 29 B–K3?, but 29 P–KB4 N–N5 30 B×N P×B 31 R–KN1 R–Q6 32 P–B5 P–N4 33 R–N2 B–B5 34 B×B R×R 35 R×P with a draw.

1 P–K4 P–K4	9 P–B3 B×N+	18 B–N5+ K–K2	26 P×Q B–B7
2 P–KB4 P–Q4	10 P×B P–QB4	19 KR–KB1	27 R–B1 B×P
3 N–QB3 KP×P	11 P×P B×P	19 . . . Q–N7	28 K–B2 P–KR4
4 N×P Q–R5+	12 Q–K1 Q–N4	20 QR–K1 R–Q3	29 B–K3 N–B3
(26)	13 Q–Q2 Q–R5	21 K–B1 B–B7	30 B–B5 P–R5
5 K–K2 B–Q3	14 Q×P Q–B7+	22 R–Q1 KR–Q1	31 P–KB4 P–R6
6 P–Q4 N–KB3	15 K–Q1 N–B3	23 B–K2 B–N3	32 R–B3 B×P
7 N–KB3 B–KN5	16 B–Q2 R–Q1	24 KR–K1 Q–B7	33 R×B
N8 ×N+ P×N	17 K–B2 N–K4	25 Q–N3 Q×Q	

Here Black's flag fell. Whom has that not happened to?

THE QP'S VOYAGE

Black: M. Kamyshov – Moscow 1947, Moscow Championship

We have all got used to the fact that in a King's Gambit White begins a sharp attack on the king right in the opening, but situations do arise in practice where White's pieces are well placed for an attack on the Q-side. What should one do then?

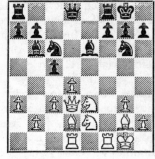

If one was to follow the normal pattern one would try, come what may, to build up a violent mating attack; but the question is whether one should be self-willed about it, or whether one should take the requirements of the position into account.

Logic tells us that we should submit to the desires of the chess pieces.

If the reader looks at the diagram he will see that most of White's pieces are directed towards an attack in the centre and on the queen's wing. The methodical siege of the strong points on the Q-side gradually led to the creating of a defended passed pawn, which, forcing its way forward, broke through on to the seventh and penultimate rank and in the final account forced Black's capitulation.

Thus it was White's pawn on Q4 which headed all White's attacks. And who was his helper? Principally the light-squared bishop.

1 P–K4 P–K4	15 B–Q2 B–K3	28 K–R1 R–K1	43 Q×N/K4 Q–Q2
2 P–KB4 P–Q4	16 P–QR3 B–B2	29 P–N5 P–QR3	44 Q×P P–N4
3 KP×P P–K5	17 QR–Q1 B–N3	30 P–QR4 P×P	45 B–K5 N–K7
4 P–Q3 N–KB3	(27)	31 RP×P R–R7	46 Q–Q5 Q–B4
5 N–Q2 P–K6	18 P–Q5	32 N/2–B3 R–R6	47 Q–K4 Q–B7
6 N–B4 N×P	18 . . . N/B3–K4	33 R–R1 R×R	48 Q–N1 Q–K6
7 N×P N×P	19 Q–B2 B–Q2	34 R×R N–Q5	49 B–Q6 Q–Q5
8 P–B3 B–Q3	20 P–B4 N–N5	35 R–KB1 P–R3	50 B–Q5 N–B6
9 P–KN3 N–N3	21 N–B5 N–K2	36 N–Q5 B–Q1	51 Q–N6+ K–R1
10 B–N2 0–0	22 N–Q6 Q–N1	37 N–B7 B×N	52 Q×RP+ K–N1
11 N–K2 N–B3	23 N–K4 N–B4	38 P×B B–B4	53 Q×P+ K–R2
12 P–Q4	24 B–B4 Q–B1	39 P–N6 Q–K3	54 Q–R5+ K–N2
12 . . . N/B3–K2	25 Q–Q3 B–B2	40 P–R3 N–B3	55 Q×P+ K–R3
13 Q–Q3 P–QB4	26 P–Q6 B–Q1	41 R–K1 B×N	56 B–B4+
14 0–0 N–B3	27 P–N4 B–N3	42 R×B N×R	Black resigns.

EXCITEMENT BEHIND THE SCENES

Black: L. Szabo – Moscow 1949, Moscow v. Budapest

28B

Chess spectators are often heard declaring delightedly 'Oh, if only I could play so calmly, I too would be a grandmaster'.

Such a view is flattering to the vanity of the masters, but alas, it is based on illusions. Firstly, tournament participants play far from calmly; they all get nervous, only they have learnt to hide their true feelings.

Secondly, in order to be less nervous at the board, they all try to play the longest variations, ones they have studied well at home.

Thirdly (and here we come to the most important point), they have all been very anxious at home, whilst preparing for the game.

All's well that ends well. Szabo made a mistake on his 5th move and got into a lost position. In my home preparation I had feared the sharp variation 5...B–KN5 6N–KB3 B×N 7 P×B P–K6: White has an extra pawn, but Black an attack. After missing this chance Black could no longer manage to equalize. In the endgame the weakness of Black's KBP and KRP allowed White to infiltrate on the 7th rank.

1 P–K4 P–K4	12 B×P R–N1	24 K×R N–K1	35 K–B2 R–Q1
2 P–KB4 P–Q4	13 R–K1+ K–Q2	25 R–K1 N–Q3	36 N–B3+ K–R4
3 KP×P P–K5	14 R–Q1 K–B3	26 R–K7 N–KB1	37 N–Q4 K–N3
4 P–Q3 N–KB3	15 B–Q4 N×P	27 B–K5 N–N3	38 N–K6 R–Q8
5 Q–K2 (*28*)	16 N–B3 N–Q2	28 B×N N×R	39 N×P R–QB8
5...Q×P	17 P–KN3 N–K3	29 B×N K–Q4	40 K–B3 R×P
6 N–QB3 B–QN5	18 B–K3 P–N3	30 K–B3 K–K3	41 N–N5 P–QR3
7 B–Q2 B×N	19 K–N2 QR–K1	31 B–N4 R–Q1	42 N–B7 P–QR4
8 B×B B–N5	20 KR–B1 P–B4	32 K–K2 K–B3	43 P–QR4 R–B8
9 P×P B×Q	21 N–R4 N–N2	33 B–B3+ K–N4	44 N–Q5 R–B8+
10 P×Q B×B	22 B–Q4 R–K7+	34 P–KR3	45 K–N2
11 K×B N×P	23 R–B2 R×R+	34...R–K1+	Black resigns.

A QUEEN OFF-SIDE

Black: W. Unzicker – Moscow 1956, Alekhine Memorial Tournament

29B

White's venturesome 6 B–K3 contained no little element of risk, but only in the event of Black being tempted by the variation 6 B–K3 Q–R5+ 7 P–KN3 N×P 8 P×N Q×R. It is easy to see that the queen in the corner would be 'off-side' for a time.

In one international tournament (Havana 1963) the Yugoslav grandmaster Trifunovic accepted the sacrifice and after 9 Q–K2 B–Q3 10 B–Q4+ played his king to Q1 and went on to win the game, although the initiator of the attack was Tal himself.

The chess sage Spassky, in a tournament in Belgrade (1964), solved the problem of the rook sacrifice and in a rather brilliant way: rejecting 8 P×N?, he preferred the solid development of the KN – 8 N–KB3!. The forced endgame that followed – 8 . . . Q–K2 9 P×N Q×B+ 10 Q–K2 Q×Q+ 11 B×Q was not in itself dangerous for Black, but the sudden switch from opening to ending sent his opponent Matanovic off balance and he lost his bearings.

Unzicker's style of play is severely classical. Defending accurately, he was able to construct an insurmountable bunker on K4. It is possible that if I had risked weakening my pawn structure by 16 P–KR3 (16 . . . N–R3 17 P–N4! or 16 . . . N–B3 17 Q–R4!) I would have had a more lasting attack, but even I do not like taking risks twice in the last round. The draw guaranteed me fifth prize.

1 P–K4 P–K4	8 B–B4 N–Q2	16 N–K2 B–Q3	24 N×N N×N
2 P–KB4 P–Q4	9 0–0 R–K1	17 N–N3 B–N3	25 B–R4 R–Q1
3 KP×P P–K5	10 R–K1 N/5–B3	18 N–K4 N–K4	26 R–K1 P–KB3
4 P–Q3 N–KB3	11 K–R1 N–N5	19 N–R4 B×N	27 P–B3 P–QR3
5 P×P N×KP	12 B–N1 N–N3	20 Q×B P–N3	28 P–KN4 P–QN4
6 B–K3 (29)	13 B–N3 B×P	21 B–Q4 N/3–Q2	29 B–N3 R–K1
6 . . . B–Q3	14 N–B3 R×R	22 R–KB1 Q–K2	Draw agreed.
7 N–KB3 0–0	15 Q×R B–B4	23 N–B3 R–K1	

HYPERMODERN CHESS

Black: M. Tal – Riga 1968, USSR Team Championship

It was under such a garish title that the brilliant work of the world's best journalist, grandmaster S. Tartakover, came out more than forty years ago.

You can find in the book's four parts information about literally anything in the world. And, not least of all, the sharpest of opening variations.

When I was accepting the congratulations of my colleagues on my convincing victory over Tal himself, I did not have the courage to confess my straightforward plagiarism. I shall now hasten to expiate my guilt: you will find all the most important moves of our game, right up to and including 12 B–R3!!, in Tartakover's book.

After 21 N–Q4 it is obvious that Black could no longer save himself; but after 20 . . . B×N 21 B×B KR–Q1 22 P–B5 QR–B1 23 P–N3 the pressure exerted by White's bishops would be extremely unpleasant.

But I, too, am not free of reproach: the simple 24 R–K1 would have won immediately: 24 . . . N–B3 25 N×BP (suggested by Tal); I saw only 25 N–N5, which for some reason did not seem much to me. To be honest, I must reveal a secret here: in my preliminary calculations I mistakenly supposed that 26 R–B7 was check and mate together, and overlooked . . . K–N3.

1 P–K4 P–K4	13 0–0–0 B–K5	23 R–N1 B–K5	34 B×R P×B+
2 P–KB4 P–Q4	14 N–N5 B×QP	24 N–B7 R–Q1	35 K×P R×P
3 KP×P P–K5	(30)	25 R×P+ K–B3	36 R×QRP R–B7
4 P–Q3 N–KB3	15 P–KN3 B×R	26 R–B7+ K–N3	37 R–R4 K–N3
5 P×P N×KP	16 P×N P–QB4	27 R–K7 N–B3	38 R–Q4 P–R4
6 N–KB3 B–QB4	17 B–B4 B–B3	28 N–K6 R–QB1	39 P–R4 P–R5
7 Q–K2 B–B4	18 N×BP P–QN4	29 P–N3 R–R4	40 P–R5 B–N7
8 N–B3 Q–K2	19 N–Q6+ K–K2	30 N–N5 B–Q4	41 P–R6 N–R4
9 B–K3 N×N	20 N×P KR–KB1	31 B–Q3+ K–R3	42 B–N7 N×P
10 B×B N×Q	21 N–Q4 B–N7	32 B–N2 P–B5	43 R×N
11 B×Q N×P	22 N–K6 R–B4	33 B–B5 P–B6	Black resigns.
12 B–R3 N–Q2			

THE HEEDLESS WHITE PAWNS

Black: V. Panov – Moscow 1947, Moscow Championship

The position in the diagram shows the triumph of the heedless white pawns. Having thought a little about it, the black king gave in.

However, this success of the pawns can equally well be celebrated by the other white pieces, whose role in preparing the decisive onslaught was extremely great, if not as noticeable.

In the very opening phase of the game Panov wisely estimated that the sober 4 ... B–KN5 would be 'like a cold shower on this young head', and so simply did not wish to test his strength in the theoretical variation 4 ... P–B4 5 BP×P QP×P 6 P–Q4 KP×P 7 B–QB4 BP×P 8 N–K5 N–KB3 9 N–B7 Q–K2 10 N×R P–Q6, where Black sacrifices a rook, but in exchange gets a dangerous attack.

Had I found a refutation of Black's idea? Yes and No. In my opinion, one should play, not 7 B–QB4?, but simply 7 BP×P!, but this would not be so much refuting, as declining.

In the following stage of the game the reader will undoubtedly discover White's strange move 13 P–N5, when he had the opportunity of opening the QN-file for an attack.

But it seemed to me then (I am not so convinced about it today) that, since one swallow does not make a summer, it would be better to delay the attack a little and first gather together a compact striking force of pawns . . .

I succeeded in putting my plan into action, and in realizing my conception. And even if the pawns were heedless, they were clever chaps all the same.

1 P–K4 P–K4	10 P–Q3 Q–K2	18 B×B Q×B	27 N×RP+
2 P–KB4 B–B4	11 0–0 0–0–0	19 K–R1 Q–K2	27 ... K–B2
3 N–KB3 P–Q3	12 P–QR4 P–QR4	20 QN–Q2 N–N5	28 N–B6 Q–K1
4 P–B3 B–KN5	13 P–N5 N–QN1	21 B–N1 P–R4	29 P–R5 N–Q2
5 P×P P×P	14 QN–Q2	22 N–B4 P–N4	30 P–N6+ K–N2
6 Q–R4+ B–Q2	14 ... B–KN5	23 N×B+ P×N	31 P–R6+ (*31*)
7 Q–B2 N–QB3	15 N–N3 P–QN3	24 N–Q2 P–B3	31 ... K×NP
8 P–QN4 B–Q3	16 B–K3 N/1–Q2	25 N–B4 K–N2	32 R–QN1+
9 B–B4 N–B3	17 QR–K1 B–K3	26 B×P N×B	Black resigns.

ALEXANDER ALEKHINE'S SCHOOL-FELLOW

Black: O. Bernstein – Paris 1954, USSR v. France

It would be as naive to study the song of the nightingale, as it would be ridiculous to try and win a King's Gambit against a representative of the old chess guard. But after an exhausting flight from Buenos Aires via Rio de Janeiro and Dacca to Paris, my thoughts were far from wins, losses and draws.

Moreover, I was happy at managing at least once in my life to play my fellow countryman who has almost the same name as myself, at being able to have even the most fleeting contact with a living chess legend and for a moment to transport myself into the world of my opponent's youth, when Steinitz and Lasker, Tarrasch and Chigorin, Capablanca and Alekhine reigned supreme.

My efforts did not go unrewarded: when the game was over, Osip Samoilovich, with a certain extraordinary pride, said, loudly, so that all could hear: 'It was the same second move, N–KB3, that I played against Chigorin! Do you know when? In 1903 at a tournament in Kiev. If I can count correctly, that was exactly half a century ago. Fifty years! And I can still play chess. What do you say to that?...'

1 P–K4 P–K4	14 P–QR3	27 P–QR4 R–Q2	40 K–Q3 B×BP
2 P–KB4 N–KB3	14 ... QR–K1	28 P–R5 P–B4	41 R–KB2 P–N4
3 P×P N×P	15 N–Q5 N–K2	29 P–B3 K–K3	42 B–Q2 K–N5
4 N–KB3 N–N4	16 N×N+ R×N	30 R–Q2 P×P	43 P×P B×B
(32)	17 B–B3 R/1–K1	31 P×P R–Q4	44 R×B K×P
5 P–Q4 N×N+	18 B–Q2 B–K5	32 R–K2 K–Q2	45 K–B4 P–N3
6 Q×N Q–R5+	19 KR–K1 P–KB4	33 P–QN4 R–N4	46 P–Q5 P×P
7 Q–B2 Q×Q+	20 P–KN3 B×B	34 R–QN2 B–K2	47 P×P R–N1
8 K×Q N–B3	21 R×R R×R	35 B–Q2 K–K3	48 P–Q6 K–B3
9 B–K3 P–Q3	22 K×B R–K5	36 K–K3 P–R4	49 K–Q5 R–KR1
10 P×P B×P	23 B–K3 B–K2	37 P–R4 B–Q3	50 K–B6 P–R5
11 N–B3 B–KB4	24 R–Q1 B–B3	38 B–K1 P–B5+	51 P–Q7
12 R–B1 P–QR3	25 R–Q3 K–B2	39 P×P K–B4	Black resigns.
13 B–K2 0–0	26 P–R3 R–K2		

5 The Vienna Game

The QN attack, 2 N–QB3 (*33*), is an opening for quiet chess players – not necessarily phlegmatic, but thoughtful. Such players wish to eliminate the weaknesses in their own camp before trying to assail their enemy's redoubts. They have seen that their KP has lost its mobility and is momentarily undefended – and they quickly strengthen it with their cavalry reserves. And only after preparation, and depending on the opponent's activities, will White decide which piece to send out on reconnaissance.

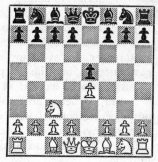

The solid 2 N–QB3 attack was a particular favourite with Viennese players, which is why it has come into theory under the name 'Vienna Game'. Numerous theoretical articles have been written about it, and in the excellent and cardinal work *Sovremenny Debyut*, which came out in 1940, there is a special chapter devoted to the Vienna Game.

Its predominant motifs are those common to all open games. Once again the QB4–KB7 diagonal, the sudden queen sortie to KR5, the inadequate defence of Black's KB2, have major roles to play. If Black manages to seize the initiative, then the situation is reversed: it is the weakness of White's KB2, the black queen's sally to KR5 and the dangerous Black QB4–KB7 diagonal.

I should like to warn those who are beginning a study of the Vienna Game against the move ... Q–B3 (1 P–K4 P–K4 2 N–QB3 N–QB3 3 B–B4 B–B4 4 Q–N4). There is no point in deliberately provoking White's N–Q5, since after 5 ... Q ×P+ 6 K–Q1 K–Q1 7 N–R3 Q–Q5 8 P–Q3 the black queen will find it extremely difficult to escape the tight clutches of the white pawns.

The main continuation of the Vienna Game is considered to be 2 N–QB3 N–KB3 3 P–B4 P–Q4 4 BP ×P N ×P and now 5 N–B3, 5 Q–B3 or 5 P–Q3.

WHITE'S WEAK KP

White: Yu. Lembersky – Kiev 1939, first category tournament

34W

Surely it is not possible that the strongest of White's pawns, that on K4, can be weak?

No, of course not. The pawn on K4 is not to blame for White's loss; it is principally the QN, which got itself pinned, that should be upbraided.

Anyone who likes pawn endings will not, I should think, miss the tiny combination 27 ... R × R by which Black forced a transposition into a won endgame.

However, even here things were not so simple! It would seem that the black king had no reason for chasing after White's KBP on B4; he had only to mark time, and, when White's supply of moves was exhausted, the QBP would fall of its own accord. But there was a trap hidden here!

In the variation 33 K–N4 K–Q5 34 P–QR4 K–Q4 35 K–R5 K × P 36 K–R6 K–N5 37 K × P K × P 38 K–N6, White would have quite real drawing chances, whilst after 37 ... P–B4 38 K–N6 P–B5 39 P–R5 P–B6 40 P–R6 the pawns would queen simultaneously!

The author requests strong players to miss out the previous paragraph, not to read it at all; I only included it for the very beginners. But they too probably can guess that after 40 ... P–B7 41 P–R7 P–B8 = Q 42 P–R8 = Q Black plays ... Q–B4 + and exchanges queens, and in the first variation he should run his king to K5: 37 K × P K × P 38 K–N6 K–N5 39 K × P K–B5 40 K–Q6 K–Q5 41 K–K6 K–K5!.

1 P–K4 P–K4	(34)	20 P–KB4 N–K5
2 N–QB3 B–B4	11 N × P P × N	21 KR–K1 P–KB4
3 N–B3 P–Q3	12 B × N B × B	22 P–KN4 P–N3
4 P–Q4 P × P	13 P–K5 N–N5	23 P × P P × P
5 N × P N–KB3	14 N–K4 B–B4	24 P–B4 QR–Q1
6 B–K2 0–0	15 N × P B × N	25 P–B5 N × BP
7 B–K3 QN–Q2	16 P × B N–K4	26 R–K7 R–B2
8 Q–Q2 P–B3	17 Q–B4 N × B	27 P–N4 R × R
9 0–0–0 B–QN5	18 Q × B Q–N4 +	28 P × R R × R +
10 B–B3 N–B4	19 Q × Q N × Q	29 K × R K–B2

30 P × N K × P
31 K–B2 K–K3
32 K–B3 K–Q4
33 K–N4 K–K5
34 K–R5 K × P
35 K–R6 K–K4
36 K × P P–B5
37 K–N6 P–B6
White resigns.

A QUIET BACKWATER

Black: L. Morgulis – Kiev 1940, Palace of Pioneers Championship

The Vienna Game does not enjoy the affection of the modern players of this minicentury.

By comparison with other quick-firing openings it appears to them to be some sort of quiet backwater, where you could try for a hundred years, but you would never arrive at a real combination.

I ask you to believe me, that this opinion is a deeply mistaken one.

The encounter on this page between two bosom-friends serves as a good illustration of the combinational possibilities of the Vienna Game. In those far-off days we were rarely allowed into serious adult tournaments and we would quench our chess thirst as best we could in endless numbers of friendly games, most of them three-minute games.

On the other hand, when it came to a tournament game, our course was obvious: there was no sounding out the opponent; it was straight into an attack on the king!

Lovers of positional play will no doubt direct their attention to the subtle 11 P–B3!, which allowed White to retain a hold for the time being on the important K4 square; whilst those who appreciate combinations will arrest their gaze on the surprising position after Black's 27th move, 27 . . . K–R1.

Both adversaries consciously aimed for this sharp position. White has a formidable attack, Black an extra rook. Moreover the tempting 28 B × P?? would have met the brilliant refutation 28 . . . B–Q6!!.

1 P–K4 P–K4	10 B–K3 N–K3	19 B–K3 N × QP
2 N–QB3 B–B4	11 P–KB3 P–Q4	20 P × P P × P
3 B–B4 N–KB3	12 B–N3 P–QR4	21 N–N3 P–N3
4 P–Q3 P–Q3	13 P–B3 P–QN3	22 B × QP N–B5
5 N–R4 QN–Q2	14 Q–K1 Q–B2	23 B × N P × B
6 N × B N × N	15 Q–B2 R–N1	24 N–K4 B × R
7 N–K2 P–B3	16 Q–R4 B–R3	25 N–N5 N–B3
8 0–0 0–0	17 QR–Q1 N–B4	26 Q–R6 Q–K4
9 B–KN5 P–KR3	18 B × RP N–K1	27 Q × P+ K–R1

(35)	
28 Q–R6+ K–N1	
29 B–K4 B–B5	
30 B–R7+ K–R1	
31 B–Q3+ K–N1	
32 B × B R–N2	
33 Q–N6+ K–R1	
34 B × P	
Black resigns.	

DREAM AND REALITY

White: A. Polyak – Moscow 1945, USSR Championship Semi-finals

The move 2 ... B–B4 could lead to a swift finale: 3 N–R4 B×P+ 4 K×B Q–R5+ 5 K–K3 Q–B5+ 6 K–Q3 P–Q4 7 K–B3 Q×KP 8 K–N3 N–QR3 9 P–QR3 Q×N+ 10 K×Q N–B4+ 11 K–N5 P–QR4 12 K×N N–K2 13 B–N5+ K–Q1 14 B–B6 P–QN3+ 15 K–N5 N×B 16 K×N B–N2+ 17 K–N5 B–R3+ 18 K–B6 B–N2+ 19 K–N5 etc., if Black did not have to play the perpetual check. Alas, this variation is but a sweet dream. For decades now no-one has wanted to play 3 N–QR4?.

It seems to me that this game contains all the reader might dream of finding: a tense opening (moves 1–14), painful jabs by both sides in the middle-game (moves 15–20) and manoeuvring by the major pieces on the threshold of the endgame (moves 21–25). Somewhere along the line there was the flitting episode of a bishop sacrifice, after which calm returned to the board.

1 P–K4 P–K4	18 P–R3 N×P	34 K–B4 R/4–K4	50 NP×P P×P
2 N–QB3 B–B4	19 B×P Q×B	35 R–K3 P–R4	51 R×P R–KR6
(36)	20 Q–N3+ K–R1	36 P–R4 R–R1	52 R–Q7 K–K4
3 N–B3 P–Q3	21 Q×N R–KN1	37 R/3–R3 R–R4	53 R–K7+ K–Q5
4 B–B4 N–QB3	22 P–KN3	38 P–B3 K–N2	54 R–K6 P–B5
5 N–QR4 B–N3	22 ... QR–K1	39 R–Q1 K–N3	55 R×P+ K×P
6 N×B RP×N	23 KR–K1 B–B2	40 R–Q5 R–R1	56 R–K6+ K–Q6
7 P–Q4 B–N5	24 Q–Q3 R–K4	41 R×R	57 R–Q6+ K–B6
8 P–KR3 B–R4	25 N–B3 R–R4	41 ... BP×R+	58 R–KR6 K–Q7
9 B–QN5 P×P	26 K–R2 B–K3	42 K–K3 K–N4	59 R–Q6+ K–B7
10 Q×P N–B3	27 N–N1 B×P	43 R–R1 R–R4	60 R–Q4 P–QB6
11 B–N5 0–0	28 N×B Q–N5	44 R–R3 K–B3	61 R×P K–Q7
12 B×QN P×B	29 K–N1 Q×N	45 P–B4 P–N4	62 K–N2 R–Q6
13 N–Q2 P–B4	30 Q–KB3	46 RP×P R×P	63 R–B2+ K–B8
14 Q–B3 N–Q4	30 ... Q–R7+	47 P–N3 R–N5	64 P–R5 P–B7
15 Q–KN3 P–KB3	31 K–B1 Q–R8+	48 R–R7	65 R–B7 K–Q7
16 B–R6 Q–K2	32 K–K2 Q×Q+	48 ... R×NP+	66 R–B2+ K–B6
17 0–0 N–N5	33 K×Q R–K1	49 K–B2 P–R5	White resigns.

OPTICAL ILLUSION

Black: A. Matanovic – Vienna 1957, European Team Championship

Black's 11th to 13th moves have one aim in view: to prevent White castling Q-side. But the white king ignored the threats and castled. Matanovic was extremely surprised. Of course, not by 14 0–0!, but by the optical illusion of which he had been a victim. The fact is that when the Yugoslav grandmaster thought up his plan of . . . B–N5, . . . B×N, . . . R–K1+, . . . Q–K2, the white bishop was on KB1 and K-side castling did not occur to him.

After Matanovic's 13 . . . Q–K2? I could not hide a little smile: I was reminded of the time when Boleslavsky made that very same mistake once in a game with me – he attacked a bishop of mine on K3 to prevent me, the idea was, from castling; but my king gave the order to castle, and then it became clear that Black's threat was illusory. Moreover, both then as now no serious battle ensued: both games came peacefully to a draw. Still, it was an amusing slip. Why not 14 . . . Q×B? Because White would reply 15 QR–K1 or 15 KR–K1 and Black would have to sacrifice his queen.

Books on theory claim that 4 P–Q3 was first used by Fenton in 1871 against Blackburne. Besides this, it is well known that Emanuel Lasker won the first brilliancy prize for his victory in the 27th round of the 1899 London tournament over the ex-world champion Steinitz, who also took the risk of playing 4 P–Q3. Nowadays there are practically no new moves left!

1 P–K4 P–K4	8 B×B Q×B	14 0–0! N–B3	19 R×R R×R+
2 N–QB3 N–KB3	9 Q–Q2 0–0	15 QR–K1	20 Q×R Q–K4
3 P–B4 P–Q4	10 N–B3 B–N5	15 . . . Q–B4+	21 Q–Q2 N–K2
4 P–Q3 KP×P	11 B–K2 B×N	16 K–R1 R–K2	22 B–B3 P–QN3
5 P×P N×P	12 B×B R–K1+!	17 P–B3 QR–K1	23 P–KN3
6 N×N Q×N	13 B–K2 Q–K2?	18 B–Q1 R×R	Draw agreed.
7 B×P B–Q3	(37)		

THE KING IN PLAY

Black: M. Tal – Amsterdam 1964, Interzonal Tournament

38W

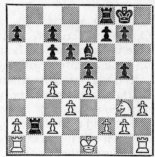

Since both Tal and I suffer from the habit of losing in the first round, neither of us was against starting the tournament with a half-point. A half-point from which we would build success.

To openly play for a draw would have been shameful for us both, but at the same time it is frightening taking risks. Therefore Tal avoided the main continuation 2 ... N–KB3, and I did not risk playing 3 P–B4.

The game took on a quiet character, rather unusual both for the Vienna Game and for the creative tastes of the players. Exchange followed exchange, but neither of us could bring himself to begin peace negotiations first. At a certain moment the pieces too became bored with being so passive. Having gained control of the open QN-file, the white rook set its sights on QN7; but at that very second the black king took the decision by itself to move closer to that square, and in so doing saved the wealth of Black's Q-side pawns from destruction.

But if I meet Tal again in the first round of an Interzonal, I shall ignore all my fears and play 3 P–B4!.

And I also advise you strongly to try your strength in the variation 3 P–B4 P×P 4 N–B3 P–KN4 5 B–B4 P–N5 6 0–0 P×N 7 P–Q4 with terrific complications. Whom to choose, Black or White? It does not matter: one can attack passively or defend aggressively, according to one's nature.

1 P–K4 P–K4	10 B–N5 Q–N4	17 N–K2 K–B1	24 N×R R–R1
2 N–QB3 N–QB3	11 N–N3 0–0	18 P–KB3 K–K2	25 N–B3 P–KB4
3 B–B4 N–B3	12 B×N P×B	19 N–B3 R–KR1	26 N–Q1 K–Q2
4 P–Q3 B–N5	13 P–QB4 QR–N1	20 KR–QN1	27 N–K3 P–B5
5 B–KN5 P–KR3	14 Q×Q P×Q	20 ... R–N3	28 N–Q1 P–B4
6 B×N B×N+	15 P–KR3 R–N7	21 R–N3 P–N3	29 N–B3 P–B3
7 P×B Q×B	(38)	22 R–R3 R–N2	30 R–N3 K–B2
8 N–K2 P–Q3	16 K–Q2 R1–N1	23 R–QN1 R×R	Draw agreed.
9 Q–Q2 B–K3			

SENSELESS CASTLING

Black: R. Teschner – Hamburg 1965, European Team Championship

39B

Is castling a good thing or a bad thing? Opinions differ. Let us listen to the long-time world champion, Emanuel Lasker. In his book *My Match with Capablanca* he said:

'I could see chess gradually losing the charm of risk and obscurity, I could see its mysteriousness being reduced to certainty, and I could see it becoming mechanised to the point of being an exercise of the memory. I deplored the impetuous pace of this process; it seemed to me unnecessarily rapid. I did not follow this path, only I could see that in the final account it was inevitable, just as death is inevitable. . . .

. . . The present development of chess does not favour the free flight of the imagination; the latter is not rewarded, but disappointed, since in the end what imagination produces serves no purpose. Of course, one can play better than one's opponent, but that is still not sufficient to win. The logical outcome of a game is often a draw, in spite of the fact that one of the players clearly outplayed the other. The advantage built up during the game is frequently too insignificant and subtle and, measured against the scoring system, is sifted and lost, like fine sand through a coarse sieve. A small advantage is insufficient to ward off the possibility of stalemate, and consequently it becomes difficult to make the game the slightest bit interesting.

The cause of this evil lies not in any weakness amongst the contemporary exponents of the game (on the contrary, it lies rather in their strength), nor in the rules of the ancient game, but in the radical reform that was carried out in the 16th century. Owing to the introduction of castling, attacks on the king became extremely difficult; in this way a major, perhaps even the most characteristic, aspect of the chess combination disappears. Further, such ancient variations as stalemate and an exposed king ought not simply to have been put on the same level as a draw. If one wishes to give games their correct value, it becomes essential to invent a scoring system which can reflect the various gradations in our evaluation of a game. The threefold assessment used at the present time – the win, the draw and the loss – is too limited. For nature's scale has an infinite number of gradations, nature makes no leaps – and we should try to take nature as our model. . . .

. . . We can get closer to this by using the method that I published four years ago: checkmate would give 10 points, stalemate 8, an exposed king 6, a draw 5, having one's king exposed 4, being stalemated 2, being checkmated 0.

A scale such as this one in no way impoverishes the game, and in many respects introduces variety into it. Anyone trying under the present rules for stalemate will still want to achieve this under the new ones, since it is still better at the moment to be stalemated than checkmated. Thus combinations that apply now will not be excluded; on the contrary, new ones will appear: first, combinations where subtle play may lead to stalemate or to preventing it, and secondly, combinations in which one exposes the opponent's king or one's own king is exposed.

. . . I do not imagine, of course, that the majority of young masters will immediately approve of my proposal. I am happy that their time has also come. For they, too, some time will come to regard as a hindrance the poverty of a scoring system which only recognizes checkmate and a draw, and which is not in a position to reward small, subtle advantages and thereby ascribe some value to the work of the imagination. . . .'

Today we know that the wise doctor was greatly dulling the colours and painting the future of chess in too sombre shades. But we all also see the ever increasing danger of the draw, so that is it not time to discuss seriously Lasker's proposals for broadening the scale for evaluating a game?

But we can leave aside for the time being the question of castling, although Teschner would probably be of rather a different opinion. . . . If he had not been able to play 17 . . . 0–0–0?? he would not under any circumstances have lost so swiftly. Lasker, then, was wrong here: the king felt perfectly comfortable in the centre and it was senseless Q-side castling which caused its downfall!

Who knows, perhaps it was not just castling that was guilty; perhaps Black should just have castled in the other direction.

1 P–K4 P–K4	8 P–QR3 B–R4	14 P–B4 N–K3	19 P × P P × P
2 N–QB3 N–KB3	9 P–QN4 B–B2	15 B–K3 P × BP	20 Q–R6 + K–N1
3 P–KN3 B–N5	10 P–Q4 Q–K2	16 N × P N–N4	21 R–N1 + B–N3
4 B–N2 P–Q3	11 Q–Q3 P–KR4	17 QR–K1 (39)	22 R × B + P × R
5 KN–K2 P–B3	12 P–R3 P–R5	17 . . . 0–0–0	23 Q × P +
6 0–0 QN–Q2	13 P–N4 B–Q2	18 P–N5 N × NP	Black resigns.
7 P–Q3 N–B1			

6 The Latvian Gambit

THE BIRTH OF AN INNOVATION

Black: V. Mikenas – Rostov 1941, USSR Championship Semi-finals

Not every chess-player likes a defensive game; one can even assume that the majority do not like to defend at all, but are keen to attack everywhere and at any time, without even taking into account the existing facts and circumstances. A good example of this is the ancient Greco Gambit, or, as it is called today, the Latvian Gambit.

In reply to White's KN attack, 2 N–KB3, Black replies with the gambit move . . . P–KB4 and offers White the choice of either pawn. Usually White will capture the KP, 3 N×P, attracted by the chance of clearing the queen's route to KR5!

Despite the negative pronouncements of theory, there still exist bold spirits wishing to revive this risky opening. I do not belong to their number. For training purposes it is often useful to play the odd game this way but, after studying Black's main difficulties, it would be more worthwhile switching one's attention and strength to other, more modern, methods of play.

People often ask: what is a theoretical innovation?

From a cursory look at this short game the main interest seems to consist of a series of effective sacrifices. If you look at it more deeply, this is not the case at all. The value of the game is contained in just one move, and that move is 6 B–K2. For the reason that this is in fact a theoretical innovation. An innovation which refutes, not one random variation, but a whole web of variations united by a common idea.

One could relate the history of this idea in a simplified form.

– What is the point of the opening?
– To attack down the KB-file.
– Which piece plays the main role in the attack?
– Black's queen.
– Which square does the queen usually go to?
– To KN3, to exert pressure on White's KN2.
– Does White have any means of preventing Black's queen getting to KN3?
– Yes, by checking with his queen on KR5.
– But after . . . P–KN3 by Black the queen will have to go away. What then?

– Then the Black queen won't be able to use its KN3. On the other hand the white queen will be well placed on K2.

Let us check it in our heads: 6 Q–R5+ P–KN3 7 Q–K2 Q×QP 8 N–QB3 with good development.

We can put this away in our memory, and it will be useful, if we find nothing better.

– Has Black not created some weak points in his position by his attacking?

– Yes, he has. For example, by advancing his KBP he has weakened the K1–KR4 diagonal.

– Does this diagonal have any significance for us?

– For White no, but for Black yes. Because Black's main aim is to establish his queen on KN3, and until he has castled both his queen and his king must stand on that diagonal.

– Both stand on a weakened diagonal? Surely this is dangerous?

– It's difficult to say. It depends on what his opponent can do.

– His opponent . . . He could give check with his bishop from QB10, if such a square existed; but Black would have a defence in B–Q0.

– Or he could try his luck from some other non-existent square on that diagonal.

– Wait a minute! Isn't it possible to transform this dream into reality?

– Yes, it is! Yes it is! – And at this point the two interlocutors shouted with one voice: 'To do this, all we have to play is 6 B–K2 Q–N3 7 B–R5!'

. . . This is how, or roughly how, a theoretical innovation is born.

1 P–K4 P–K4	8 0–0 N×N	14 Q×P B×P	21 B×P P×B
2 N–KB3 P–KB4	9 B×N Q–N3	15 B–N5+ N–B3	22 N–N5+ (40)
3 N×P Q–B3	10 B–QN5+	16 QR–K1 P–B3	22 . . . P×N
4 P–Q4 P–Q3	10 . . . K–Q1	17 B×N+ Q×B	23 Q×NP R–K1
5 N–B4 P×P	11 B–KB4 P–KR4	18 Q–K2 Q–Q5+	24 R–K7+
6 B–K2 N–B3	12 P–KB3 B–B4	19 K–R1 B–N3	Black resigns.
7 P–Q5 N–K4	13 N–B3 P×P	20 R×B+ K–B2	

7 The Black QP Gambit

EXCLAMATION MARK

White: A. N. Other – Moscow-Kislovodsk Express, friendly game

41W

Readers generally do not like to hear truisms of the type: keep your pawns, do not sacrifice them for nothing!

And it would be especially strange to read a call for thriftiness on this page, when the author as early as the second move moved his QP into the fight, without worrying first about defending the more valuable pawn on K4.

It would be ridiculous to justify myself by saying that I had a weak opponent – a fellow traveller on the Moscow-Kislovodsk train. One should play well against any opponent. How else can weak players learn to play well themselves?

Any move which contributes in the first stage of the game, when both sides are developing, to the opening of lines for pieces could be given an exclamation mark.

From this point of view ... P–Q4 is simply excellent! Lines for the queen and both black bishops are immediately opened up.

Those who do not want to be the victim of their more widely-read acquaintance's book learning, those who believe in their own creative strength and have nothing against turning aside from well-trodden theoretical paths on the second move – these bold players should be allowed to use the double-edged gambit of the Black QP.

I hope that these cunning people have understood my suggestion properly: before playing it yourselves, it is essential that you try out alone the various most probable attacking lines for White, and supply yourself with an antidote beforehand. . . .

1 P–K4 P–K4	4 B–B4 Q–N4	8 K–K2 R×B	11 Q×B B–N5+
2 N–KB3 P–Q4	5 B×P+ K–K2	9 Q–B7+ K–Q3	12 K–K3 Q–K8
(41)	6 Q–R5 Q×NP	10 Q×R K×N	Mate!
3 N×P P×P	7 B×N Q×R+		

8 Philidor's Defence

42W

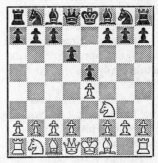

Rarely seen in modern tournaments, the defence 2 ... P–Q3 was founded in theory and introduced into practice by the famous musician and chess-player, the uncrowned world champion, André Danican François Philidor (1726–95).

In his manual, which appeared in 1749, he declared grandiosely: 'My principal intention is to offer the public something new. I have in mind pawn-play. Pawns are the soul of the game. They alone create attack and defence; the way they are deployed decides the fate of the game.'

The move 2 ... P–Q3 complies entirely with the ambitious aspirations of the black pawns. Apart from the pawn on K4, all the other seven still have the right to move, whilst six of them can even choose – to advance one square or two!

In his book Philidor gave a series of instructive variations. He was particularly attracted by the possibility of an audacious pawn attack by means of the bold ... P–KB4.

The inquisitive reader may wish independently to study the variations arising after 1 P–K4 P–K4 2 N–KB3 P–Q3 (*42*) 3 P–Q4 P–KB4. For the lovers of classical antiquity I can recommend the games, which are saturated with sharp combinations, of Paul Morphy, who gave a lot of consideration to ... P–Q3.

But my most sincere advice is not to believe the leading figures of chess but to try and bring this opening into your own personal tournament practice. Experience will tell you how you should go from there, but there can be no doubt that many of you will come to like Philidor's defence, perhaps for ever.

The latest tournaments have shown that interest in the Philidor Defence is reviving and it is possible that we shall yet live to see it flourish again.

ONE AND ONLY ONE

Black: R. Pyatnitsky – Kiev 1940, First Category Tournament

In contrast to athletics competitions where each participant has three attempts, in chess any piece, including the king, has the right to one, and only one attempt. . . .

You have guessed of course that I am referring to castling.

If one is taking a first look at the diagram, it is incomprehensible why the black king stubbornly refuses to take cover: 12 . . . 0–0!.

The fact is that our chess diagrams are far from complete. Not only are we not able to tell from them how many moves one piece or another has made, but on the whole we are unable to make out whether a piece has moved at all!

And here the black king has already moved twice.

It is quite probable that this book will fall into the hands of a complete beginner. For his sake I will reveal a little secret of mine. In almost every simultaneous display I give one game goes as follows: 3 P–Q4 B–N5 4 P×P B×N 5 Q×B P×P 6 B–QB4 N–KB3 7 Q–QN3 Q–K2 8 N–B3 etc., but, alas, I have never once managed to copy that famous masterpiece by Morphy: 8 . . . P–B3 9 B–KN5 P–N4 10 N×P P×N 11 B×NP+ QN–Q2 12 0–0–0 R–Q1 13 R×N R×R 14 R–Q1 Q–K3 15 B×R+ N×B 16 Q–N8+ N×Q 17 R–Q8 mate.

On the other hand games of the type 3 . . . P×P 4 Q×P N–QB3 (now will White suddenly overlook something?!) 5 B–QN5 B–Q2 6 B×N B×B 7 N–B3 N–B3 8 B–N5 B–K2 9 0–0 0–0 I have played hundreds of in displays.

And every time my attention is divided at this point: whether to play 10 KR–K1 or defend the bishop on KN5 by 10 P–KR4, to be on the safe side.

1 P–K4 P–K4	6 N–B4 P–Q4	11 Q–KR4+	13 P–KR4 N–Q2
2 N–KB3 P–Q3	7 B–KN5 B–K2	11 . . . K–K1	14 B–N5 Q–K2
3 P–Q4 N–KB3	8 B×B K×B	12 Q–KB4 (43)	15 0–0–0
4 P×P N×P	9 N–K3 B–K3	12 . . . N–K5	Black resigns.
5 QN–Q2 N–B4	10 Q–Q4 P–QN3		

THE SLEEPING BEAUTY ROOK

White: M. Bertok – Lvov 1962, USSR v Yugoslavia

In chess there are two players. Moves are made alternately – White, Black, White, Black, etc.

Sometimes, distracted by the familiar rhythm of 'I, you, I, you, I, you' both players play the opening stage of the game so quickly that they forget in their haste about the development of one or other sleeping piece.

The one that suffers most frequently in this respect is the handsome rook – at times a white one, at times a black one. Why? All the four rooks are positioned in the corners and are practically immovable during the first moves. Moreover, it is hard to free them so that they can engage in the hand-to-hand fighting which the pawns and minor pieces are involved in in the opening. And when the fighting is at its height . . . the rooks are forgotten.

Bertok did not forget about his rooks, but strove hard to clear all the ranks for them quickly, exchanging a large number of minor pieces in the process.

Such a single-minded strategy is worthy of praise in itself, but realising it required too much 'chess time', or, as the specialists say, too many tempi.

So one should find nothing strange in the fact that the open K-file prepared for the white rook was first used by Black's KR, whilst the freed QR1–KR1 rank was first penetrated by the black queen!

What the consequence was the reader can easily surmise from the position in the diagram.

To sum up: it is essential to castle, and that at all speed!

1 P–K4 P–K4	8 P×P B×P	15 Q–B1 Q–R5	22 R×P B–QB4+
2 N–KB3 P–Q3	9 KN–Q4 QN×N	16 Q–Q1 P–QB4	23 R–Q4
3 P–Q4 N–KB3	10 N×N 0–0	17 Q–R4 R–K5	23 . . . Q–QB8+
4 P×P N×P	11 B–QB4 Q–B3	18 P–B3 P×B	(44)
5 QN–Q2 N–B4	12 P–QB3 N×N	19 P×R Q–B5+	24 K–B2 Q×R
6 N–N3 N–K3	13 B×N R–K1+	20 K–N1 B–K3	White resigns.
7 B–K3 N–B3	14 K–B1 Q–B5	21 R–Q1 P–Q6	

9 Petroff's Defence

Petroff's Defence, or the Russian Game, is an extremely peace-loving opening.

By choosing a symmetrical move, Black is as much as saying: whatever you do, I'll follow you; I'm a meek and mild-tempered fellow.

If White responds to Black's peace initiative, then the moves flow like water off a duck's back – a dozen exchanges, and the clocks are stopped. Draw.

But White has only to show a touch of arrogance and obstinacy, and go in for an open fight, when Black immediately replies blow for blow, and then for a long time it is difficult to tell who is attacking and who is defending.

But that rarely happens.

More often White complies; one exchange, then another – and then the judge rushes to the table. . . .

The theory of Petroff's Defence has been well worked out. However, to point out a single best attacking system for White and the most reliable defensive plan for Black is not so much difficult, as impossible: everything depends on the minutest subtleties.

The most frequent move is 3 N ×P. In reply to 3 . . . P–Q3 the knight retreats to KB3, although no weaker, in the author's opinion, is the bold 4 N ×BP!. After 4 . . . K ×N 5 P–Q4 White has two mobile pawns in the centre, which promises him a lasting advantage. I once tried this move out in a simultaneous display. My opponent – it was during a tour of the cities of Holland – took the knight, and my KP as well: 4 N ×BP K ×N 5 P–Q4 N ×P. I then checked on KR5 (again that KR5 square!) and after 6 Q–R5 + K–K2 I retreated my queen to K2. Black found himself faced with insoluble problems, since his knight on K5 is attacked and his queen on Q1, too, because of the threat of B–KN5 +!

You must certainly try the knight sacrifice on KB7!

THE THEORY OF MINOR MISTAKES

White: P. Trifunovic – Leningrad 1957, USSR v Yugoslavia

46W

R. Fine expressed the view that a game would be lost in the last century after four mistakes, at the beginning of the present century after only two, and in the middle of the 50's only one mistake would be needed.

This inevitably suggests the conclusion that we are approaching the time when it will be possible to lose a game without making a single mistake!

The famous grandmaster-journalist S. G. Tartakover warned us, not against making mistakes in general, but against making the last mistake, as he was convinced that the person who makes the last mistake loses the game. I should like to develop his idea.

Avoid minor mistakes! Most often he loses who makes the first minor mistake, because it signifies the beginning of an incorrect strategical plan.

A quiet opening, an early exchange of queens, a leisurely . . . P–KN3 lulled Trifunovic's imagination to sleep and when he saw that the black-squared bishop wanted to occupy the great KR1–QR8 diagonal, instead of the usual K2 square, he thought: why should I castle K-side? And he castled Q-side.

Two more minor mistakes followed on this one. First the KRP advanced one square, to make room for the bishop on KB4, and then the white bishop took advantage of this haven.

Three minor mistakes probably equal one full mistake.

1 P–K4 P–K4	11 0–0–0 B–N2	20 P–Q4 P–QN4	28 . . . R–QB5+
2 N–KB3 N–KB3	12 P–KR3 N–N3	21 P–Q5 N–R2	29 K–N1 N–B1
3 N×P P–Q3	13 N–Q2 KN–Q4	22 N–N3 P–N5	30 R–K6 K–B2
4 N–KB3 N×P	14 N×N N×N	23 RP×P P×P	31 P–N4 N–K2
5 Q–K2 Q–K2	(46)	24 P×P KR–N1	32 P×P N×BP
6 P–Q3 N–KB3	15 B–R2 0–0	25 R–K4 B–R5	33 R–KB3
7 B–N5 QN–Q2	16 B–B3 N–N5	26 R–Q3 P–KB4	33 . . . R–QN1
8 N–B3 Q×Q+	17 P–R3 N–B3	27 R–K7 R×P	34 B–B2 R×B
9 B×Q P–KR3	18 P–B3 P–QR4	28 B–Q1	White resigns.
10 B–B4 P–KN3	19 KR–K1 B–Q2		

AND THE KNIGHT CAME TO LIFE!

Black: I. Zaslavsky – Kiev 1938, First Category Tournament

What is the most interesting thing for the curious reader?

A queen sacrifice!

Just when Black was certain that White's knight on K6 had fallen into a fatal pin, it turned out that all was not lost: the knight came to life and wreaked havoc in Black's camp.

Is 5 P×P playable? As you can see, it is. Any move connected with a definite plan of play, even for only one move ahead, is good. But this is an obvious truth as well-known to the reader as to the author.

If you are not too lazy to play this game through, on a board, you will come across the strange move 12 ... Q–Q2, when there was the chance of going 12 ... Q–Q4.

Perhaps Black had foreseen the manoeuvre 13 P–KR3 B–R4 14 P–KN4 B–N3 15 N–N3! and decided to take steps to defend his KB4?

My opponent of long ago has today given up serious play, but in previous years he was a very clever and tough opponent.

And as soon as I qualified for the third category, without delaying a second I challenged the second-category Zaslavsky to a six-game match, and he, contrary to the example of the present generation, agreed immediately.

This was probably my first successful match experience – 3–3 – and it sowed in me the poisonous seed of dislike for tournaments and of respect for the open duel of the equal match situation!

1 P–K4 P–K4	8 P×N B–KN5	15 KR–K1	20 N×R R×Q
2 N–KB3 N–KB3	9 B–K3 P–Q5	15 ... P–KR3	21 R×R K×N
3 P–Q4 N×P	10 B–B4 B–K2	16 P–R3 P–B4	22 R/1–K1 P–B3
4 B–Q3 P–Q4	11 QN–Q2 0–0	17 P×Pep B×BP	23 B–Q6+ K–B2
5 P×P N–QB3	12 N–K4 Q–Q2	18 N–B5 Q–B1	24 N–K5+ B×N
6 Q–K2 N–N4	13 P–KR3 B–K3	19 N×B N–Q1	25 R×B
7 0–0 N×B	14 B–N3 QR–K1	(47)	Black resigns.

BISHOPS OF THE SAME COLOUR

White: E. Geller – Riga 1968, USSR Team Championship

48B

How often we talk of the usefulness of bishops of opposite colours and how rarely we refer to bishops of the same colour! Such an injustice can only be put down to our short-sightedness. If we manage to draw an ending one, or even two, pawns down, we naturally extol our 'opposite-coloured bishop' and thank our opponent's bishop! But then if we get a draw thanks to there being bishops of the same colour on the board, we take all the credit for the valiant efforts of the pieces and pawns for ourselves. This was exactly how events transpired in my game with Geller. But, having merited half-a-point for my play, I want to point out the exceptionally valuable help given to me by my dark-squared bishop, which had such ease of movement behind the chain of pawns that it totally eliminated any attempts to break through on the part of my opponent.

In a position where many would automatically castle, Geller used a slight innovation of his own preparation 6 N–Q2!, and the game went along an unknown course. If Black were now to capture this knight, then after 6 ... N×N 7 B×N 0–0 8 Q–B3 and 9 0–0–0 White would have too much space. Therefore the black knight retreated to Q3 and somewhat moderated White's appetite. But even then White's game became highly promising, and if it had not been for the good black bishop, I would have come to a sorry end in this game.

1 P–K4 P–K4	9 B×B N×B	16 Q×Q P×Q	23 K–K1 K–N3
2 N–KB3 N–KB3	10 R–K1 0–0	17 B–Q2 K–N2	24 K–Q1 K–B4
3 P–Q4 N×P	11 Q–N4 P–KN3	18 R–K2 QR–K1	25 B–B1 R–KN1
4 B–Q3 P–Q4	12 N–B1 N–Q2	19 QR–K1 R–K5	26 P–QN3 R–N3
5 N×P B–K2	13 N×N Q×N	20 P–B3 R×R	27 P–B4 P–N4
6 N–Q2 N–Q3	14 N–N3 (*48*)	21 R×R P–B5	28 P×QP
7 P–QB3 P–QB3	14 ... B–Q3	22 K–B2 P–KR4	Draw agreed.
8 0–0 B–B4	15 N×N Q×N		

EXCESSIVE IMPUDENCE

White: V. Ragozin – Moscow 1957, Moscow Championship

49B

The unexpected queen check took Ragozin unawares, and he decided to reply with blow for blow; but his K–Q1 was perhaps excessive impudence.

The secret is a simple one: the black queen can afford to shift its base to another square, whilst the white king at one stroke deprives itself for good of the two possibilities of castling, K-side and Q-side.

The further course of the game confirmed the riskiness of the king move – the king in the end was unable to find a comfortable refuge.

In addition, in the process of the struggle White had his K-side pawns broken up, and one of them soon fell.

It is true that for some time the KN-file was opened up for White's rooks, but the threats against Black's KN2 did not prove very terrible: there were too few fighting units on the board for an attack.

White realized this himself – how else is one to explain his offer of the exchange of queens on move 24?

Had the black KBP on KB4 not been blocking the path to KR7 of White's bishop on Q3, the two open files (the KN- and KR-files) might have given White a strong attack. But rooks on their own are not as a rule adequate to breach a pawn line.

Moreover, White was without his KNP, which might have gone to KN4 to undermine Black's KB4; that was the disadvantage of 17 P ×B.

1 P–K4 P–K4	12 N ×B+ Q ×N	23 Q ×QP+	32 K–N1 N–K3
2 N–KB3 N–KB3	13 B–KN5 P–B3	23 ... K–R1	33 P–R4 P–N3
3 P–Q4 P ×P	14 R–K1 Q–B2	24 Q–B4 Q ×Q	34 B–R6 R–B2
4 P–K5 N–K5	15 B–KB4 B–N5	25 B ×Q	35 B–N5 P–KR4
5 Q ×P P–Q4	16 B ×N B ×N+	25 ... QR–Q1+	36 K–R2 P–R5
6 P ×Pep N ×QP	17 P ×B P ×B	26 K–B1 P–KN3	37 B–B1 N–B5
7 B–Q3 Q–K2 +	18 P–KB4 P–Q4	27 P–QB3 K–N2	38 R–K8 R–Q7
8 K–Q1 (*49*)	19 K–Q2 Q–R4	28 R/1–K1 R–Q3	39 P–B3 R ×BP
8 ... N–B3	20 R–K3 Q ×P	29 K–B2 R–B1	40 R–KB8+
9 Q–QR4 Q–Q2	21 R–KB1 P–B4	30 B–B1 K–B3	40 ... K–N4
10 N–B3 B–K2	22 Q–N5 Q ×P/5	31 P–R3 N–Q5+	White resigns.
11 N–Q5 0–0			

A WHITE KNIGHT OR A BLACK KNIGHT?

Black: G. Borisenko – Moscow 1961, USSR Championship

Because of the situation in the tournament (which was nearing its close) only a win was any good to me. And even then it remained unclear whether I would be able to catch up with the leaders, so badly had I played the tournament middlegame! On the other hand, whether I drew or lost made no difference, which is why White committed a grave oversight out of excessive zeal when playing on after the adjournment and in a fit of temper began playing recklessly and could not even stop himself when he saw quite clearly that the KRP was openly aspiring to queen. It was a pity, of course. The position at the adjournment on move 40 was won.

Look for a moment, please, at the diagram. What a silly printing error! Even two. The black knight is white and the white one black.

Alas, the diagram is correct; it was exactly so. How did the white knight come to be on QN8?

To find that out, you will have to play through the game; I shall not prompt you at all.

Or perhaps just a little. Would you in Black's place have played 10 ... P–KB3 too?

1 P–K4 P–K4	18 P–KB3 N–B2	35 P–QN3 K–B2
2 N–KB3 N–KB3	19 N–B4 B–Q3	36 N–N7 K–K1
3 P–Q4 P×P	20 B–N3 QR–K1	37 N–B5 K–K2
4 P–K5 N–K5	21 N–N3 B×B	38 N–K4 N–Q2
5 Q×P P–Q4	22 P×B R–K7	39 P–B3 K–B2
6 P×Pep N×QP	23 R–Q2 R×R	40 P–N3 K–K2
7 N–B3 B–B4	24 K×R B–K3	41 N–B5 N–K4
8 Q–K5+ Q–K2	25 N/4–R5 B×N	42 P–B4 N–B2
9 N–Q5 Q×Q+	26 RP×B N–Q1	43 N–R6 N–Q3+
10 N×Q P–KB3	27 P–QN4 P–R4	44 K–B4 N–N2
11 N–KB3 K–Q2	28 R–R4 R–R3	45 P–B5 N–Q1
12 B–KB4 N–B3	29 P–N4 P×P	46 K–B5 N–K3
13 O–O–O R–Q1	30 R×R P×R	47 N–N8 N–Q5+
14 N–K3 B–K3	31 P×P K–Q2	48 K–K4 N–K7
15 B–QN5 K–B1	32 K–K3 N–B2	(50)
16 B/5×N P×B	33 K–B4 N–K4	49 N×P+ K–Q2
17 N–Q4 B–Q2	34 K–B5 K–K2	50 N×P N×P+

51 K–Q5 P–B4
52 P×P N×P
53 P–B6+ K–Q1
54 K–K5 N–K6
55 P–N5 P–R4
56 P–N6 P×P
57 K–K6 P–R5
58 N–N5 P–R6
59 P–B7+ K–B1
60 K–Q6 N–B4+
61 K–B6 N–K2+
62 K–Q6 P–R7
63 N–R7+ K–N2
64 K×N K×P
White resigns.

THE WHITE KING'S SPURT

Black: L. Maslov – Moscow 1959, USSR Team Championship

Those who are not too lazy to play this game through will see that the hero of the battle was not the king at all, but the humble white pawn on QR2.

Nevertheless, the pawn would not have had the least chance of coping with the black knight if it had not been for the king's bold spurt.

It is only thanks to the manoeuvre K–K2–Q3–B4–N5–R5–N6 that the pawn on QR4 became passed and in due course set off to queen. It is curious that it made its first step on move 33 and then waited a full sixteen moves for a favourable moment.

In the variation 49 . . . K ×N 50 P–R6 White's king keeps the black knight at bay.

They were both fine fellows, the king and the pawn.

'But what about me, surely I deserve a good word', quietly asks the knight on KB4, who by a miracle is still alive. 'Of course; please forgive me.'

It was the knight with its nimble jumps hither and thither, N–QB3 –QR4–QB3–K4–QB5–K4–QB5–K6–QB7–K6–KB4, who prepared the ground for the decisive manoeuvre: P–QR4–R5–R6–R7–R8=Q! It fell to this knight's lot to make exactly a quarter of all the moves – 12 out of 48!

1 P–K4 P–K4	14 B ×B K ×B	26 N ×B N ×N	39 N–K6 + K–N5
2 N–KB3 N–KB3	15 KR–K1	27 N–K4 + K–N2	40 N ×P K–N6
3 P–Q4 P ×P	15 . . . R ×R +	28 N ×P R–Q7	41 N–K6 N–B7
4 P–K5 N–K5	16 R ×R Q–B3	29 R–QB1 N–Q5	42 K–K2 (51)
5 Q ×P P–Q4	17 Q ×Q + K ×Q	30 N–K4 R ×QBP	42 . . . K ×P
6 P ×Pep N ×QP	18 P–QN3 B–B4	31 R ×R N ×R	43 K–Q3 N–K8 +
7 N–B3 N–B3	19 N–Q4 B–Q2	32 K–B1 N–N5	44 K–B4 N–B7
8 Q–KB4 P–KN3	20 N–R4 N–N2	33 P–QR4 P–KB4	45 K–N5 K–B6
9 B–N5 B–N2	21 N–K2 P–B4	34 N–B5 K–B3	46 K ×P K–K5
10 B ×N+ P ×B	22 N/4–B3 B–B3	35 P–B4 P–R3	47 K–N6 K–Q6
11 0–0 0–0	23 N–B4 R–Q1	36 P–R4 P–N4	48 N–B4 + K–K5
12 B–K3 P–QR4	24 N–Q3 R–Q5	37 RP ×P + P ×P	49 P–R5
13 B–Q4 R–K1	25 N–K5 N–Q1	38 P ×P + K ×P	Black resigns.

A BOOK MOVE

White: L. Stein – Tiflis 1967, USSR Championship

52W

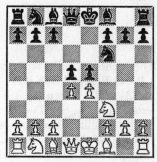

Since the starting positions of the pieces and pawns are not only symmetrical with each other, but are also considered completely equal, Black might unwittingly find himself wanting to maintain this symmetry and prolong it for some time. A dangerous symptom!

But it is well known that every rule has its exceptions. And so when I read in a reliable openings book that after 1 P–K4 P–K4 2 N–KB3 N–KB3 3 P–Q4 Black can play without fear 3 . . . P–Q4, I was very happy and concluded that I had happened upon one such rare exception.

Stein was surprised, thought for a long time and played 4 KP×P P×P 5 B–QN5+ P–B3 6 P×P P×P 7 B–K2!. I immediately realized I had been wrong to avail myself of the book suggestion.

If White had gone 7 B–QB4, then Black would have had at his disposal the cunning manoeuvre 7 . . . B–QN5+ 8 P–B3 Q–K2+ 9 B–K2 P×P 10 N×P 0–0 with a satisfactory game; but after the subtle B–K2 Black was in a bad way.

Neither the tricky . . . B–Q7, nor the final effort . . . B×RP could help me – all was in vain: my opponent's pieces worked pitilessly and amazingly harmoniously, like a well oiled machine.

I learnt a useful lesson from this game: book moves are fine, but one's own moves are even better. And my advice to you is not to use book suggestions without checking them thoroughly first.

1 P–K4 P–K4	10 N×P K–K2	18 R–B2 B×B	27 R–B7 N×P
2 N–KB3 N–KB3	11 0–0 R–Q1	19 P×B N–K4	28 B–B4 N–N5
3 P–Q4 P–Q4 (52)	12 R–K1 K–B1	20 P–KR3 R×P	29 N–K5 P–KR3
4 KP×P P×P	13 B–KB4 QN–Q2	21 R–Q1 N–Q4	30 B×P+ K–R1
5 B–QN5+ P–B3	14 N–QR4 B–N5	22 N–QB5 B×P	31 R/1–QB1
6 P×P P×P	15 KR–QB1	23 P×B R×P	31 . . . R–KN6+
7 B–K2 B–QB4	15 . . . R–K1	24 N×P N×N	32 K–R2
8 P–B3 P×P	16 N–Q4 R–K5	25 N–Q7+ K–N1	Black resigns.
9 Q×Q+ K×Q	17 B–K3 B–Q7	26 R/2×N N–N5	

10 The Chigorin Counter-Attack

This is how I propose to call the opening 1 P–K4 P–K4 2 N–KB3 N–QB3 3 B–QB4 N–B3! (*53*), which up till now has been wrongly called the Two Knights' Defence.

The brilliant tournament and match practice of M.I. Chigorin, the long time champion of Russia and very strong challenger for the world chess throne, not only helped this opening to gain recognition amongst large sections of chess-players in all corners of the earth, but also completely reversed the old treatment of 3 . . . N–KB3 as a defensive move.

The most dangerous reply for Black is 4 N–N5. For quite a number of years Black really did little else than defend himself, since the threat of 5 N×BP is not particularly pleasant.

At the same time, the attempts to block White's QB4 – KB7 diagonal by . . . P–Q4 came to a lamentable end: 4 . . . P–Q4 5 P×P N×P 6 N×BP K×N 7 Q–B3 + and the king is forced to make the risky move to K3, where it has often died under the fire of White's pieces.

Chigorin's merit was that he was the first to show convincingly that Black has no need to capture White's pawn on Q5 with his knight – he can himself launch a counter-attack with 5 . . . N–QR4!.

Chigorin's basic variation 6 B–N5 + P–B3 7 P×P P×P 8 B–K2 P–KR3 9 N–KB3 P–K5 10 N–K5 Q–B2 is still not refuted today, although various theoreticians persistently search for improvements in White's attack.

But neither are the proponents of improvements in Black's play sleeping. Alongside 5 . . . N–QR4, they are examining such complicated attacks as 5 . . . P–QN4 and 5 . . . N–Q5.

As a result of many trials the first conclusion has been drawn: in reply to the paradoxical 5 . . . P–QN4 White should not play 6 B×P, but 6 B–B1, and only after 6 . . . N×P take the QNP with the bishop.

MORPHY THE MAGICIAN

Black: A. Rojahn – Moscow Olympiad 1956

54W

When I have to play too many severely positional games (such is chess life today) then for relaxation I take my collection of the best games of players of the nineteenth century down from my book-shelf, and find amongst the first, of course, the games of the magician, Morphy. The uncrowned world champion, Paul Morphy, loved a fast, sharp game and would choose corresponding openings. The move 3 B–QB4 was one of his favourites.

Whilst preparing for my game against the Norwegian master Rojahn, I stumbled upon a curious idea based upon the power of mobile pawns. Then I remembered that Morphy liked to play the variation with 6 P–Q3. I eagerly opened a collection of his games; there was not a word about the move 8 P×P and not a single game played in that way. Good, I shall risk it and be its originator. I got permission from my team colleagues and rushed into the fight.

White's bold idea proved a formidable weapon. The onslaught of the closely linked White pawns made Black's pieces tremble and they began gradually crawling back to rearguard positions. The first to change its mind was the dark-squared bishop, which, ashamed to play 32 ... B–N1, thought it better to die immediately on the field of battle. Its example was soon followed by the black knight.

After the game I was regally rewarded: my opponent asked in a very quiet voice: 'You of course overlooked the bishop on QB4?'

1 P–K4 P–K4	11 Q–Q3 B–N5	21 P–K5 Q–B4	31 K–R1 Q–Q1
2 N–KB3 N–QB3	12 QN–Q2 B–K2	22 P–B4 B–N3	32 P–N6 B×P
3 B–B4 N–B3	13 0–0–0 0–0	23 N–K4 QR–N1	33 P×B P–N4
4 N–N5 P–Q4	14 N–K5 B–R4	24 Q–B3 B–R2	34 P–Q6 Q–N3
5 P×P N–QR4	15 P–QN3	25 P–KN4 Q–N3	35 P–Q7 N×QP
6 P–Q3 P–KR3	15 ... N/N3–Q2	26 P–B5 Q–N3	36 P×N QR–Q1
7 N–KB3 P–K5	16 B–N2 N×N	27 Q–N3 P–B3	37 N×KBP
(54)	17 B×N N–Q2	28 P–K6 N–K4	37 ... Q–B3+
8 P×P N×B	18 B–B3 B–B3	29 P–KR4 K–R1	38 Q–N2
9 Q–Q4 N–N3	19 QR–K1 B×B	30 P–N5 QR–B1	Black resigns.
10 P–B4 P–B4	20 Q×B Q–B3		

THE OLYMPIC DÉBUT IN HELSINKI

Black: V. Smyslov – Moscow 1952, Training Tournament

55B

In 1968 the USSR chess team won the World Chess Olympiad for the ninth time in succession, but in 1952 we had still to make our début in the 'tournament of nations'.

In order that all those taking part in the Olympic team should arrive at the competition theoretically well-prepared and in good health, the Chess Federation of the USSR organised a training get-together in a holiday house in one of Moscow's suburbs. And where you have chess-players, you inevitably get a tournament. Quite honestly, we were playing tournaments daily, from after breakfast till supper; but lightning, five-minute tournaments are one thing, and the training tournaments which took place at the end of the teaching session with a strict time-control were quite another. During the training games I was able to try out several interesting opening moves, one of which the reader can see in my game with Symslov.

The manoeuvre N–K5–KN4 does not enjoy popularity perhaps wrongfully. Of course play becomes extremely tense, but is 11 P–Q4 really better than 11 N–N4?

I draw your attention to the capacity for work of White's bishop which made ten moves.

1 P–K4 P–K4	13 B–R3 0–0	24 N–B3 (55)	34 P–Q5 N–N4
2 N–KB3 N–QB3	14 P–KN3 N–Q4	24 ... Q × P	35 B–N2 R–Q3
3 B–B4 N–B3	15 0–0 QR–K1	25 N × R Q × N	36 Q–Q3 Q × Q
4 N–N5 P–Q4	16 P–Q3 P–K6	26 Q–B5 B–N3	37 R–K8+ K–R2
5 P × P N–QR4	17 P × P Q–N3	27 Q–B3 N–N2	38 R × Q K–N3
6 B–N5+ P–B3	18 N–B3 N × P	28 QR–Q1 N–B4	39 R–QB3 P–B3
7 P × P P × P	19 B × N R × B	29 B–N2 R–Q1	40 P–R4 N–B2
8 B–K2 P–KR3	20 K–R1 Q × P	30 KR–K1 Q–N5	41 R–B6 R–Q2
9 N–KB3 P–K5	21 N–K4 B–B2	31 B × P Q–N3	42 B–K4+ K–R4
10 N–K5 Q–B2	22 R–QN1	32 B–B3 Q–B4	43 K–N2
11 N–N4 B × N	22 ... Q × RP	33 P–Q4 N–K3	Black resigns.
12 B × B B–Q3	23 Q–B1 R–K7		

VICTORY IN THE CALM OF MY STUDY

Black: B. Baranov – Moscow 1953, Moscow Championship

56W

Chess is so rich in interesting combinations that no amount of preparatory work can save a player from the need to work hard at the board. And yet there are the odd exceptions. If one has a certain degree of luck one can sometimes play a game in which the most difficult moves have been foreseen during one's preparatory reflections. My game with Baranov is precisely one such pleasant exception.

Black was rather naively tempted by White's KNP and apparently hoped that he might queen his KRP. However, winning the KNP and KRP cost him several tempi. And when a quiet endgame came about, it emerged that White's central pawns were stronger than Black's passed pawns on the wing.

The basic culprit in Black's defeat was his QN. After its bold leap to QR4 it could not find a quiet haven for itself for the rest of the game. Each time the knight prepared itself for the attack, the white pawns took one square or another away from it – see the moves P–QB5 and P–KB5.

After 20 ... Q ×Q + Baranov proposed that we consider the game drawn. He would probably have kept silent if he had guessed that the whole variation up to 19 ... Q–B6 had been minutely analysed by me in the calm of my study. And the ensuing endgame too.

1 P–K4 P–K4	11 N–N4 N ×N	20 N ×P Q ×Q +	29 QR–N1 P–R3
2 N–KB3 N–QB3	12 B ×N Q–N4	21 K ×Q P–B3	30 P–R4 QR–K1
3 B–B4 N–B3	13 P–KR3 P–R4	22 P–QB4 K–B2	31 K–Q3 R–K2
4 N–N5 P–Q4	14 P–Q4 Q–N3	23 P–B4 B–N1	32 P ×P P ×P
5 P ×P N–QR4	15 B ×B Q ×P	24 P–QB5 N–Q1	33 R ×P R/1–K1
6 B–N5 + P–B3	16 R–B1 R ×B	25 P–B5 N–N2	34 B–B4 N–Q1
7 P ×P P ×P	17 Q–K2 Q ×RP	26 P–N4 QR–Q1	35 R ×B R ×N
8 B–K2 P–KR3	18 B–Q2 N–N2	27 B–K3 P–R5	36 R ×N
9 N–KB3 P–K5	19 N–B3 Q–B6	28 P–N5 P ×P	Black resigns.
10 N–K5 B–Q3	(56)		

A PAGE FROM A MAGAZINE

White: N. Rossolimo – Munich Olympiad 1958

57B

It is an intriguing thing, the memory of a chess-player.

No sooner had Rossolimo 'screwed' his bishop into KN5 than 'something' told me: You're being caught in a variation.

Suddenly, as if by the wave of a magic wand, my visual memory dragged from goodness knows what recesses of my mind a clear outline of a page of the American Magazine 'Chess Review' where the move 9 B–N5 was analysed in detail. The author of the analysis – and I remembered that, too, perfectly clearly – was my opponent that day, Rossolimo.

At first I wanted to find a refutation on my own at the board, but when I began to study a typical variation of the attack, 9 ... P–B3 10 R×N+ K–B2 11 Q–Q3 P×B 12 QR–K1 P×N 13 Q–B4+ K–N3 14 R–K6+ B×R 15 R×B+ Q–B3 16 N×P Q×R 17 Q×Q+ K×N 18 P–R4+ K×P 19 P–N3+ K–N4 20 P–B4+ K–R4 21 Q–B5+ K–R3 22 Q–N5 mate, or 10 N×N K–B2 11 Q–Q3 P×B 12 N/4×P, I came up against insoluble problems.

As a result – a quick draw and ... a not very happy reaction from the team captain Kotov: 'I myself won against Rossolimo in Venice'. He had forgotten that only an hour earlier he had been warning me: 'Look out and be careful, particularly in the endgame, he's a dangerous player. ...'

Of course, if there had been the slightest hope of a win in the position, I would have played this endgame too, but, alas, after 13 ... 0–0–0! White would have had to play only tolerably well to guarantee the draw.

Moreover, after the 1952 Olympiad I had become more experienced and more cautious. I had twice got myself into lost positions then by trying to go in for complications in drawn positions.

1 P–K4 P–K4	5 0–0 N×P	9 B–N5 (57)	12 Q×P Q×Q
2 N–KB3 N–QB3	6 R–K1 P–Q4	9 ... B–K2	13 N×Q
3 B–B4 N–B3	7 B×P Q×B	10 B×B N×B	Draw agreed.
4 P–Q4 P×P	8 N–B3 Q–Q1	11 N×N B–N5	

DUMMY ATTACK ON BLACK'S KB2

White: V. Lyublinsky – Moscow 1963, 'Dinamo' Team Championship

Why does White play P–K5, inviting return fire against himself and completely killing his own attack on KB7?

The subtlety of White's idea is that he has no intention at all of attacking KB7! By means of this dummy attack White wants to lure Black's KN onto the central K5 square, where it will subsequently find itself in the thick of White's pawns and will succumb!

You do not believe me? You want concrete proof, as always?

All right, listen carefully. 6 ... N–K5 7 N × P B–Q2 8 B × N P × B 9 0–0 B–QB4 10 B–K3 0–0 11 P–KB3 N–N4 12 N–B3, and the serious threat of the pawn attack P–KB4–B5–B6! hangs over Black's position. And where will the black knight go?

There exist very detailed analyses of this complex opening variation, but I always like, if I get the chance, to go my own way. That is why I chose an original route for the KN – not to the vulnerable central K5 square, but to the well guarded rear square, QN1.

From looking at the diagram you would not guess at all, without knowing the pre-history of the game, that Black's knight on QN1 had already made three moves!

1 P–K4 P–K4	14 P–B4 B–K3	27 R–B3 RP × P	41 K × R P–B6
2 N–KB3 N–QB3	15 N/3–K2 P–QB4	28 RP × P R–N5	42 K–K2 N–N5
3 B–B4 N–B3	16 N × B P × N	29 R–QB2 N–N3	43 B–R4 P–B5
4 P–Q4 P × P	17 P–B4 P–B3	30 R/2–B2 P × P	44 K–Q1 K–B2
5 P–K5 P–Q4	18 B–Q2 N–Q2	31 P × P R × P	45 B–Q8 K–N3
6 B–QN5 N–Q2	19 P–QN3 B–Q1	32 P–R3 N–Q2	46 B–R5 N–Q4
7 0–0 B–K2	20 P–N3 P–N4	33 K–N3 R–Q5	47 B–Q8 P–R3
8 R–K1 0–0	21 K–N2 NP × P	34 R–QR2 P–N5	48 K–B2 P–R4
9 B × N P × B	22 N × P B–N4	35 R–R6 N–B4	49 P × P + K × P
10 N × P N–N1	23 R–K2 B × N	36 B–K3 N × R	50 P–R4 K–N5
11 Q–B3 Q–Q2	24 B × B P–QR4	37 B × R P–B4	51 B–N5 K–B4
(58)	25 R–KB1 P–R5	38 B–B2 R–N1	52 B–B6 N × B
12 N–B3 Q–N5	26 P–KN4	39 K–B4 R–N6	53 P × N K × P
13 Q × Q B × Q	26 ... QR–N1	40 K–K4 R × R	Draw agreed.

11 The Hungarian Defence

WHEN THE QUEEN TAKES A REST

Black: L. Scherbakov – Moscow 1955, Moscow Team Championship

59W

In the early stages of learning to play chess we all make a lot of mistakes, but perhaps the most widespread is the desire to avoid the exchange of queens at all costs.

It is obvious to everyone: what attack is there without queens?

And yet pawns, knights, bishops and rooks, too, are perfectly capable of, and, what is important, enjoy, making concerted and insistent attacks on enemy redoubts. Of course, the person commanding the battle must have a clear conception of which problems each fighting unit should be given to solve.

Seen in the light of this very general and diffuse reasoning, I am pleased with my play in this game. Its principal heroes are, in White's camp, the KP and the KN, and in Black's, the king himself. But what else could the brave monarch have done, when someone had precipitously played his KNP to N3 and purposelessly exchanged the black-squared bishop?

The presence of weak squares in the centre of Black's camp allowed White to develop a decisive attack without much difficulty. Particularly worthy of praise were the bold activities of the pawns on moves 18–20.

It remains for me to add that Leonid Vasilevich Scherbakov, a teacher in the Palace of Pioneers on the Lenin Hills, no longer plays like that himself, and will not let his pupils do it either!

1 P–K4 P–K4	10 B×Q N–Q5	19 P–K5 P–KB4	28 N–K6+ K–B2
2 N–KB3 N–QB3	11 N–R3 P–QB3	20 P–K6 B×P	29 N–B7 R–N1
3 B–B4 B–K2 (59)	12 B–N3 N×B	21 KR–K1 K–B2	30 N×B K×N
4 P–Q4 P–Q3	13 RP×N P–B3	22 N–K5+ K–B3	31 R–Q8+ K–B2
5 P×P P×P	14 B–K3 N–K2	23 N×BP R–K1	32 P–B4 R–R1
6 B–Q5 B–Q2	15 N–B4 N–B1	24 P–R4 B–B2	33 P–B5 N–N3
7 N–N5 B×N	16 0–0–0 P–N3	25 B–N5+ K–N2	34 P×N
8 Q–R5 P–KN3	17 B–R6 R–KN1	26 R×R B×R	Black resigns.
9 Q×B Q×B	18 P–B4 P×P	27 N–Q8 P–N4	

12 The Italian Game (Giuoco Piano)

The Italian game, 3 B–QB4!, is the sharpest branch of the open games. It might be said that only the King's Gambit can compete with it for the quantity of various kinds of combinations, but in that opening, too, one cannot get by without B–QB4. Setting his sights on KB7, White lets his opponent know immediately that he is faced with a struggle, not for life, but to the death, and he forces Black to take essential defensive measures without wasting a moment.

There is no need in this brief survey to dwell in detail on separate variations – any book on openings will tell you much more. My aim is different: to understand the main methods of attack and defence, after which to construct White's play and Black's correspondingly.

It is for players with fantasy, imagination, a thirst for adventure and a love of the unknown that the attacks of the Italian school were invented. You can sacrifice, dare, combine – each time differently, today better than yesterday, and tomorrow better and with greater confidence than today.

It might be asked why Black loses so often.

The dormant Q-side – there's the rub! Moreover, that is almost always how one can answer the question, why, in positions of an open type, does White triumph more frequently than Black? Of course, that is on condition that the attacking side is not mean with his pawn and piece sacrifices.

It is the sleeping black pieces which are guilty of the death of their king. They should not remain onlookers, but should rouse themselves into action, rush onto the stage without worrying about the loss of a pawn – time is the important thing.

If this advice can stir the pride of Black's QR, QN and QB, my goal will have been achieved.

LEARNING FROM EXPERIENCE

White: E. Eliskases – Mar del Plata 1960, International Tournament

By the last round of the 1936 Moscow International Tournament the ex-world champion J. R. Capablanca was only a half-point ahead of Mikhail Botvinnik. To avoid having to share first prize Capablanca had to beat Eliskases.

And in the same way as the great Emanuel Lasker in St. Petersburg in 1914 had prepared a quiet variation of the Ruy Lopez for his decisive game with Capablanca, so Capabalanca himself chose a harmless variation of the Giuoco Piano. Eliskases was very pleased at this and accepted all the piece exchanges that were offered him quite willingly, only to realize, when the major-piece ending came around, that he had been the victim of skilful mystification.

Naturally Eliskases cherished for many a year the hope of playing the same trick on someone else, and here I can understand him. But why he decided to try out Capablanca's 'play-acting' on me, that I cannot explain.

1 P–K4 P–K4	15 Q–N3 Q–K3	31 R×Q R–N1	46 K–R3 R–KB7
2 N–KB3 N–QB3	16 R–Q3 QR–K1	32 R–B7 P–KR3	47 R–B7+ K–Q1
3 B–B4 N–B3	17 N–Q2 P–B4	33 R–B6 R–N5	48 R–B7 B–B4+
4 P–Q3 B–B4	18 K–B1 Q–R3	34 P–B3 R×BP	49 K–N3 R–B6+
5 N–B3 P–Q3	19 P–N3 P–B5	35 R×RP P–N4	50 K–B2 B–K6
6 B–KN5 *(61)*	20 P–KB3 P×P	36 R–N6 P–N5	51 B–B7+ K–B1
6 ... N–QR4	21 P×P B–KR6+	37 P×P R×P	52 R–K7 B–N4
7 N–Q5 N×B	22 K–K2 P–B4	38 K–B2 R–K5	53 R–R7 P–Q5
8 P×N P–B3	23 P×P B×P	39 P–KN4	54 B–R5 P–Q6+
9 N×N+ P×N	24 N–K4 B×N	39 ... R–K7+	55 K–N2 P–K6
10 B–R4 R–KN1	25 P×B R–N5	40 K–N3 K–Q2	56 R–QB7+
11 0–0 B–K3	26 K–Q1 Q–N3	41 B–N5 B–Q5	56 ... K–N1
12 Q–Q3 Q–K2	27 R–KB3 R×KP	42 B–B1 P–K5	57 R–B5 R–B7+
13 QR–Q1 0–0–0	28 R×R Q×R	43 B–B4 P–Q4	58 K–N3 P–Q7
14 KR–K1	29 Q–Q3 Q–N3	44 R–Q6+ K–K2	White resigns.
14 ... B–KN5	30 Q–B5+ Q×Q	45 R×BP R×P+	

THE CHAMELEON TRAP

White: V. Korchnoi – Moscow 1952, USSR Championship

The famous trap in the Two Knights' Defence 1 P–K4 P–K4 2 N–KB3 N–QB3 3 B–B4 N–Q5 4 N×P Q–N4 is well known to every chess player, but even the most self-assured of grandmasters would be unable to tell you with complete confidence for whom it is a trap, for White or for Black.

Here there is the move 6 ... N–QR4, which I took the risk of trying out against Korchnoi; it was very little known in theory at that time and completely untested in practice. People were frightened off by the variation 7 N–Q5 N×B 8 P×N B×P+ 9 K×B N×P+ 10 K–N1 N×B 11 N×N P–QB3 12 Q–R5 P–KN3 13 Q–B3 etc. with wild play.

But I had practically no choice: Korchnoi, previous to our game, had crushed one opponent after another with the standard 6 ... P–KR3 7 B×N Q×B 8 N–Q5 etc.

Not so long ago, when Korchnoi had already become a serious contender for the world chess crown, I happened to ask him: 'Why don't you play the Two Knights' any more these days?' The grandmaster looked at me in amazement and muttered: 'Because of 6 ... N–QR4, of course. You mean to say you didn't know that yourself? ...'

1 P–K4 P–K4	14 ... P–QR4	27 BP×P P×P	40 K–B2 R–K8
2 N–KB3 N–QB3	15 B×B Q×B	28 P–B4 P×BP+	41 N–Q3 R–K5
3 B–B4 B–B4	16 Q–K3 Q×Q+	29 N×P R–R1	42 K–Q2 R–Q3
4 P–Q3 N–B3	17 P×Q R–N5	30 N×RP	43 R–B8+ K–K2
5 N–B3 P–Q3	18 N–Q2 R/1–N1	30 ... R–Q1+	44 R–B3 B–K3
6 B–KN5 N–QR4	19 P–N3 K–Q2	31 K–B3 R×KP	45 P–R4 R/5–Q5
(62)	20 K–N2 K–K2	32 P–KR4	46 K–B2 P–K5
7 N–Q5 N×B	21 K–B3 P–KR4	32 ... R×KP+	47 N–K5 B–B4
8 P×N P–B3	22 KR–B1 P–KR5	33 K–N2 P–KB4	48 R–K3 K–B3
9 N×N+ P×N	23 P×P R×RP	34 P–R5 P–B5	49 N–B4 R–Q1
10 B–K3 Q–N3	24 R–B2	35 P–R6 R–KR1	50 P–R5 K–N4
11 Q–Q2 B–K3	24 ... R/1–KR1	36 N×P B–Q4	51 K–N2 K–B5
12 0–0–0 0–0–0	25 R–KR1	37 R–QB1 R×RP	52 R–B3 B–K3
13 P–QN3	25 ... R/1–R3	38 R–B7+ K–B1	53 N–K3 R–Q6
13 ... KR–N1	26 K–Q3 P–Q4	39 N–B5 P–B6	White resigns.
14 KR–N1			

THE ENDGAME THEORETICIAN

Black: Yu. Averbakh – Moscow 1961, International Tournament

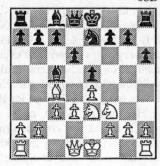

63B

Grandmaster Averbakh, an acknowledged specialist on the endgame, does not care much for experimenting in the opening, where he often follows well trodden paths. And when Averbakh, in my game with him, willingly started repeating all Eliskases's moves from the latter's Moscow encounter with Capablanca, I was rather pleased: at last I would find out how exactly Eliskases could have saved his difficult rook ending against the Cuban!

Alas, I discovered nothing.

Perhaps Averbakh will reveal this secret in a new edition of his three volume work on the endgame?

But in my game he simply deviated from Eliskases's move 10 . . . B–K3; he quietly castled and gradually consolidated the position of Black's pawns in the centre.

There was to be no replica of the famous Capablanca-Eliskases game. Whether I liked it or not, I had to think all the time on my own.

When I began 'playing without prompting', I was unable to think up anything better than the routine taking control of the Q-file. Unfortunately Black's two powerful bishops defended all the avenues of approach and, taking advantage of a lull in the fighting, Averbakh himself set purposefully about bringing the game to an ending. A slight slip, 36 . . . P–KB3, allowed me to put up all the shutters for good.

1 P–K4 P–K4	11 0–0 N–N3	22 P–KN3 N–R4	33 N–Q2 P–QN4
2 N–KB3 N–QB3	12 P–Q4 B–N3	23 B–Q3 N–B3	34 B–N3 B–Q2
3 B–B4 B–B4	13 P–QR4 P–QB3	24 N–Q2 QR–Q1	35 P–R4 B–N5
4 N–B3 N–B3	14 P×P P×P	25 B–B2 N–N5	36 K–B1 P–B3
5 P–Q3 P–Q3	15 Q×Q R×Q	26 N/2–B1 B–N3	37 P–B3 B–B1
6 B–KN5 P–KR3	16 QR–Q1 R–K1	27 N×N B×N	38 P–R5 B–K6
7 B×N Q×B	17 KR–K1 K–B1	28 R×R R×R	39 K–K2 B–N4
8 N–Q5 Q–Q1	18 N–B5 B–B2	29 K–N2 K–K2	40 B–B2 P×P
9 P–B3 N–K2	19 B–N3 N–N5	30 P–R3 B–K3	41 B×P
10 N–K3 (*63*)	20 N–K3 P–QR4	31 R–Q1 R×R	Draw agreed.
10 . . . 0–0	21 B–B2 B–K3	32 B×R B–R2	

A TECHNICAL WASTE

Black: B. Ivkov – Amsterdam 1968, International Tournament

The struggle developed neither in the centre nor on the K-side, as is usually the case in this opening, but on the Q-side, where Black's black-squared bishop, which had carelessly got stuck on QN3, was the object of attack.

And only on the fifteenth move did White make a sharp change in the tempo of the game, when he played the programmed advance P–Q4!.

Black had hurriedly to take counter-measures to defend against the threatened pawn-storm, hence the sorties of his bishop to KN5 and his knight to Q5.

But Ivkov was unlucky: when playing 15 P–Q4, I had calculated the possibility 15 ... B–N5 16 P–Q5 B × N 17 Q × B N–Q5 and had prepared the immediate sacrifice: 18 P × N Q × B 19 B × P!. It is clearly bad to take the bishop, because of 20 Q–N4 +.

During my preparation at home I dared not even dream of getting the position shown in the diagram. The weakening of Black's pawn chain could have best been taken advantage of by 22 QR–B1 and 23 R–B7, after which there seems to be no defence against the threat of Q–Q7, × KBP!.

Did I see this move? Of course. What was wrong with it then? I wanted to spare my bishop. Black could easily have defended his KBP by ... R–KB1: I was not going to give my bishop away for this rook! After the game, however, Ivkov and I established that this variation was favourable for White. In short, the move 22 P × P? was a technical waste.

1 P–K4 P–K4	9 P–QR4 0–0	17 Q × B N–Q5	24 B–K3 R–K2
2 N–KB3 N–QB3	10 0–0 R–K1	18 P × N Q × B	25 Q–R4 R–B2
3 B–B4 B–B4	11 B–B2 N–Q2	19 B × P N–B3	26 P–N4 N–B3
4 P–B3 N–B3	12 P–R5 B × N	20 Q–KN3 N–R4	27 QR–N1 Q–K4
5 P–Q3 P–Q3	13 RP × B B–K3	21 Q–N4 P–KN3	28 KR–Q1 N–R2
6 QN–Q2 B–N3	14 P × BP Q × P	(64)	29 QR–B1 R × R
7 B–N3 B–K3	15 P–Q4 B–N5	22 P × P R × P	Draw.
8 N–B4 P–KR3	16 P–Q5 B × N	23 P–B3 Q × QNP	

13 Captain Evans' Gambit

The inventor of the three-coloured identi-
fication lighting used by ships, the Englishman, Captain Evans, never became world
chess champion. He never even tried to
contend for the title. Nevertheless, chess
players will always remember with gratitude
a man who has given the world such a
remarkable opening as the renowned Evans
Gambit – 1 P–K4 P–K4 2 N–KB3 N–QB3
3 B–B4 B–B4 4 P–QN4!.

The patent on 4 P–QN4 was taken out in
1824, and almost immediately the Evans' Gambit became the most
popular opening in various areas of the world. Wherein lies the strength
of this opening?

In those far-off years tournaments were rarely organized; matches were
preferred, so that opponents knew each other well and had no need to
sound each other out. The main problem was how to engage close battle
as quickly as possible. The Evans' Gambit suited this style of play down to
the ground, and for more than half a century it served faithfully and
truthfully more than one generation of lovers of chess.

A serious blow was struck against 4 P–QN4 by the world champion of
1894–1921, the author of a series of lectures 'Common Sense in Chess', a
man of outstanding intellect, Dr Emanuel Lasker. He offered the world
a fundamentally new approach to the problem of gambits. One should
accept the sacrifices, but at the earliest convenient moment return them
with advantage. Nowadays such advice would be considered natural, but
then it was equivalent to blasphemy: during the period when the art of
combination was flourishing it was counted a question of honour both that
one should sacrifice generously when attacking, and give nothing back
when defending.

Is this opening refuted today? No, it is not, although safer methods of
conducting the attack have also been found.

MY MEMORY JOGGED

White: A. Sokolsky – Kiev 1944, Masters Tournament

66W

When people talk about the need to marry theory and practice, they usually mean by this taking part in serious tournaments and reading chess literature. But is not the most essential thing forgotten in this? Namely, the most valuable element in any field of work: daily training and training in conditions that approximate most closely to the practical situation.

For the chess-player the most difficult moment in his work is playing in time-trouble. And so for the chess-player it is vitally necessary to practise almost every day at playing fast.

I have been lucky in this respect. The chess-club instructor in the Kiev Palace of Pioneers was a man of rare spiritual qualities, a player of great practical strength and an excellent teller of stories. Having already reached a respectable age, Semen Abramovich Sauskan did not take part in serious tournaments but, as it turned out, would willingly play three-minute games with me.

It was about then that I came upon the idea of 7 . . . N–KR3, but it was only in my game with Sokolsky that I was first presented with the opportunity of testing this move seriously.

Black's overbold plan was wrecked.

Quite honestly, I had fancied that things would turn out differently: after the loss of his KBP Black would have an extra line of attack, and the menacing black rooks would surge relentlessly and irresistibly into White's camp.

Everything happened as Black had wanted, except with colours reversed!

1 P–K4 P–K4	9 B×P+ K–B1	17 N–Q2 B–N5	24 Q×QP+
2 N–KB3 N–QB3	10 P×P Q–K2	18 K–R1 R–K1	24 . . . R–K2
3 B–B4 B–B4	11 B–Q5 N×P	19 P–KB4 Q–QB4	25 Q–B6+ K–K1
4 P–QN4 B×NP	12 N×N Q×N	20 Q–N2 B–K7	26 Q×R/8+
5 P–B3 B–R4	13 0–0 P–B3	21 KR–K1 B–Q6	26 . . . K–Q2
6 P–Q4 P–Q3	14 Q–R4 B–Q1	22 P–K5 Q–B7	27 QR–Q1
7 Q–N3 N–R3	15 B–N3 P–N4	(66)	Black resigns.
8 B×N P×B	16 Q–R3 B–N3	23 Q–R3 Q×N	

A KING WITHOUT AN ESCORT

White: V. Ragozin – Moscow 1945, USSR Championship

Wherein lies the charm of the Evans' Gambit for White? A quick and varied attack, in which courage, impudence and, not least, knowledge are required.

But what attracts Black to this opening? To some degree, of course, it is the chance of winning a pawn as early as the fifth move, but this is not the main point.

Black, whilst still preparing for the game, can invent, on the basis of available experience, some extremely interesting plan or complex system of defence.

I too could not help wanting to make my contribution to this general stock of theory, and the sad experience of my encounter with Sokolsky (completely in keeping with my obstinate nature) not only failed to dampen my ardour, but even whipped it up more: dare for a second time, perhaps now I will be more successful!

Moreover, I had prepared specially for my game with Ragozin what seemed to me then an improvement on my play, a crafty new pawn move.

Alas, the open position of the black king, which had literally nowhere to hide from the scorching rays of the attack, meant that Black could not take sufficient advantage of the open KB- and KN-files. Black could only re-emerge as the attacking side at the very end of the game.

1 P–K4 P–K4	11 B–Q5 N×P	21 P×P+ K×P	31 N–K5+ K–B2
2 N–KB3 N–QB3	12 N×N Q×N	22 N–Q4 K–B2	32 Q–R5+ K–B1
3 B–B4 B–B4	13 Q–R3 B–N3	23 QR–Q1 B–Q3	33 N–Q3 Q–R4
4 P–QN4 B×NP	14 N–Q2 B–QB4	24 KR–K1 Q–N4	34 P–R3 K–N2
5 P–B3 B–R4	15 Q–N2 P–B3	25 B–K6 R–B3	35 P–QB4 R–B6
6 P–Q4 P–Q3	16 B–N3 P–N4	26 B×B K×B	(67)
7 Q–N3 N–R3	17 0–0 K–K2	27 P–QR4 P–R3	36 N–B4 R×N
8 B×N P×B	18 N–B3 Q–N2	28 P×P BP×P	37 R×B Q–B2
9 B×P+ K–B1	19 K–R1 B–Q2	29 Q–R2 R–R1	38 Q–N6+
10 P×P Q–K2	20 P–K5 QR–KB1	30 N–B3 Q–QB4	Black resigns.

14 The Scotch Game

That combinations are sometimes similar, the reader knows. But does he know that there are closely-related openings?

He probably does not know, but I myself have only realized this now, at this very moment.

The Englishman, Captain Evans, invented his gambit in 1824, and in the same year a correspondence match took place between London and Edinburgh. The Scots were White and after 1 P–K4 P–K4 they chose the attack 2 N–KB3, and in reply to 2 ... N–QB3 played 3 P–Q4!.

Usually moves with which beautiful victories are gained become very popular and immediately give rise to valuable theoretical research. This is what happened on this occasion too. The Scots triumphed in fine style, the move 3 P–Q4 came firmly into practice, whilst the whole opening 1 P–K4 P–K4 2 N–KB3 N–QB3 3 P–Q4 (*68*) received the name 'The Scotch Game'.

Who can say now that the Evans' Gambit and the Scotch Game are not related openings, if not twin-openings! Both were born in 1824 and both can be ascribed the respectable age of 146. It is not every opening that can boast such a long life.

There are various interpretations as to which is the best method of attack for White and which is the most reliable defence for Black. Those who want to make closer acquaintance with 3 P–Q4 should have a look at reference books on the opening.

There are various ways of conducting the attack. Considered the most dangerous for Black is the variation 3 P–Q4 P×P 4 P–B3 P×P 5 B–QB4 P×P 6 B×NP. But Black is not forced to accept the sacrifice of the pawns, and he ought only take the QBP when he is in a fighting mood. He does better to restrict himself to 3 ... P–Q6 or 3 ... P–Q4.

ONE MUST COLLECT AND READ THEM

Black: A. Fuderer – Kiev 1959, USSR v Yugoslavia

69B

What I am thinking about are books on chess theory. Those who wish to be counted in the ranks of chess theoreticians are obliged to read and know by heart all the books on theory, from Adam and Eve to today.

When the game analysed on this page was played, I was confident that I had devised an original attack, in the moves Q–N3, N–KN5, B–QN5, P–KB4 and P–KR3. . . .

But in the spring of 1960, whilst returning to Moscow from Mar del Plata, I acquired in the capital of Argentina, Buenos Aires, several old Spanish books and on one of the pages I discovered the opening of my game with Fuderer from move 1 to move 11! As the Spanish book bore witness, then, these moves had already been played in 1890. . . .

The aim of Black's 13 . . . P–N5 is to remove the white queen from the QN3–KB7 diagonal, so that the black bishop could have the chance to go to K2.

Now I see clearly that the correct retort was 14 Q ×NP B–K2 15 Q–N3, and to allow Black to castle K-side.

In this case White need not fear for the fate of his knight on KN5: Black will hardly risk opening the KR-file for the white rook. But at the time I was indeed afraid of losing the knight: Fuderer is a player of an extremely sharp style; he is not frightened by the slightest thing.

1 P–K4 P–K4	11 ... P ×B	22 B–B5 Q–B2	32 R ×B R–K7
2 N–KB3 N–QB3	12 P ×N P–KR3	23 P–QN4 RP ×P	33 R–KB1 R/1 ×P
3 P–Q4 P ×P	13 B–K3 P–N5	24 B ×P B–N2	34 P–Q7 Q–N1 +
4 P–B3 P ×P	14 Q ×NP B–K2	25 P ×P P–B3	35 N–K5 + R ×N
5 B–QB4 P–Q3	15 N–B3 N ×NP	26 KR–K1 +	36 P–Q8 = Q
6 N ×P N–B3	16 B–Q4 P–Q4	26 ... K–B2	36 ... R–K6 + +
7 Q–N3 Q–Q2	17 B–B5 N–K6	27 P–Q6 Q–N3 +	37 K–N4 R ×P +
8 N–KN5 N–K4	18 B ×B N–B7 +	28 K–N3 KR–K1	38 K–B5 Q ×Q
9 B–N5 P–B3	19 K–B2 N ×Q	29 KR–Q1 P–N4	39 R ×Q R–K4
10 P–B4 N/4–N5	20 B ×N P–QR4	30 P ×P RP ×P	Mate.
11 P–KR3 (69)	21 B–R3 P–QN4	31 N–Q5 B ×N	

EXCHANGES, EXCHANGES...

White: R. Letelier – Mar del Plata 1960, International Tournament

If I tell you that Black could easily have won the central pawn on K4 as early as the fourth move, will the reader take me at my word or will he require proof?

This variation – 4 . . . Q–R5 – was invented by Steinitz. The most curious feature of it is that the White KP does in fact fall.

And I have proof of this: 5 N–QB3 B–N5 6 Q–Q3 B×N+ 7 P×B N–B3 8 N–N5 K–Q1, and there is no defence against . . . Q×KP. Clever, eh?

But for some reason I have never met any bold fellow prepared to chase after such spoils!

Besides, on move 7 White could play Q×B and on 7 . . . Q×KP+, reply 8 B–K3, or 8 N–K2, or 8 B–K2 – any way White gets a formidable attack.

Finally, and this is the essential point, White has at his disposal the simple and very strong 5 N–N5!.

I will give one variation by way of example: 5 . . . Q×KP+ 6 B–K2 B–N5+ 7 B–Q2 B×B+ 8 Q×B Q–K4 9 P–KB4 Q×NP 10 0–0 Q×R 11 N/1–B3 Q×R+ 12 K×Q K–Q1 13 N–Q5!.

But what should I say about the present game?

I should have played 6 . . . Q–R5! instead of the passive 6 . . . P–Q3?, but I was afraid of long theoretical variations after 7 Q–K2 KN–K2 8 P–QR4 etc.

I succeeded in turning the game into a quiet channel, but simultaneously any chances of complicating were lost; exchange after exchange and in the end I myself was glad when a draw was proposed.

1 P–K4 P–K4	6 N–B3 P–Q3	12 B–K3 B×B	17 N–Q4 N×N
2 N–KB3 N–QB3	7 P–QR4 P–QR4	13 N×B N–KB3	18 Q×N KR–K1
3 P–Q4 P×P	8 N–Q5 B–R2	14 R–K1 0–0	19 P–QB4 QR–Q1
4 N×P (70)	9 B–QN5 B–Q2	15 N–Q5 N×N	20 P–QN3 P–QN3
4 . . . B–B4	10 0–0 N–K4	16 Q×N N–B3	Draw agreed.
5 N–N3 B–N3	11 B×B+ Q×B		

GRANDMASTER GÖSTA STOLTZ

White: G. Stoltz – Stockholm 1948, Interzonal Tournament

Unfortunately this player was not very active in the international arena in the later years of his life. But in the thirties his name was pronounced alongside those of such aces as Flohr, Nimzowitsch, Reti, Ståhlberg, Liliental and Botvinnik.

Apparently modern, deeply scientific play did not arouse any special emotions in Stoltz, and he did not strive to maintain an active chess life.

The game with Stoltz we shall look at below took place in the middle of the tournament. I had thought that in a game between two lovers of the King's Gambit the opening would be predetermined, but the Swedish grandmaster preferred the Scotch Game.

When the black knight on QB3 went to the strong K4 square, it seemed that White's position was on the point of collapse: he could not defend his KB3 satisfactorily! All the more so in that in answer to 15 N–Q2 I had prepared the forceful refutation 15 ... R×N 16 Q×R R–Q1 17 N–Q5 R×N 18 Q×R N–B6+ 19 B×N Q×B.

But on more thorough examination it turned out that there was a hole in Black's combination: 19 K–R1 N×R 20 P–KB4 P–B3 21 Q×P/B5!.

But when Black's pressure had weakened and the game was moving quickly towards a draw, Stoltz faltered and fell into a trap.

1 P–K4 P–K4	12 0–0 N–N3	21 P–KB4 Q–K7	31 P–B5 N–K2
2 N–KB3 N–QB3	13 P–KN3 B–R6	22 N/2–B1 B×N	32 P–B6 P×P
3 P–Q4 P×P	14 R–K1	23 Q×Q B×Q	33 N–B2 B–N4
4 N×P B–B4	14 ... N/B3–K4	24 R–Q6 B–B6	34 N–Q4 B–K1
5 B–K3 Q–B3	(71)	25 R×P B×P	35 N–B2 R–N1
6 P–QB3 KN–K2	15 N–Q2 P–B3	26 R×P P–QR3	36 N–N4 R×N
7 N–B2 P–Q3	16 QR–Q1 P–N4	27 P–QR4 P×P	37 P×R B–N4
8 B×B P×B	17 N–N3 R×R	28 R–QR5 B–B3	38 P–N3 P×P
9 N–K3 0–0	18 R×R N–B6+	29 N–B5 K–B1	39 R–R3 B–B5
10 B–K2 R–Q1	19 B×N Q×B	30 N–Q4 B-K1	White resigns.
11 Q–B2 B–K3	20 N–Q2 Q–R4		

AN ENDGAME WILLY-NILLY

White: Yu. Randviir – Parnu 1947, Training Tournament

I doubt whether the black queen's cowardly move from K5 to K4, which forced the game into a boring endgame, will appeal to anyone.

If you want to suggest 14 ... N–N5 to me, then excellent! If the white queen takes the rook, Black will mate in two with his knight and bishop: 15 Q×R? N–B7+ 16 K–K2 B–B5 mate!

However, after the black knight has left QB3 the white KB gets the chance to give check and simultaneously free a square for his king's escape: 14 ... N–N5 15 B–QN5+! P–QB3 16 Q×R N–B7+ 17 K–B1.

Perhaps Black should have chosen this variation? I do not think so. Instead of 16 ... N–B7+?, it is true that 16 ... Q×P! 17 R–KB1 N–B7+! 18 K–K2 B–N5 mate is stronger, but White here too need be in no hurry to take the rook. The correct defence would be to check first, 15 B–QN5+, but then hastily to castle: 15 ... P–QB3 16 0–0!, since Black's KR in the corner cannot run away from the white queen. I spent quite a bit of time, I remember clearly, looking for some decisive combination in the variation 14 ... N–N5 15 B–QN5+, but just could not find one.

In short, an endgame willy-nilly.

1 P–K4 P–K4	13 N×B RP×N	22 R×R N–B3	32 P–B3 P–B3
2 N–KB3 N–QB3	14 Q×NP (72)	23 B–QN5 K–B2	33 B–K2 B–B5
3 P–Q4 P×P	14 ... Q–K4	24 N–B1 R–KN1	34 B×N B×B
4 N×P B–B4	15 Q×Q N×Q	25 N–K2	35 R–B2 P×B
5 N–N3 B–N3	16 B–KB4 P–KB3	25 ... N/N3–K4	36 R×B K–K3
6 P–QB4 P–Q3	17 B–K2 N–K2	26 B–K3 N–QN5	37 K–B2 P–B5
7 N–B3 Q–R5	18 0–0 0–0	27 P–QR3 B–N6	38 P–KN3 P–N4
8 P–B5 P×P	19 KR–K1	28 R–KB1 N–Q4	39 K–K3 R–QR1
9 B–K3 B–N5	19 ... N/2–N3	29 N–B4 N×N	40 R–QB2 P–B4
10 Q–Q2 R–Q1	20 B–KR6	30 B×N B–Q4	41 P–B4 R–Q1
11 N–Q5 B–K3	20 ... KR–K1	31 B–N3 P–R4	White resigns.
12 Q–B3 Q×KP	21 QR–Q1 R×R		

15 The English Game (Ponziani)

PROUD CHESS HORSES

Black: Yu. Balashov – Moscow 1967, Grandmaster and Masters Tournament

73B

I wonder if amongst the readers there is even one trusting fellow who will take me at my word that the tempting piece sacrifice 3 ... N–B3 4 P–Q4 N×KP 5 P–Q5 B–B4 6 P×N B×P+ is absolutely harmless for the white king?

On the other hand if *you* were to have asked *me* about this, then I would only have shaken my head in doubt. ... I could not allow it! No, however much *you* might want to, *I* would not go chasing such a piece. It is a serious matter that the king loses the right to castle and remains in the centre, with an avalanche of black pawns descending upon him!. ...

But if White had not wanted to play 4 P–Q4, why did he go 3 P–B3?

This question is very easily answered: White was counting on the sharp reply 3 ... P–Q4.

1 P–K4 P–K4	18 QR–B1 P–KN3	35 Q–K2 R–KB1	52 R–QN1 B–K2
2 N–KB3 N–QB3	19 P–QR4 B–R3	36 N–N3 Q–B7	53 N–K4 K×P
3 P–B3 N–B3	20 K–N1 Q–Q1	37 Q×Q R×Q	54 K×P K–B1
4 P–Q3 P–Q4	21 N–N3 Q–B2	38 R–K1 N–Q2	55 R–KB1 R–N2
5 QN–Q2 B–K2	22 B–KB3 N–KB3	39 N×RP P–N3	56 P–R6 B–N4+
6 P–QN4 P–QR3	23 P–R4 N–B1	40 N–N3 K–B2	57 K–K2 B×P
7 P–QR3 0–0	24 P–R5 P–N4	41 P–R5 P×P	58 R–B8+ K–B2
8 B–N2 R–K1	25 B–B1 N–N3	42 N–R4 K–K2	59 N/3–B5 R–K2
9 Q–B2 B–B1	26 B–KN2 N–N5	43 N×RP R–Q7	60 R–B6 B–N2
10 P–N3 B–N5	27 B–KR3 B–K3	44 N–N3 R×P	61 R×P K–Q1
11 B–N2 Q–B1	28 P–B3 N–K6	45 K–B2 R–Q5	62 R–QN6 K–B1
12 P–R3 B–Q2	29 B×N P×B	46 K–B3 K–Q3	63 N–K6 (73)
13 P–B4 P–Q5	30 B×B P×B	47 P–N6 R×KP	63 ... K–Q2
14 N–KN1	31 N/3–B1 P–N5	48 P–N7 N–N1	64 N/6–B5+
14 ... P–QR4	32 P×P R–KB1	49 P–N5 B×P	64 ... K–B1
15 P–N5 N–K2	33 N–B3 R–B2	50 N/4×P R–N5	65 R–Q6
16 N–K2 P–B4	34 R×R Q×R	51 K–Q3 K–B3	Black resigns.
17 0–0–0 N–R4			

16 Konstantinopolsky's Opening

THE INDIAN FIANCHETTO

Black: L. Lengyel – Amsterdam 1964, Interzonal Tournament

74B

Chess was born in India and in the early stages of its development it was an extremely slow game. One had no reason then to fear sudden attacks, since no piece could cross the whole board at one go, just as two thousand years ago no ship could cross the Indian Ocean in under twenty-four hours. And chess is nothing other than a miniature model of ancient battles, where the fierce fighting would be preceded by many days or years of transferring and shifting military units about.

These days, when all the pieces have considerably increased their firing power, the bishop operates excellently from any cover, but, as in years gone by, it is extremely active when developed on a flank.

The fianchettoed bishop here coped wonderfully with the task entrusted to it: the defence of the pawn on K4, and it thereby freed the other white pieces for an offensive in the Q-side region.

Having seized a certain amount of space, White forced his opponent to defend hard, but he could not make a breach in Black's fortress wall.

I leave it to the reader himself to check if the exchange sacrifice, R ×N, would have achieved the desired objective.

1 P–K4 P–K4	8 0–0 P–QN3	16 P–QN4 B–Q5	24 P–R4 R–Q3
2 N–KB3 N–QB3	9 R–K1 B–N2	17 Q–B2 B×B	25 B–B1 P×P
3 P–KN3 (74)	10 P–N3 B–B4	18 Q×B B–K3	26 P×P Q–B1
3 ... N–B3	11 B–N2 N–KN5	19 P–B5 Q–Q2	27 B–K2 R/1–Q1
4 P–Q3 P–Q4	12 R–KB1 B–R3	20 P–N5 N–R4	28 Q–B3 Q–B2
5 QN–Q2 B–K2	13 P–B4 P–B3	21 P–B6 Q–B1	29 N–R2 Q–K2
6 B–N2 P×P	14 P–QR3 B–B1	22 P–KR4 R–Q1	30 Q–B2 N–B2
7 P×P 0–0	15 P–R3 N–R3	23 KR–Q1 P–R3	Draw agreed.

17 The Three Knights' Opening

75B

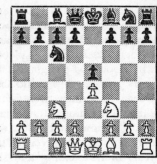

If you are not in the mood for a drawn-out fight, if you have toothache, or if you have tickets for an interesting show in your pocket – in all of these cases the most desired outcome of the game for you is a quick draw!

But what if your opponent does not share your peaceable intentions?

That is not too great a worry: choose the Three Knights' Opening, and then the most competitive opponent will find himself in psychological zugzwang. Either he will have to settle for the boring Four Knights' Opening, where you will have no difficulty in getting a draw, or . . . he will be stuck in the Three Knights'.

The latter is even better for you. You can attack boldly, seize the initiative and, having infiltrated into your opponent's half . . . immediately propose a draw from a position of strength.

I assure you that no-one will refuse. And you will still have time to get to the opening night at the theatre.

Does this seem ridiculous to you? To us grandmasters, it is not at all. When we play 2 . . . N–QB3, we always risk running aground . . . in the Three Knights'!

There is only one way of avoiding standard variations: one must look for some unusual move. Then one's opponent will straight away forget his peaceable intentions and rush headlong into the attack!

And if he still will not attack but follows his drawing line as before? Or if you have been so eager in your attempts to 'avoid' that you have got a bad game?

One needs to 'avoid' carefully.

But do not try to confuse your opponent with 3 . . . P–KN3. The variation 4 P–Q4 P×P 5 N–Q5 B–N2 6 B–KN5 N/3–K2, although it is not bad for Black, has nowadays been studied thoroughly too. There's no escape!

BISHOP OR PAWN

White: A. Sokolsky – Moscow 1949, USSR Championship

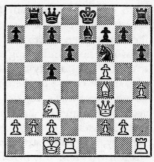

76W

The question is not which is the stronger – the reply to that is already well-known: the bishop, if it commands the board, the pawn, if it can become a queen.

The interesting question is this: Black's bishop on K2 and White's pawn on QN2 – which of them is more in need of protection?

It would seem the bishop, since after 15 Q–K2! Q×P+ 16 K–Q2 there is no defence against the two threats 17 R–K1 and 17 R–QN1 Q–R6 18 R×R+.

However, Black can disregard the threat of Q×B, and calmly castle: 15 Q–K2? 0–0!, since bad is 16 Q×B? R–K1!.

There is one further undisclosed secret in the position: the variation 15 Q–K2 Q×P+ 16 K–Q2 0–0 17 Q×B. White has won a piece but will he be able to maintain his advantage after 17 ... Q–N5 ?

Therefore White did not try to find a refutation of Black's plan, but exchanged queens and kept an advantage in the endgame.

1 P–K4 P–K4	19 P–QB4 R–K1	38 K–B4 K–B3	55 R–N8 R–N8
2 N–KB3 N–QB3	20 K–B2 R–QN1	39 R–K8 R–R4	56 K–B4 P–B5
3 N–B3 P–Q3	21 R–Q3 R–K5	40 R–QR8	57 B–R7
4 P–Q4 P×P	22 P–N3 B–K2	40 ... R–KB4	57 ... R–QB8+
5 N×P N–B3	23 N–B3 R–KN5	41 R–K8 K–N2	58 K–Q3 K–Q4
6 B–QN5 B–Q2	24 B×P P–R3	42 R–K4 R–R4	59 R–Q8+ B–Q3
7 B×N P×B	25 B–K3 R–KR1	43 P–R4 B–N5	60 R–KN8
8 Q–B3 P–B4	26 P–B5 N–B5	44 R–B4 P–KB4	60 ... R–QN8
9 N–B5 P–KR3	27 R/3–Q1 RP×P	45 R–B3 R–R5+	61 K–B2 R–N8
10 B–B4 B×N	28 BP×P B×P	46 R–B4 R–R6	62 K–Q3 P–N4
11 P×B R–QN1	29 P×P R×R	47 R–Q4 K–B3	63 P–B3 R–N7
12 0–0–0 B–K2	30 R×R R×P	48 R–Q8 R–R8	64 B–Q4 R–N6
13 P–KR4 Q–B1	31 P–B6 P–N3	49 R–K8 R–R5+	65 B–B3 R×P+
(76)	32 R–R8 R–KB4	50 K–Q3 K–Q4	66 K–Q2 R–N6
14 P–KN4 Q–N2	33 R–R8 P–R4	51 R–Q8+ K–K3	67 B×P P–B6
15 Q×Q R×Q	34 N–K4 N–Q4	52 R–K8+ K–Q2	68 R–N7 B–B5+
16 P–N5 N–R4	35 K–Q2 N×P	53 R–KN8 R–N5	69 K–Q3 R–N8
17 B–K3 K–Q2	36 N×N R×N	54 R–N7+ K–B3	White resigns.
18 N–Q5 B–Q1	37 K–Q3 R–B4		

AN AVALANCHE OF BLACK PAWNS

White: L. Kanevsky – Kiev 1939, Kiev Team Championship

I am still not indifferent today to mobile pawn chains, but there was a time when I liked them even more.

I would not mind losing a valuable tempo in the opening if only to get a mobile pawn mass in the centre of the board.

And the pawns repaid me generously. Even when queens had been exchanged, Black's attack in no way relented – even the contrary, it became stronger.

But if (in chess this invisible 'if' is always present) in the diagrammed position it had been White to move, he could have torn open the strong point of his opponent's defence with a knight sacrifice: 1 N×P P×N 2 Q×KP with the threat of 3 N–Q5. Curious variations would have arisen:

a) 2 ... R–B1 3 N–Q5 R–N2 4 P–KB4 K–B2 5 N×B Q×N 6 Q–Q5+ B–K3 7 Q×R.

b) 2 ... 0–0! 3 Q–Q5+ R–B2 4 Q×B B×P+.

But, as the reader can see, not even these variations favour White.

I probably ought to say something too about similar positions where pawn-type hedgehogs rob the knights of their best squares: in such situations one can rarely achieve something decisive with a simple variation – a sacrifice is always necessary. That is why in my commentary I have tried to destroy Black's camp by N×P; but, as you have already seen, nothing came of my efforts.

1 P–K4 P–K4	11 P–KN4	18 ... P–B3	27 N×B+ K–B2
2 N–KB3 N–QB3	11 ... R–QN1	19 Q–Q2 0–0	28 R×Q K×N
3 N–B3 P–Q3	12 P–N5 KP×P	20 Q–K3 B–K3	29 K–Q2 P–B5
4 B–N5 P–QR3	13 B×P N–K4	21 P–R3 R–N2	30 P–QB3 P–B4
5 B×N+ P×B	14 Q–K2 P–QB4	22 QR–N1 Q–R4	31 KR–N1 B–Q2
6 P–Q4 P–B3	15 B×N BP×B	23 N–Q1 R/1–N1	32 P–B3 B–R5
7 B–K3 N–K2	16 Q×P B–K2	24 N–R4 P–Q4	33 R–N2 R×P+
8 Q–Q2 N–N3	17 Q–B4 R–N5	25 N–B5 P–Q5	34 K–B1 R×R
9 0–0–0 B–N5	18 Q–Q5 (77)	26 Q–K1 Q×Q	White resigns.
10 P–KR3 B–Q2			

EVERYONE KNOWS, YOUNG AND OLD ALIKE

White: R. Gorenstein – Dniepropetrovsk 1939, Ukrainian Championship

78B

One should not play one's RPs forward unnecessarily – everyone, young and old alike, knows this truth today.

I know it too, but when you are fighting with might and main, do you have time to observe all the strict rules of chess etiquette?

Black, for example, by ... P–QR3 prepared a pawn attack on White's bishop on QB4, whilst White, by P–QR3, prepared a safe shelter for the bishop.

With P–KR3 White took KN5 away from Black's bishop in revenge for ... P–KR3, which deprived the white knight of the tempting route N–N5–KB7.

In the end both players played so over-cautiously that they got into terrible time-trouble right in the opening and ... in their fear, agreed on a draw.

What was the point of Black's putting his QB on Q2? There was none!

But at the time when this game was being played the author feared more than anything else in chess ... the exchange of queens. 4 ... B–Q2 was a defence against the variation 5 P×P P×P 6 Q×Q+ etc.

Many years were to pass before, not from somebody else's experience, but from by own, I realised that one can sometimes play a lively, attractive game without the queens on.

But in those days I dreamt only of intricate and complicated combinations in the Evans' Gambit, the King's Gambit, and other openings, invariably from the Italian school. And who knows, perhaps in chess too one ought to organise tournaments based not only on the number of points but also on 'the greatest number of cheerful combinative games'. . . .

1 P–K4 P–K4	7 P–KR3 P–R3	11 P×N N×P	16 KR–K1 R–B1
2 N–KB3 N–QB3	8 P–R3 (78)	12 N×N P×N	17 QR–Q1 P–N5
3 N–B3 P–Q3	8 ... B–K2	13 B×QP 0–0	18 P×P P×P
4 P–Q4 B–Q2	9 Q–Q2 P–QN4	14 0–0 P–QR4	19 N–R2 R–N1
5 B–QB4 P–KR3	10 B–Q5 N×B	15 Q–B4 P–KB4	Draw agreed.
6 B–K3 N–B3			

I WAS SIMPLY FRIGHTENED

White: V. Simagin – Parnu 1947, Training Tournament

The pitiful 42 . . . B–R1 nullified all the preparatory work done by Black's pieces.

Was I really simply frightened of the variation 42 . . . B–N8   43 N×B Q×P 44 Q–Q6?

I cannot remember.

But today I regret that I let this chance slip. If the bishop had penetrated to QR7, White's pawns would not have held out!

Alas, there is nothing one can do about it afterwards.

And yet it is interesting to know why I did not play my bishop to QN8. I can only plead . . . time-trouble.

But who would believe that? . . . B–R1 was played on the 42nd move, after the resumption, and I had had sufficient time to analyse it at home.

But anyone who has been to Parnu will understand that in this holiday resort the last thing one is drawn to is the home analysis of adjourned games, in addition to which the tournament was a semi-official, training one. So that both players came fresh to the game and to the resumption of it after the adjournment. Now I can offer a clearer explanation of the timid 42 . . . B–R1?. I was simply frightened!

The game in itself is also interesting: the white knights tried this way and that way to break up Black's pawn chain, but this duel too culminated in a draw.

1 P–K4 P–K4	14 B–R6 N–N2	27 Q×R P–R4	40 Q–N3 B–K5
2 N–KB3 N–QB3	15 QR–Q1 P–QB4	28 N–Q3 R–K3	41 N–K1 P–R4
3 N–B3 P–Q3	16 N/4–K2 P–QB3	29 Q–Q2 Q–R2	42 P–B3 B–R1
4 P–Q4 P×P	17 P–B4 P–Q5	30 P–QR4 Q–N3	(79)
5 N×P N–B3	18 P–N3 P–B3	31 R×R N×R	43 N–Q3 P–R5
6 B–QN5 B–Q2	19 P–K6 B×P	32 Q–Q1 N–Q1	44 Q–K1 B–N2
7 0–0 B–K2	20 Q×QBP R–N3	33 B–B4 B–K3	45 B–B1 B–B1
8 P–KR3 0–0	21 Q–B3 Q–R1	34 N–KB1 N–B2	46 Q–Q1 B–Q2
9 B×N P×B	22 Q–Q3 P–B4	35 Q–K2 B–Q2	47 N–B1 B–K1
10 Q–B3 N–K1	23 N–B4 B–B2	36 B–B1 K–N2	48 B–Q2 B–B2
11 P–K5 P–Q4	24 KR–K1 B–B3	37 N–Q2 N–Q1	49 N–R2 B–K1
12 N/3–K2 R–N1	25 R–K2 R–K1	38 B–R3 N–K3	50 N–KB1
13 N–KN3 P–N3	26 R/1–K1 R×R	39 Q–B3 B–B3	Draw agreed.

18 Four Knights' Opening

80W

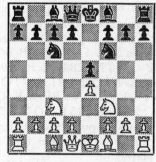

The Four Knights' Opening is a derivative of the Three Knights' which, in its turn, is a derivative of the Vienna Game or the Petroff Defence. The Four Knights' cannot be separated at all from these openings: they are all made up of only 'knight' moves! Here we have touched upon a detail of some importance – how to name openings?

Since many openings frequently, as the game unfolds, imperceptibly take on characteristics of related, but different openings, theoreticians find it difficult to say in many cases which opening has been played. FIDE even created a special commission, whose duty was to work out an openings nomenclature, but the problem has not only not yet been solved, there is not even news of the commission beginning work. One can understand the hitches the experts are finding: everything is so complicated and confused that one cannot know how to set about it.

For example, take a very simple case: 1 P–K4 P–K4 2 N–QB3 N–QB3 is the Vienna Game; 3 N–B3 is the Three Knights'; 3 . . . N–B3 the Four Knights'. The author thought a lot about this and decided, at his own risk, to arrange the openings arbitrarily, and also to name this or that variation at random, and more by intuition, either after the names of great masters, or on purely chess grounds.

So I beg strict lovers of chess theory not to complain: after all, my book is a collection of games, not an openings book!

I have tried as far as possible to choose more lively games. So, for example, there are few games from the Four Knights'. And this is correct, since this opening is a convenient platform for peace negotiations, with White showing the initiative.

A GRANDMASTER DRAW

White: G. Levenfish – Moscow 1948, USSR Championship

81W

Rubinstein's defence 4 ... N–Q5! is only called a defence out of a misunderstanding. It is a good defensive move, given that its main aim is to mate the opponent's king!

If you require proof, open a book on openings theory. In any of them analysis of the move 4 ... N–Q5 begins with the variation 5 N×P Q–K2 6 P–B4 N×B 7 N×N P–Q3 8 N–KB3 Q×P+ 9 K–B2 N–N5+ 10 K–N3 Q–N3 11 N–R4 Q–R4 12 P–KR3 N–B3 13 N×BP+ K–Q1 14 N×R

Q×N+(*81*) 15 K×Q N–K5; Black has sacrificed a queen and rook, but in return has put the white king in a difficult position. But arriving at such a concise variation has required the efforts of a whole number of chess-players.

And it was only after many people had suffered at the hands of the defensive ... N–Q5 that theoretical manuals began to accompany the knight thrust with the international sign '!', which signifies in all languages: 'Look out, be careful on the bend!'

In the light of the above it is clear why Black, on the seventh move of the variation which occurred in the game, was wise to take the pawn on KB3 and not the pawn on Q7. Why develop your opponent's pieces?

After 7 ... P×QP+? 8 B/1×P Q×P 9 0–0 B–K2 10 B–B3, the attack by White's pieces seems irresistible.

And in conclusion, the most important thing. The fact that this game ended in a draw suited me well ... and would have done even before the game began. When you think that it was my first official encounter at the highest rank of international grandmaster, and with whom? With Grigory Yakovlevich Levenfish himself, on whose games I had been brought up!

1 P–K4 P–K4	8 QP×P Q–K4+	14 K–B1 B–Q3	19 P–B4 R×R
2 N–KB3 N–QB3	9 Q–K2 Q×Q+	15 B–K5 B×B	20 R×R P×P
3 N–B3 N–B3	10 K×Q P–QB3	16 R×B P–KR3	21 B×P R–K1
4 B–N5 N–Q5	11 B–Q3 P–Q4	17 P–KB4	22 R×R+ B×R
5 N×N P×N	12 R–K1 B–K3	17 ... QR–K1	23 K–K2
6 P–K5 P×N	13 B–KB4 0–0–0	18 R/1–K1 B–Q2	Draw agreed.
7 P×N Q×P			

A SHARP ENDGAME

White: A. Renter – Parnu 1947, Training Tournament

Black set the transparent trap: 20 Q–Q2?
R ×N!, but his opponent saw it.

After the black king reached the fourth
rank first and the black rook fatally pinned
White's QRP to its place, it seemed that
Black's win was not far off. This impression
was strengthened in particular after the
energetic 32 ... P–Q4.

It is interesting that this signal of attack for
Black also served as a signal of defence for
White. My opponent obviously remembered
that it was not the rook's job passively to defend the QRP and he immediately embarked on a counter-attack.

It was difficult during play to decide whether 43 R ×RP R ×BP
44 R–QB6 K–K4 45 R × P/B7 K ×P was sufficient for the draw. However,
after the game a draw was found: 46 R–KN7 P–N4 47 P–N4 P–N5
48 P–N5 P–N6 49 P–N6 R–QN5 50 R–Q7+ K–K3 51 P–N7 R–N5
52 R–N7 P–B5 53 K–K3 K–B3 54 P–N8 = Q R ×Q 55 K–Q4 R–N5+
56 K–B3!, and the king gets there in time.

White would not have had to calculate this variation at all if instead of
42 R–K6 +? he had played more decisively: 42 R ×RP R ×BP 43 P–R4
K ×P 44 P–R5.

1 P–K4 P–K4	16 P–B4 P ×P	29 R–R2 K–B2	43 R–QB6 R ×BP
2 N–KB3 N–QB3	17 R ×P Q–K4	30 N–B3 K–K3	44 R ×P/B7 P–N4
3 N–B3 N–B3	18 R/4–B1	31 N ×B R ×N	45 P–Q6 K–K3
4 B–N5 B–N5	18 ... QR–N1	32 R–R1 P–Q4	46 P–Q7 K–K2
5 0–0 0–0	19 N–N3 Q–B6	33 R–K1+ K–Q3	47 K–K3 P–R4
6 P–Q3 B ×N	(82)	34 P ×P R ×P	48 P–N3 P–N5
7 P ×B Q–K2	20 KR–Q1 R–N3	35 P–B4 R ×P	49 R–N7 R–B6+
8 B ×N NP ×B	21 Q–Q2 Q ×Q	36 R–K6+ K–Q2	50 K–K4 P–N6
9 B–N5 P–KR3	22 N ×Q R/1–N1	37 R–N6 R–Q5	51 K–Q5 P–B5
10 B–R4 P–Q3	23 R ×R RP ×R	38 R ×KNP+	52 K–B5 R–B7
11 R–N1 Q–K3	24 P–QR3 R–R1	38 ... K–B1	53 K–B6 R–Q7
12 B ×N Q ×B	25 R–R1 P–B4	39 R–N8+ K–Q2	54 P–Q8 = Q++
13 P–B4 Q–K2	26 P ×P B ×P	40 R–N7+ K–Q3	54 ... K ×Q
14 Q–K2 P–QB4	27 K–B2 B–Q2	41 R–N6+ K–K4	White resigns.
15 N–Q2 B–Q2	28 N–K4 B–R5	42 R–K6+ K–B4	

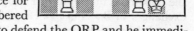

THE STALEMATED ROOK

White: G. Uusi – Moscow 1953, Moscow Championship

I succeeded in this game in repeating a well-known stratagem: pawns keeping a bishop out, as well as excluding one of the enemy pieces for a time from the game. Our generation observed this means of attack most frequently in the games of the great Capablanca.

Having played the opening stage of the game quietly White could have achieved the maximum of simplification by one more exchange: 11 B ×N Q ×B. However, he was attracted by another plan, that of provoking . . . P–KN4 and, after the necessary regrouping, tearing down Black's fortifications with a decisive P–KB4. But Black introduced his own correctives into White's plan.

And when the nomadic bishop returned to active service, its army was already in a difficult position which it was no longer possible to rectify.

The bishop was not the only guilty party. The Q-side pawns got split up, and the QR somehow strayed on to a square forgotten by everyone, QR3, from where its visibility was nil.

All these troubles started from the moment when, having made the firm decision to play for a draw, White did not take Black's knight on KB3 with his bishop. Perhaps he deliberately wanted to provoke . . . P–KN4 so as to take advantage of the black king's denuded position.

It was a sensible idea, but Black had reliable defenders in the light-squared bishop and the fiery KN.

The manoeuvre N–KB3–K1–KN2! was introduced into serious tournament practice by Emanuel Lasker.

So that I find myself having willy-nilly to repeat the already stated truth: the experience of our elders is no hindrance!

1 P–K4 P–K4	9 B ×QN P ×B	16 R–K1 Q–B2	23 Q–N4 P–QB4
2 N–KB3 N–QB3	10 R–N1 P–KR3	17 R–R3 P–QR4	24 P ×BP P ×P
3 N–B3 N–B3	11 B–R4 Q–K3	18 P–B3 B–R3	25 B ×P B–K1
4 B–N5 B–N5	12 N–Q2 P–N4	19 B–B2 B–N4	26 Q–B4 R ×R +
5 0–0 0–0	13 B–N3 N–K1	20 Q–N1 KR–N1	27 N ×R R–Q1
6 P–Q3 P–Q3	14 P–Q4 P–B3	21 Q–N3 N–K3	(83)
7 B–N5 B ×N	15 R–N3 N–N2	22 R–N1 P–R5	White resigns.
8 P ×B Q–K2			

INTERFERENCE AND OBSTRUCTION

White: I. Bondarevsky – Moscow 1945, Semi-Finals USSR Championship

84W

If I had not been an eye-witness to this game, I would not have believed that Black could play anything other than 27 ... Q×RP!.

I considered this move inadequate because of 28 Q×P! and paid no attention to the possibility of 28 ... N×R!.

The position in the diagram is a dream for lovers of compositions. The theme of 'interference and obstruction' is brought out most clearly in the variation 30 Q–N7 Q–Q5 31 Q–R1 P–QB3 32 B×P Q–B4.

Nor would 30 B–Q5 have saved the game – but with both of us in terrible time-trouble Black wrongly declined the queen sacrifice, since the variation 30 ... P–QB3 31 P–K6 R×B 32 Q×R P×Q 33 P–K7 Q–N7+ 34 K–Q1 Q–N8+ 35 K–K2 Q–N4+ 36 K–Q1 Q–K1 37 R–K3 P–B3 38 K–K2 K–B2 39 K–Q3 Q–N4+ 40 K×P K–K1 would have allowed Black to stop the white pawn and activate his queen.

As the game was being adjourned, a miracle occurred: my opponent thought for a long time and ... sealed in the envelope the horrible move 41 Q–Q3??, after which either he would lose his rook or mate would be unavoidable.

For many years the best move has been recognised to be 7 B–Q3, when Black is still faced with a difficult task.

1 P–K4 P–K4	13 N×B N–Q2	25 N–N1 Q–B5	36 R–K3 P–N3
2 N–KB3 N–QB3	14 P–KB4 R–N1	26 N×P P×N	37 Q×RP R–Q7
3 N–B3 N–B3	15 Q–B3 N–N3	27 R×B N×R	38 Q–K4 R×RP
4 P–Q4 P×P	16 Q–QR3 Q–B3	28 B×N Q×NP	39 R–Q3 Q–B4
5 N×P B–N5	17 P–KN3 Q–B3	29 B×R R–Q1	40 R–Q7+ K–B1
6 N×N NP×N	18 P–N3 P–QR4	(*84*)	41 Q–Q3 R–Q7
7 Q–Q4 Q–K2	19 B–Q3 P–R5	30 B–Q5 P–QB3	42 R–Q8+ K–N2
8 P–B3 P–Q4	20 P–K5 B–K3	31 P–K6 P×P	43 R–Q7+ K–B3
9 B–Q2 0–0	21 KR–K1 R–R1	32 Q–K4 Q–R6+	44 P–N4 Q–B7+
10 0–0–0 P–B4	22 P–QN4 P–B5	33 K–Q1 R×B+	45 K–K4 R–K7+
11 Q–B2 P–Q5	23 B–K4 B–Q4	34 K–K2 Q–Q3	White resigns.
12 N–N1 B×B+	24 Q–KB3 P–B6	35 K–B3 K–B2	

19 The Ancient Spanish Game - Ruy Lopez's Opening

It would be very good if the reader could interrupt his reading for a few minutes and study the position after 3 B–N5 carefully.

He will see that the most important difference between White's and Black's positions is the degree of danger which the kings can be subjected to – this is clearly in White's favour. His king is ready to castle immediately at the slightest signs of a storm, whereas Black's king has his way barred by his own pieces.

Top chess-players will possibly think such a view naive – what? pieces getting in the way! We will play ... N–KB3, and ... B–K2 and the king's path is free. That is right – but, my friends, this will cost you two tempi!

It is curious, by the way, that the Spanish priest Ruy Lopez, whose name is associated with 3 B–N5, himself thought this method of attack weak.

But since he was the first, in his manual which appeared in 1561, to give examples of several variations with 3 B–N5, there is no basis for depriving this remarkable player and theoretician of the rights of discovery.

Over four centuries the theory of the Ruy Lopez has developed extraordinarily. And yet the fundamental question, what is the best defence, has still not been decided; an answer has not been found to this day! But do we need such an answer?

Chess is played by people of different characters, age and tastes. It seems to me that the many methods of defence which the reader will come across in the pages of this, the main, section of the book, will help him to form his own opinion as to the most advisable piece routes and the most advisable pawn moves in the Ruy Lopez. And this, in fact, is the author's basic idea.

THE SPANISH MOVE IN REVERSE

Black: V. Gaevsky – Dniepropetrovsk 1939, Ukraine Championship

One might ask, for what pressing reason does the Spanish bishop return to KB1? Did he not like it on QN5? Or was he simply homesick?

One can find the most varied justifications for the bishop move, but the most convincing would be this: by leaving KB1 for QN5, the bishop allowed the king and rook to be connected – to castle, – and when he saw that the rook had returned his kind favour and vacated KB1 for him, he interpreted this as an invitation to return to his native dwelling.

If this light-hearted explanation is enough for the reader, that is fine; but for those who want something more serious, I can only sorrowfully say: alas, the whole of this variation, including White's ninth move, B–B1, can be found in any book.

The waiting move by the king, from KR1 to KN1, contained a small trap, which Black surprisingly fell into.

It remains for me to add that this game was played in the first round and, one might say, was my debut in 'adult' tournaments beyond the bounds of my native Kiev.

1 P–K4 P–K4	13 N/4–K2	24 R–Q1 P–QB3	37 KP×Pep+
2 N–KB3 N–QB3	13 ... N–KR4	25 K–R1 B–B3	37 ... R×P
3 B–N5 P–Q3	14 P–KN4 N–B3	26 N–Q3 N–B1	38 P–B5 B–B2
4 P–Q4 B–Q2	15 N–N3 P–KR3	27 N–N3 N/1–Q2	39 R/1–K1 N–B1
5 N–B3 N–B3	16 B–N2 B–K3	28 P–KR3 B–N4	40 P–N5 RP×P
6 0–0 B–K2	17 R–N1 N–R2	29 R–K2 N×N	41 Q×P R–R1
7 R–K1 P×P	18 N/B3–K2	30 P×N N–N3	42 K–N1 R–Q3
8 N×P 0–0	18 ... N–K4	31 P–Q4 P–Q4	43 R–K6 R×R
9 B–B1 (*86*)	19 N–B4 Q–R5	32 B–N4 Q–Q2	44 P×R B×P
9 ... R–K1	20 N–B1 N–N4	33 B–Q2 B×B	45 Q–K5+ K–R2
10 P–QN3 B–KB1	21 R–K3 QR–Q1	34 Q×B K–N2	46 Q×B Q×Q
11 B–N2 P–KN3	22 B–B3 N–R2	35 P–K5 R–KB1	47 R×Q R–B1
12 P–B3 B–N2	23 Q–K1 Q–K2	36 P–B4 P–KB4	48 B–B1 R–B5

and, without waiting for the reply, Black resigned, as he saw that time-trouble was over.

THE PERFIDIOUS BLACK KNIGHT

Black: P. Romanovsky – Moscow 1945, Semi-Finals USSR Championship

Everything, classical ideas and the like, suggests the benefit that can accrue from a study of the heritage of chess.

I agree, but why does no one point out the harm which is caused by drumming games into one's brain? I have in mind the weak games of champions of the past.

Now, for example, whenever as White I am playing against the variation 3 ... N–B3, I cannot free myself from a feeling of fear ... I fear the move ... N–KN5 +!

Where do such strange associations come from? From a game in the Lasker-Capablanca match. When the black knight landed on KN5 giving check, Lasker realised that he had to resign the match.

The reader too is probably afraid – lest I should advise him again to go to the library.... Have no fear, you have a game here. It would be good if you just noted this mistake; for if you were to come across some other, who knows what moves you would then start fearing?

The reader has perhaps already surmised that I was not in real earnest when I deployed my pieces with rooks on Q3 and KB3 and my queen on KN4 ... but I was on the alert. So that if instead of 20 ... P–Q4 Black had played 20 ... B×N, I would not have taken the bishop with my pawn (21 P×B? Q–K8+ 22 K–R2 N–K4!) but I would have limited myself to the variation 21 R×B Q–K3 22 R–N3 K–R1 23 P–KR4.

1 P–K4 P–K4	12 B×B Q×B	22 Q×B Q×Q	33 P–R6 R–QR8
2 N–KB3 N–QB3	13 P–KR3 N–K4	23 R×Q R–K8+	34 R–K2 P–B3
3 B–N5 N–B3	14 Q–N3 Q–B3	24 K–R2 N–K2	35 N–B4 R–Q4
4 0–0 B–K2	15 QR–Q1 N–N3	25 R–B4 P×P	36 N–R3 R–R4
5 R–K1 P–Q3	16 R–K3 R–K2	26 R–QR4 K–B1	37 P–KN3 K–Q1
6 P–Q4 B–Q2	17 R–B3 Q–K4	27 R×RP P–QB3	38 P–KB4 N–Q2
7 N–B3 P×P	18 N–B5 R/2–K1	28 P–QR4 P–Q5	39 R–K6 R–Q4
8 N×P 0–0	19 Q–N4 QR–Q1	29 P–R5 K–K1	40 R–N7 P–Q6
9 B×N P×B	20 R/1–Q3 (87)	30 N–R4 N–N3	41 P–R7
10 B–N5 R–K1	20 ... P–Q4	31 N–N6 N–K4	Black resigns.
11 Q–Q3 N–N5	21 P×P B×N	32 R–Q2 P–N4	

THE LOPEZ CHAMPION

White: I. Boleslavsky – Moscow 1950, Eighth Match Game

88B

My match with Isaac Efremovich Boleslavsky was the first match in FIDE's long elimination system adopted in 1947.

To use modern terminology, it might be called the Final Candidates' Match. We were both playing extremely hard and showing the greatest respect for each other. It seems to have been the only occasion in the history of chess contests when players have exchanged bouquets of bright flowers before the first move of the first game!

Boleslavsky's play is in no need of my compliments. He is overall one of the subtlest and strongest players in the world, and when it comes to playing the Ruy Lopez as White, his favourite occupation, he is the undisputed world champion.

Note carefully the amazing manoeuvres by the white pawns in the middlegame and the sudden composition-study-like finale to the ending, where the heroes were no longer the pawns, but the knight and the rook.

1 P–K4 P–K4	16 Q×Q N×Q	30 R×R R–R4	43 K–B4 R–N5+
2 N–KB3 N–QB3	17 P–B3 P–QR4	31 P×P R×P+	44 K–B3 R–N6
3 B–N5 N–B3	18 P–QR3 P×P	32 K–B3 (88)	45 K–N4 R–N5+
4 0–0 P–Q3	19 P×P N–Q2	32 ... K–K2	46 K–R5 R–K5
5 P–Q4 B–Q2	20 N–Q5 R–R2	33 R–R8 B–B5	47 N–N6 P–N5
6 N–B3 B–K2	21 R/1–Q1 N–K4	34 N–B5+ K–Q2	48 N–B8+ K–Q1
7 B×N B×B	22 B×N R×B	35 R–R8 R×P	49 P–N6 R×R
8 Q–Q3 P×P	23 N–K3 B–Q2	36 R×P+ K–B1	50 P–N7 B–K7+
9 N×P 0–0	24 R–B3 B–K3	37 R–R6 R–QN7	51 K–N5 R–K5
10 B–B4 N–Q2	25 R–Q4 P–N4	38 R×P R×P	52 K–B6 R–N5
11 QR–Q1 B–B3	26 P–N3 K–B1	39 P–N5 B–Q6	53 N–N6 R×N+
12 P–QN4 R–K1	27 K–B2 P–KB3	40 R–K6 P–Q4	54 K×R B–Q6+
13 KR–K1 B×N	28 R/4–Q3 P–N5	41 N–K7+ K–Q2	55 K–R6
14 Q×B P–QN4	29 R–R3 R×R	42 P×P R–N6	Black resigns.
15 R–Q3 Q–B3			

EXACTLY À LA TARRASCH

White: I. Boleslavsky – Moscow 1950, Fourth Match Game

89B

A perfect model for those studying the Ruy Lopez attack!

The play of White's rooks, bishops, knights, pawns, in fact all the pieces, was of the highest order. Here we see both the straightforward transfer of the rook from QR1–Q1–Q3–KN3 and the heroic cavalry thrust, N–QB3–Q5.

Also deserving acknowledgment is Boleslavsky's courage, when in the endgame and still the exchange down, he nevertheless refused the draw that was offered him.

What factors permitted White to dispose of his material valuables so generously, and did he conduct the fight correctly?

Very much so! After the KR-file became open the KBP gained considerably in strength and began actively to threaten the black centre. In these conditions the powerful knight on Q5 and the menacing bishop on QN3 more than compensated for White's small losses.

The bishop, the light-squared Lopez bishop, was the piece which guaranteed Boleslavsky favourable playing conditions. The bishop manoeuvre B–QN5–QR4–B2–R4–N3–R4 used up after all one fifth of the allowed 'move limit'!

I want finally to remind you of Tarrasch's famous formula: 'A knight in the centre, supported by its own pawn and not subject to attack from enemy pawns, is no weaker than a rook'.

1 P–K4 P–K4	11 P×P N–N5	20 R–Q3 QR–B1	28 N–B4 Q–R3
2 N–KB3 N–QB3	12 B–R4 P–QN4	21 P–B4 Q–R3	29 K–N2 Q–B3
3 B–N5 N–B3	13 B–N3 P–B4	22 R–N3 B–Q1	30 Q×NP Q–Q5
4 0–0 B–K2	14 P–QR3 N–B3	23 Q–K3 N–R4	31 R–K2 K–B1
5 R–K1 P–Q3	15 N–B3 P×P	24 N–Q5 (*89*)	32 Q–Q5 Q×Q
6 P–B3 0–0	16 B×QP N×B	24 ...N×R	33 N×Q R–B8
7 P–Q4 B–Q2	17 Q×N B×N	25 RP×N B–N3	34 K–B3 R–N1
8 B–R4 Q–K1	18 P×B Q–Q2	26 Q–Q3 Q–R6	35 B–R4 B–Q5
9 B–B2 B–N5	19 QR–Q1 Q–R6	27 P–B5 KR–K1	Draw agreed.
10 B–K3 P×P			

A FLASH OF TEMPERAMENT

Black: A. Bannik – Moscow 1963, USSR Team Championship

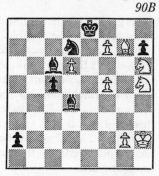

Nowadays grandmasters no longer study their opponent's games so much, but they study his character, his behaviour and his temperament in the most thorough fashion.

Master Bannik is reputed to be a man of a cold temperament. Could I have guessed that, having set up his pawns for defence, he would suddenly create a breakthrough in the most fortified part of the board?

I am talking about Black's 20 ... P–Q4, which is as like as two pins to Fuderer's ... P–Q4. Do you remember it? If you don't, then turn to page 76.

Even after the centre had been opened up, White still retained an excellent attack; however, I was no longer thinking about the game, but about my opponent. It would seem that even a cold temperament has some explosive force!

When Black's attack had been successfully concluded and his pieces began abandoning important squares, then Bannik himself remembered about defence; his move 25 ... R–N6!, which took KN3 away from White's pieces, looked particularly good.

By the way, there are no mistakes in the diagram: the pawn on White's KB7 is white, not black. On the other hand, the pawn on White's QR2 is, more's the pity, a black one.

1 P–K4 P–K4	14 Q–Q2 N–Q2	27 P–B5 P–N4	39 R–QB1 R–R8
2 N–KB3 N–QB3	15 N–R2 P–QN4	28 P×P B–Q1	40 R×R B×R
3 B–N5 N–B3	16 P×P B×NP	29 Q–Q2 Q–N5	41 B–N7 P–R4
4 P–Q3 P–Q3	17 P–B4 P–KB3	30 N–B3 Q–Q5+	42 N–R6+ K–K1
5 P–B4 B–N5	18 P–QR4 B–B3	31 K–R1 Q×Q	43 K–R2 P–R5
6 QN–Q2 B–K2	19 P–Q4 P×QP	32 R×Q B–R4	44 P–R4 P–R6
7 P–KR3 B–Q2	20 Q×P P–Q4	33 R–K2 R×R	45 P×P P–R7
8 N–B1 P–QR3	21 QR–B1 R–N5	34 N×R K–B2	46 P×P B–Q5
9 B–R4 0–0	22 Q–Q2 B–R1	35 R–Q1 R–N5	47 P–B7+ (90)
10 N–N3 P–KN3	23 KR–Q1 Q–N1	36 P–Q6 R×P	47 ... K–Q1
11 0–0 R–N1	24 N–N4 R×NP	37 N–N3 B–B3	48 B×B P×B
12 B×N B×B	25 Q–K1 R–N6	38 N–R5 B–B6	White resigns.
13 B–R6 R–K1	26 N–K2 P–QB4		

TO RISK OR NOT TO RISK

White: E. Geller – Moscow 1967, Grandmaster Tournament

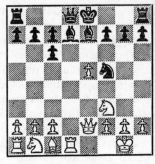

This game sticks in my mind for two reasons. The first was the terrible time-trouble, in which I only just managed to counter my opponent's threats. And the second was the agonising hesitations: to risk or not to risk, which took up seventeen minutes before 1 ... P–K4, twenty-one minutes before 4 ... B–K2 and eighteen minutes before 7 ... QP×B, although I had specially prepared all this variation for the present game.

But if the variation had been carefully prepared, why the fear?

What a variation I had looked at! I wanted to try Trifunovic's audacious opening idea: 10 P–K6 P×P 11 N–K5 B–Q3 12 Q–R5+ P–KN3 13 N×NP N–N2 14 Q–R6 N–B4 15 Q–R3 R–KN1 16 Q×P R–N2 17 Q–R8+ K–B2 18 Q×Q R×Q.

Fortunately, Geller is not quite a clairvoyant: coming up against this variation for the first time he could not assess the combinations that arise from it accurately, and sensibly he decided not to take any risks. It is interesting that he did not come to this decision immediately. He hesitated. Though my opponent had spent only six(!) minutes on moves 1 to 9, the second-hand of his clock completed altogether thirty-five full revolutions before, of the two moves 10 P–K6 and 10 N–B3, Geller plumped for the second. Six minutes, and thirty-five!

1 P–K4 P–K4	12 P–KR3 P–B4	23 ... R–QB1	34 P–KR4
2 N–KB3 N–QB3	13 B–N5 B–QB3	24 P–KB4 R/4–K1	34 ... R×R/Q8
3 B–N5 N–B3	14 B×B N×B	25 P–B5 N–K2	35 R×R/1 N–K4
4 0–0 B–K2	15 N×P N–N3	26 N–KB4 P–N3	36 N–Q5+ K–N2
5 P–Q4 N×KP	16 N–Q3 R–K1	27 P–B4 B–Q2	37 N×BP R–QB1
6 Q–K2 N–Q3	17 R–K1 P–N3	28 P×P P×P	38 N–Q5 R×P
7 B×N QP×B	18 N–R2 Q–B4	29 QR–Q1	39 R–K1 N–B3
8 P×P N–B4	19 Q–N4 Q×Q	29 ... R/B1–Q1	40 P–KN3 R–B7
9 R–Q1 B–Q2	20 N×Q B–N4	30 N–B2 K–B2	41 P–QN4 P–N4
(91)	21 N–N4 P–KR4	31 N–Q4 B–B4	42 P–R3
10 N–B3 0–0	22 N–K3 R×P	32 N–B3 N–B3	Draw agreed.
11 N–K4 Q–B1	23 N/4–Q5	33 N–N5+ K–B3	

A GAMBIT WILLY-NILLY

White: H. Pilnik – Amsterdam 1956, Candidates' Tournament

Every time as White I play my bishop to QN5 and not QB4, the same thought worries me: what if suddenly 3 ... N–B3?

'So what?' you ask. Surely this move holds no particular threat for White? Yes and no.

Although the KP is under attack, White can quietly castle: 4 0–0.

In itself the threat to take the KP is not a terrible one, but after 4 ... N×P 5 P–Q4 N–Q3, whether you want to or not, you must sacrifice a pawn in the sharp variation 6 P×P N×B 7 P–QR4 P–Q3 8 P–K6 P×P 9 P×N N–K2 10 N–N5 with complicated play. In other words, a gambit willy-nilly.

And if you are not in the mood for sacrificing, then you can expect a quick draw. My game with Pilnik is a model for this.

But do not expect that the draw will just fall from the sky: Black still has to fight for it.

This should be kept in mind and pointless exchanges should be scrupulously avoided. The correct way is to aim for an endgame with opposite-coloured bishops.

My last recommendation for White in this variation is the QN route N–QB3–K2–KB4. This is how Fischer plays it.

But Black too has his supporters. I once saw Spassky confidently gain half a point in this opening variation. At the same time he thought carefully about his every move!

If you have time, check if the pawn ending is won. That's a very difficult problem, although there is a solution.

1 P–K4 P–K4	8 Q×Q+ (92)	14 P–KR3 N–K2	20 N–K3 R×R
2 N–KB3 N–QB3	8 ... K×Q	15 B–N2 P–QN3	21 R×R R–Q1
3 B–N5 N–B3	9 N–B3 K–K1	16 R–Q2 P–KR3	22 R×R K×R
4 0–0 N×P	10 P–QN3 B–K3	17 R/1–Q1 N–B3	23 P–KB4 N–Q5
5 P–Q4 N–Q3	11 B–N2 B–N5	18 N–R2 K–K2	24 K–B2 N–B4
6 B×N QP×B	12 KR–Q1 B×N	19 N–B1 KR–Q1	Draw agreed.
7 P×P N–B4	13 B×B P–B4		

A BORING VARIATION

White: A. Chistyakov – Moscow 1956, Moscow Championship

The peaceful variation chosen by the players here is in no way indicative of their chess tastes and inclinations.

Chistyakov, for example, is in his element in a sharp, combinative struggle, and he has achieved significant successes in this area.

But why did I play this boring variation 3 ... N–B3? Because one cannot always be making the same moves! In our search for variety, we sometimes stumble in the dark on such variations as 3 ... N–B3 4 0–0 N × P.

Those who like burrowing in the dust of archives can ask at the library for the 1908 Lasker-Tarrasch match, where several games were played in the so-called Rio de Janeiro variation: 5 P–Q4 B–K2 6 Q–K2 N–Q3 7 B × N NP × B 8 P × P N–N2 9 R–K1 0–0 10 N–B3 P–Q4 11 P × P ep B × P – White has the better pawn formation, Black the two bishops.

And if you do not trust old games, look at the games of the Keres-Unzicker match played in 1956. You will find this variation there too.

What also needs to be pointed out to those studying the Ruy Lopez is the sharp variant 5 R–K1 N–Q3 6 N × P B–K2 7 B–Q3 0–0 8 N–B3 N–K1, which, in the opinion of the books, is an excellent way of achieving equality, e.g. 9 N–Q5 B–B3 10 N–KN4 P–Q3.

My advice to you in this mini-section is to play 3 ... N–B3 and leave it to your opponents to do the attacking! In as much as you have read this page carefully and are now armed to the teeth with knowledge, all your opponents' attacks will be beaten off.

1 P–K4 P–K4	6 B × N QP × B	12 QR–Q1 R–Q1	17 B–N2 P–KR3
2 N–KB3 N–QB3	7 P × P N–B4	13 R × R + K × R	18 N × B P × N
3 B–N5 N–B3	8 Q × Q + K × Q	14 N–KN5 B × N	19 P–QB4 R–B1
4 0–0 N × P	9 N–B3 K–K1	15 B × B N–K2	20 P–B3 P–B4
5 P–Q4 N–Q3	10 P–QN3 B–K3	16 R–Q1 + K–K1	Draw agreed.
(93)	11 B–N2 B–N5		

MIGUEL? – HERE! NAJDORF? – THERE

Black: B. Spassky – Mar del Plata 1960, International Tournament

The resort of Mar del Plata, where the traditional tournaments take place, is linked with the most resounding of the young Miguel Najdorf's triumphs: six first places on the run!

I myself had occasion to play in one of these tournaments. Fischer and Spassky emerged winners, but I was satisfied with my third place.

The move 10 B–KN5 was something of a chess joke: I was pleased at the possibility of provoking . . . P–KB3.

On move 15 White could have taken Black's KRP, but that would have been playing for a win, and I was only out to draw.

'Only draw?' asks the disbelieving reader. 'Why 8 B–Q3 then?'

This move certainly does need some thinking about. For example, can Black play his knight to QB4 or not? Is the bishop sacrifice (8 . . . N–B4 9 B ×P +) dangerous?

I remember once, in Budapest in 1950, Paul Keres thought over the position after 1 P–K4 P–K4 2 N–KB3 N–QB3 3 B–N5 B–B4 4 0–0 N–B3 for something like two hours (!!), when in answer to 5 N ×P Szabo made the quietest of replies, 5 . . . N ×P. Everyone spends time thinking like that, experienced players and beginners alike. I myself am not averse sometimes to pondering this or that opening problem, and, what is most interesting, I do it not at home but during actual play.

This is all very well, but what has Miguel Najdorf to do with it all? Surely he wasn't playing? No, he wasn't, but he was at the tournament. He came from Venezuela . . . as a tourist, for a rest.

1 P–K4 P–K4	9 P ×Pep N ×QP	17 N/3–Q2 B–N3	24 R ×R R ×R
2 N–KB3 N–QB3	10 B–KN5 P–B3	18 B ×B P ×B	25 R–Q1 P–KB4
3 B–N5 N–B3	11 B–KB4 B–N5	19 Q–K4 Q ×Q	26 K–B1 R–R4
4 0–0 B–B4 (94)	12 QN–Q2 P–N4	20 N ×Q KR–K1	27 P–QR3 R–R5
5 P–B3 0–0	13 B ×N Q ×B	21 KR–K1 N–K4	28 R–Q8 R–KB5
6 P–Q4 B–N3	14 Q–B2 K–N2	22 N ×N R ×N	29 P–B3 R–KR5
7 P ×P KN ×P	15 B–B5 B–KR4	23 N–N3 R/1–K1	Draw agreed.
8 B–Q3 P–Q4	16 N–B4 Q–B5		

THE BLUE SEA OF AZOV

Black: A. O'Kelly – Hastings 1953–4, International Tournament

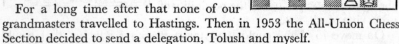

I read a story in one of the English magazines of how grandmaster Flohr, on hearing
a lift-boy at Nottingham in 1936 say 'First
floor, second floor, third floor', got the
impression he was expected to win all the
prizes.

This amusing incident occurred in 1935
on the closing day of the annual Hastings
tournament. Botvinnik was taking part then
for the first time.

For a long time after that none of our
grandmasters travelled to Hastings. Then in 1953 the All-Union Chess
Section decided to send a delegation, Tolush and myself.

The tournament proved to be a tough one. The unusual system of play,
with three sessions and short breaks for food, the absence of days for
adjourned games, a solitary free day, play from morning to midnight – all
this made our task more difficult. And, the main thing, our opponents
were strong. Each half-point had to be got with a fight. My conscience
pricks me even today when I recall that I refused the peace overtures
initiated by Savely Grigorevich Tartakover; but what could I do – I had
my duty!

I wanted to try and expiate my guilt, and began peace negotiations at
the book-stall; but to my question: 'Is your latest book good?' Savely
Grigorevich only smiled sadly and made a helpless gesture: 'I'm just a
hack!'

Growing bolder, I made a second step, and offered my old idol . . . a
tin of Azov bullheads, and here, it seems, we found grounds for reconcili-
ation.

If you are born in Roston-on-Don you have an eternal liking for
bullheads. I know this from my own experience. In my childhood I spent
four happy years on the edge of that bluest sea in the world, the Sea of
Azov.

In those far-off days I did not even dream that I would be entering
1954 in completely different latitudes. True, in spite of the closeness of
the North Sea, the weather in Hastings in winter is exceptionally mild.
However, I only noticed this afterwards, since I and O'Kelly spent the
whole of January 1st at the board. We began at 9 a.m. and finished around
midnight. The opening was played sharply, and the position did not seem
to be one of those where equilibrium could be maintained indefinitely.
However, I did not get caught in any home preparation of O'Kelly's, nor
would he consent to be the victim of the concerted attack from White's
bishops: B–QN5–Q3 and B–KN5–R4.

Gradually the game evened out and took on positional characteristics. A series of exchanges on White's K4 allowed White to penetrate first on the weak QR2–KN8 diagonal; however, even the check, 27 Q–K6 +, contrary to my expectations, did not break open my experienced adversary's solid defences.

Then I reprogrammed myself and decided to squeeze the maximum out of the minimum: I exchanged queens and began gradually to improve the position of each White piece and pawn individually. But even my new tactics remained for a long time unrewarded: my opponent defended remarkably accurately. In the endgame Black was close to drawing for some time, but then we were reminded of the New Year's banquet. In short, youth proved the hardier.

1 P–K4 P–K4	20 B–N5 Q–Q3	37 R–QB1 K–B3	54 R–Q5 K–N5
2 N–KB3 N–QB3	21 P–KN3	38 P–QN4 P–KR4	55 K–K2 R–N2
3 B–N5 B–B4	21 ... QR–K1	39 P–B4 P–KN4	56 K–B2 N–K2
4 P–B3 N–B3	22 P–QR3 N–K5	40 P×P+ N×P	57 R×QP N–B4
5 P–Q4 B–N3	23 B–B4 Q–Q1	41 R–B2 N–K3	58 R–B4 K–R6
6 0–0 0–0	24 N×N P×N	42 R–B2+ K–N3	59 R–B3 K–N5
7 P×P KN×P	25 R×P R×R	43 R–K2 N–Q1	60 R–B4 K–R6
8 Q–Q5 N–B4	26 Q×R Q×P	44 B–B4 N–B3	61 R–B8 R–KB2
9 B–N5 N–K2	27 Q–K6 + (95)	45 R–K6 + K–B4	62 R–KN8
10 Q–Q1 N–K5	27 ... R–B2	46 R–R6 K–N5	62 ... N×RP
11 B–KR4 P–Q4	28 Q–N3 Q–Q4	47 R–N6 + K–B6	63 R–N5 R–B4
12 QN–Q2 P–QB3	29 Q×Q P×Q	48 P–KR4 P–Q5	64 R–N7 N–N7
13 B–Q3 P–KB4	30 R–Q1 R–Q2	49 R–N5 R–R2	65 K–B3 R–QN4
14 P×Pep	31 K–B1 N–N2	50 B–Q6 R–Q2	66 R–Q7 P–R5
14 ... N×P/KB3	32 K–K2 K–B2	51 R–KB5 +	67 R–Q1 K–R7
15 Q–B2 P–N3	33 K–Q3 N–K3	51 ... K–N5	68 R–Q2 P×P
16 QR–K1 B–KB4	34 B–K5 N–Q1	52 R–KN5 +	69 R×N + K–R6
17 N–Q4 B×N	35 B–B4 N–K3	52 ... K–B6	70 R–N1
18 P×B B×B	36 B–N8 P–QR3	53 B–B4 R–R2	Black resigns.
19 Q×B N–B4			

Did O'Kelly really blunder away his knight? That is possible, only not at the time of 68 ... P×P, but some time earlier. On move 68 he too saw that after the normal 68 ... P–R6 White's dark-squared bishop enters the game with great force: 69 P–N4 + K–R8 70 R–Q1 + N–K8 71 R×N mate!

But perhaps my opponent deliberately presented me with the knight as a New Year's gift?

A FORGOTTEN VARIATION

White: G. Ravinsky – Moscow 1954, Moscow Team Championship

96W

In the 1945 USSR Championship, in the 1946 Moscow Championship, in the 1947 USSR Championship – in all these crucial competitions I used the King's Gambit successfully, and this was not due to luck.

In those years I was earnestly occupied by the purely theoretical problem of how best to attack Black's KP on K4.

Putting a lot of mental effort into propaganda for 2 P–KB4!, I was at the same time very keen to prove the harmlessness of the Ruy Lopez attack – 2 N–KB3 N–QB3 3 B–N5.

Then I also came across the move 3 . . . P–B4, which corresponded more closely than anything to my combinative tastes. And I began to study this variation. But I just got no chance to try out my own innovations: everyone avoided the main variation.

The manoeuvre . . . Q–Q4–Q3 was then already well-known to people, but I thought that Ravinsky more than anyone would not want to risk his fate in the giddy variation 6 N × P P × N 7 N × N P × N 8 B × P + B–Q2 9 Q–R5 + K–K2 10 Q–K5 + B–K3 11 P–KB4 P × Pep, the assessment of which was changing from day to day.

Somewhere after the opening stage the position began to look like a draw, but it was a team encounter, and we fought with all our might.

1 P–K4 P–K4	11 B × N Q × B	21 P–N3 R–B6	31 P × R R–N1 +
2 N–KB3 N–QB3	12 B–N5 P–KR3	22 K–N2 P–K5	32 K–B1 P–R4
3 B–N5 P–B4	13 B × N P × B	23 N–Q4 R–Q6	33 R–Q7 R–N5
4 N–B3 P × P	14 P–B4 P × P	24 N–K6 B–N5	34 R–Q8 + K–N2
5 QN × P P–Q4	15 Q × Q P × Q	25 N–B4 R–KB6	35 R/1–Q2 R × BP
(96)	16 P × P R–Q5	26 R–Q4 P–KB4	36 K–N2 R × RP
6 N–N3 B–KN5	17 P–N3 P–KR4	27 R/1–Q1 B–B4	37 R–K8 R–N5 +
7 P–KR3 B × N	18 QR–Q1 R–B5	28 R/4–Q2 B–N5	38 K–R3 R–B5
8 Q × B N–B3	19 N–K2 R–B4	29 R–Q4 B–B4	39 K–N2 P–KR5
9 P–Q3 Q–Q3	20 P–KR4 B–B4	30 R/4–Q2 R × N	40 R–KR8 B–Q3
10 0–0 0–0–0			

The game was stopped for adjudication. The jury's conclusion: a draw.

THE BISHOP OR THE KNIGHT

White: R. Kholmov – Moscow 1949, USSR Championship

'The bishop or the knight, which is the stronger piece?' beginners often ask. Anyone who is still unsure about the answer can look at the diagram.

And do not try to convince yourself that if the knight was a bishop and the bishop a knight. . . .

Then the bishop would escape, whilst the knight did not: he was powerless to.

The theoretical refutation of 3 . . . P–B4 was for many years considered to be the reply 4 N–B3. The variation 4 . . . P × P 5 QN × P P–Q4 6 N × P P × N 7 N × N Q–N4 8 Q–K2 Q × NP 9 Q–R5 + ! is a good illustration of the dangers awaiting Black if he plays along normal lines. I worked for a long time on strengthening Black's defence and came up with the active system 7 . . . Q–Q4 and 8 . . . Q–Q3!.

In 1952 during some friendly training games with our Olympiad Team I took the risk of disclosing my secret weapon. One of my lightning games with Smyslov developed as follows: 8 P–QB4 Q–Q3 9 N × P + B–Q2 10 B × B + Q × B 11 N–N5 N–B3 12 0–0 P–B3 13 N–B3 B–B4 14 P–Q4 P × Pep 15 R–K1 + K–B2 16 B–K3 B × B 17 R × B QR–Q1 18 Q–Q2 KR–K1 19 R/1–K1 R × R 20 R × R Q–Q5 21 P–QN3 Q × N 22 Q × Q P–Q7 23 R–K1 P–Q8 = Q – the triumph of a home preparation, without a single move of my own. The most amusing aspect was that my opponent did not even notice the innovation 7 . . . Q–Q4!, nor that I had given away a secret.

1 P–K4 P–K4	13 0–0 B–QB4 +	24 B–Q2 B–K2
2 N–KB3 N–QB3	14 K–R1 KR–B1	25 P–KN3 P–N4
3 B–N5 P–B4	15 N–B3 Q × KP	26 K–N2 B–B3
4 P–Q4 BP × P	16 Q–K1 Q × Q	27 K–B2 P–B5
5 N × P N × N	17 R × Q B–KN5	28 P–B3 K–B3
6 P × N P–B3	18 B–K3 P–Q5	29 N–N2 B–B7
7 B–QB4 Q–R4 +	19 B–N5 QR–K1	30 K–K2 B–Q6 +
8 N–Q2 Q × KP	20 R × R + R × R	31 K–Q1 B–B8
9 B × N R × B	21 R–K1 R × R +	32 N–B4 P × P
10 Q–K2 P–Q4	22 N × R K–Q2	33 B × P B × B
11 P–KB3 B–K3	23 P–KR3 B–Q8	34 P × B P–KN4
12 P × P 0–0–0		

35 N–K6 P–KR3	
36 P–KR4 K–Q4	
37 N–Q8 P × P	
38 P × P P–N3	
39 N–B7 B–R6	
40 K–Q2 B–K3	
41 N × P K–K5	
42 K–K2 P–N4	
(97)	
43 P–R3 P–R4	
White resigns.	

A FORCED MANOEUVRE, OR A COMBINATION?

White: J. Szily – Moscow 1949, Moscow v Budapest

Where does the king feel safest at the height of the battle?

This question can be heard almost daily.

And we always reply with the same patter, as if even a fool did not know: in the corner of the board; castle as quickly as possible, to the right or the left, only do not keep your king in the centre long.

If we allow for a second that the rules permit us to make two moves in succession, then I would have had a reliable move ready if White had castled on move 23. But it was my turn to move and I had to keep the blow I was preparing secret.

But if . . . And I quietly brought my bishop further away from its visible target, White's KRP.

'I see!' my opponent probably decided. 'Black wants to increase the pressure on my KBP, so I must castle to protect it with my rook.'

The rest of the game does not require my commentary.

Only, what is interesting is this. The variation from move 23 to move 29 was quite easy to calculate: both sides' moves were forced. But I just cannot say which chess weapon it was that helped me to break the white king's resistance. Was it cunning, a combination or a forced manoeuvre?

1 P–K4 P–K4	12 N–R4 R–QN1	22 N–K2 N–Q2	31 R × R Q × R +
2 N–KB3 N–QB3	13 P–Q4 P–B5	23 Q–B3 B–K3	32 K–N1 N × N
3 B–N5 P–B4	14 N/3–B5 B–Q3	(98)	33 P × N Q–N6 +
4 P × P P–K5	15 P–QN3 0–0	24 0–0 B × P	34 K–R1 R–KB1
5 Q–K2 Q–K2	16 P–KR3 B × P	25 N–N3 Q–N3	35 Q–K1 Q–B6 +
6 B × N NP × B	17 B–K3 N–Q2	26 P × B B × N	36 K–N1 R–B3
7 N–Q4 N–B3	18 Q–Q2 N–N3	27 K–R1 Q–R4	37 B–B2 R–N3 +
8 N–QB3 P–B4	19 N–B3 Q–K1	28 P × B Q × P +	38 K–B1 Q–R6 +
9 N–N3 P–Q4	20 P–QR4 P × P	29 K–N1 Q × P +	39 K–K2 Q–Q6
10 Q–N5 + Q–Q2	21 P × P P–B3	30 K–R1 R–B6	Mate!
11 Q–R5 Q–B3			

THERE SHOULD BE A SECOND EDITION

White: R. Nezhmetdinov – Tiflis 1959, USSR Championship

99B

Black's psychological mistake is there – the move 14 ... K–R1?. The exchange of queens by 14 ... Q–B2 15 Q×Q+ R×Q would have retained for Black all the advantages he had accrued in the opening: better pawn structure, the open operational KB-file, and a mobile pair of knights.

Later, with the brilliant manoeuvre B–Q2–K3!, White equalized the position and presented Black with a choice between hurrying after a draw in the variation 18 ...

N×P 19 B–N6 N–B6+ and continuing the piece manoeuvres in the hope that the other might make a mistake.

As was to be expected, the one who dug the pit (and that was me!) duly went and fell in it.

The idea of provoking the advance P–KR4–R5 was perhaps not a bad one: the pawn did in fact succumb!

On the other hand, the blatant provoking of 30 B×P by the careless ... N–B3 was nothing short of foolhardiness.

Black had quickly calculated the variation 30 B×P P×B 31 Q×RP+ N–R2 32 P–KN4 Q–B2 33 P–N5 R–KN1 34 R/1–R1 N/3–B1 but had forgotten about the possibility of inserting 33 R/1–R1.

The inventive strategy of the most interesting draughts- and chess-player, Nezhmetdinov must, as always, receive the highest acclaim.

What a pity that the book of Nezhmetdinov's best combinations has only been printed in an edition of 3,000!

1 P–K4 P–K4	12 B–B4+ B–K3	22 P–R5 R–B3	33 R/1–R1
2 N–KB3 N–QB3	13 KR–K1 B×B	23 N–R4 N–K2	33 ... R–KB1
3 B–N5 P–B4	14 Q×B+ (99)	24 Q–Q2 Q×P	34 Q–Q1 N–B5
4 P–Q3 P×P	14 ... K–R1	25 R–R1 N–N1	35 P–KN4 Q–K3
5 P×P N–B3	15 Q–K2 N–Q2	26 N–B5 Q–N3	36 B×N KP×B
6 N–B3 B–N5	16 K–N1 P–QN4	27 P–KB3 R×N	37 Q–Q3 K–B2
7 Q–Q3 P–Q3	17 B–Q2 N–B4	28 P×R Q×BP	38 Q–N6+ K–K2
8 B–Q2 B×N	18 B–K3 N–K3	29 R–R4 N–B3	39 Q×P Q–K4
9 B×B 0–0	19 P–KR4 Q–R4	30 B×P K–N1	40 Q×Q+ P×Q
10 0–0–0 Q–K1	20 Q–Q2 P–R3	31 B–K3 P–N4	41 R–K1
11 P–KR3 P–QR3	21 Q–Q5 Q–K1	32 R–R6 K–N2	Black resigns.

THE KNIGHT'S CUNNING FORK

White: L. Szabo – Moscow 1956, Alekhine Memorial International Tournament

The term 'fork' is usually used referring to a knight move whereby two pieces come under fire, but the danger of the knight really lies in the fact that its appetite knows no bounds: this piece is capable of attacking eight targets in one move!

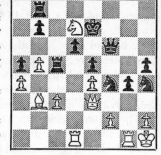

Let us for a minute leave the real game aside.

Look at the diagram. With the move, the white knight would be entitled to gobble up any of three black pieces – even the queen! The most vexing thing for Black is that he cannot even retaliate with a check.

And yet the white knight on QN6 went to QB4 and not Q7! Why? The talented tactician and creator of numerous combinations, grandmaster Laszlo Szabo, sensed an insidious trap which the black pawn on Q3 and the knight on KB5 were wanting to catch him in. Hidden behind 29 N–Q7? (*100*) K × N 30 Q × R was the downfall of the white queen . . . or king. Instead of Szabo falling into the trap, Liliental did, when he suggested in his commentary to the game published in *Pravda*, that 29 N–Q7 was an easy win.

I hope that, after analysing this fragment of the game, many readers will believe in the strength of the knight, all the more so since the move 30 . . . N–Q4 is also a fork, one move containing two terrible threats, . . . P × Q and . . . Q–B6 +.

1 P–K4 P–K4	12 Q–N3 B × N	23 N–B4 KR–QB1	32 R–N3 N–R6
2 N–KB3 N–QB3	13 B–B7 + K–B1	24 N × NP R–B4	33 B–B1 P–R5
3 B–N5 P–B4	14 P × B N–N3	25 P–KB4	34 R × N/R3 P × R
4 P–Q3 P × P	15 B–K3 N–R4	25 . . . N × P/B5	35 B × P Q–B5
5 P × P N–B3	16 N–Q2 Q–B3	26 QR–Q1 P–N4	36 Q–B7 + K–K1
6 B–QB4 B–B4	17 B–Q5 N/4–B5	27 R–KN1 P–R4	37 K–N2 N–N4
7 0–0 P–Q3	18 K–R1 N–R5	28 B–N3 P–N5	38 R × P Q–B6 +
8 P–B3 B–KN5	19 Q–B4 N–R6	29 N–B4 R × N	39 K–B1 Q × B +
9 P–N4 B–N3	20 Q–K2 R–QN1	30 B × R N–B6	40 K–K1 R × R
10 P–QR4 P–QR4	21 B × P P × B	31 Q–N6 R–Q1	White resigns.
11 P–N5 N–K2	22 Q–K3 K–K2		

A MOVE TO SUIT ALL TASTES

White: V. Smyslov – Moscow 1944, USSR Championship

101B

The defence of the English Master, Bird, 3 ... N–Q5, is rather unpopular nowadays, but unjustly so.

Firstly, it is not a defence at all, but an attack; secondly, its spirit is close to every lover of chess: the black pawn on K4, having transferred itself to Q5, will hold up the development of White's QN and help Black's pieces.

Are you asking for concrete variations? Why do you need them? You surely do not seriously think that all chess ideas can be expressed in concrete moves? Then chess itself would not have lasted for more than two to three years!

The inventor of this method of play, H. Bird, occasionally created attacks with the moves ... P–KR4 and ... Q–R5. Why the move with the KRP?

When White sees the black knight that will have advanced to KN5 he will undoubtedly want to chase it away with P–KR3, but the impudent knight will not even move!

In my game with Smyslov there was nothing like that. However, when White imprudently exchanged rooks on Q5, it suddenly awoke dangerous attacking forces in Black, and the KR-file, which had only been opened by chance, became important.

If I had not thought all evening solely about defending my weak pawns, then I would certainly have noticed the obvious manoeuvre 29 ... K–N2 and 30 ... R–KR1!. It is hardly possible to give the white king any good advice as to how to defend KR1.

Lest any reader did not take me at my word, I repeat: 3 ... N–Q5 is an attacking move, but it is also good for defence.

1 P–K4 P–K4	10 N–R3 P–Q4	18 P–R5 Q–N4	25 R×R P×R
2 N–KB3 N–QB3	11 B×N P×B	19 R–K5 Q–R3	26 Q–Q4 R–R1
3 B–N5 N–Q5	12 BP×P P×P	20 R/1–K3 RP×P	27 N–K5 P–QB4
4 N×N P×N	13 Q–B2 B×P	21 QRP×P	28 Q–N2 P–Q5
5 0–0 N–K2	14 R×P B×B	21 ... QR–Q1	29 R–K1 (101)
6 R–K1 P–KN3	15 Q×B B–K3	22 Q–B3 R–Q4	29 ... R–N1
7 P–QB3 N–B3	16 R/1–K1	23 P×P RP×P	30 Q–B2
8 P–QN3 B–N2	16 ... P–QR4	24 N–B4 R/1–Q1	Draw agreed.
9 B–N2 0–0	17 P–R4 P–R5		

A BEGINNER'S TRAP

White: J. Szily – Helsinki Olympiad 1952

... When the Black QP, forgetting its duty, made its advance, the role of the white bishop on QR4 immediately became crucial.

Here even the most level-headed of players could not help but play P–Q4, so as to threaten P–Q5.

This is, of course, not such a dangerous threat for Black. But in fact, 5 P–Q4 pursues completely different aims; White has not the least intention of winning the knight! He wants to frighten Black, to force him to advance his QNP and weaken his Q-side needlessly.

If you want proof, here it is:

5 P–Q4 P–QN4 6 B–N3 N×P 7 N×N P×N 8 Q–R5 P–N3 9 Q–Q5 with a simultaneous attack on Black's KBP and his QR – a direct result of ... P–QN4 is the fact that the Q5–QR8 diagonal is weakened. In answer now to 9 ... B–K3 White can either force a draw by 10 Q–B6 + B–Q2 11 Q–Q5, or develop an attack by 10 Q×P/Q4, setting his sights on Black's KR!

Szily considered this variation inadequate for White and chose another means of attack – 8 P–QB3, inviting Black to gorge himself on one or even two more pawns; but such generosity seemed to me dangerous. ...

Whoever wants to can allow himself to be cramped after 8 ... P×P 9 Q–R5 Q–K2 10 N×P or 9 ... P–N3 10 Q–Q5 B–K3 11 Q–B6 + B–Q2 12 Q×P/B3.

My opponent had a better move in 9 P–QR4!, and then a very weak move would have been 9 ... B–Q2, because of 10 P×P P×P 11 Q–R5!.

1 P–K4 P–K4	7 N×N P×N	13 N–Q2 R–K1	19 B–B4 B–Q4
2 N–KB3 N–QB3	8 P–QB3 P–Q6	14 QR–Q1 B–N2	20 B×P B–B5
3 B–N5 P–QR3	9 Q×P N–B3	15 QR–K1 P–Q4	21 B–B6 P–N4
4 B–R4 P–Q3	10 0–0 B–K2	16 P–K5 N–K5	22 B×R P×B
5 P–Q4 (102)	11 B–N5 0–0	17 N×N P×N	23 B–B6
5 ... P–QN4	12 B–B2 P–N3	18 Q×Q QR×Q	Draw agreed.
6 B–N3 N×P			

A THREE-MOVER OF SAMUEL LOYD'S

White: M. Matulovic – Belgrade 1964, International Tournament

103B

A picture of a position! Black's queen and both kings are under attack. One could not choose a more suitable moment to agree a draw.

You may ask why both kings are under attack, when only the black king is in check?

That check is a clearly visible one, but the white king is threatened with even greater unpleasantnesses, for example, mate. In one move. Or in three moves, if White allows Black the move: 39 K–N1?? R–R8+! 40 K×R Q–R6+ 41 K–N1 Q–N7 mate.

Matulovic would have retained real winning chances if he had ventured out into uncharted waters with his king – 33 K – Q2!!, but to have such impudence, one must be a chess composition fan and know the three-mover by Samuel Loyd, with the solution 1 K–K2!!, which he dedicated to Steinitz (White: K/KB1, R/QR5, R/KB6, B/QN5, B/QR7, N/QN6, N/K4, P/QN4, Q2; Black: K/K4, R/K1, R/KR7, B/KN1, B/KN6, N/QR7, N/KR8, P/QR3, QN2, QB6, KB7, KR5).

But no-one can like and know everything! Matulovic struck me by the speed with which he moved in the opening, when for the first ten moves I was just not able to press the button on my clock down, from which I concluded that the variation I had chosen was better known to my opponent than to me.

It happens sometimes.

1 P–K4 P–K4	12 Q–K2 P–R4	23 Q–R5 P×N	32 ... K–N1
2 N–KB3 N–QB3	13 0–0–0 B–R3	24 Q×B P×P	33 R×N P–B6
3 B–N5 P–QR3	14 Q–K1 Q–Q2	25 KR–K1 N–K4	34 Q–N6+ (*103*)
4 B–R4 P–Q3	15 P–B4 N–N5	26 RP×P P–B4	34 ... K–R1
5 B×N+ P×B	16 P–QN3 K–B2	27 N×BP B–R3	35 Q–R6+ K–N1
6 P–Q4 P–B3	17 P–B5 R–K1	28 B×B P×N	36 Q–N6+ K–R1
7 B–K3 N–K2	18 B–B4 P–N3	29 B–B4 R–R1	37 Q–R5+ K–N1
8 N–B3 N–N3	19 N–K6 Q–K2	30 Q–N5	38 Q–N6+ K–R1
9 P–KR4 P–KR4	20 N–K2 P×P	30 ... KR–QN1	Draw agreed.
10 Q–Q3 P×P	21 P×P P–R5	31 Q–K2 P–B5	
11 N×P N–K4	22 N/2–Q4 P–B4	32 Q×RP+	

A CENTURY SINCE HIS BIRTH

White: M. Schöneberg – Berlin 1968, Lasker Memorial Tournament

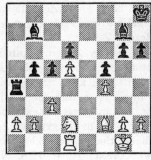

December 1968 saw the completion of 100 years since the birth of the famous German player, Emanuel Lasker. The world champion of many years enjoyed a huge following in the chess world and was a sought-after guest in every country.

It is particularly pleasurable to recollect that during the very different periods of his unparalleled career, Dr. Lasker did not miss a single major tournament that took place in our country. And for the venue for his return match with Steinitz in 1896 he chose Moscow.

All my life I have studied deeply and carefully the work of this great player and, as well as I can, I have tried to convert the best of it to my own use. Therefore I was grateful to accept the invitation to take part in a tournament dedicated to the memory of Lasker.

The Ruy Lopez was also the German champion's favourite opening, both as White and as Black.

My opponent played very confidently for some time, and I could detect no weak point or other object of attack. Then I remembered Lasker's advice and I began setting my opponent various difficult problems, even at one point sacrificing a pawn out of purely psychological considerations.

1 P–K4 P–K4	12 Q–Q3 0–0	22 N–Q5 N×N	(*104*)
2 N–KB3 N–QB3	13 Q–B4+ K–R1	23 P×N R×R+	32 P–QR3 B–KB1
3 B–N5 P–QR3	14 N–Q4 Q–K1	24 B×R R–K1	33 P–QN3 R×RP
4 B–R4 P–Q3	15 P–B4 Q–B2	25 Q–Q4 P–KB4	34 P–B4 B–R3
5 B×N+ P×B	16 Q–Q3 P–QB4	26 Q×P P–B4	35 R–QB1 P–N4
6 P–Q4 P×P	17 N–B3 B–B3	27 Q–Q3 R–K5	36 KBP×P
7 N×P B–Q2	18 B–K3 B–N2	28 P–B3 Q–K1	36 ...RP×P
8 0–0 P–N3	19 QR–Q1 P–B5	29 B–B2 Q–N4	37 P–QN4 BP×P
9 N–QB3 B–N2	20 Q–Q2 KR–K1	30 Q×Q P×Q	38 P×P B×P
10 R–K1 N–K2	21 B–B2 P–R3	31 N–Q2 R–R5	39 B–Q4+.
11 N–B3 P–B3			

At the second of making this move White's flag fell.

THE QUEEN'S COMMAND

White: I. Zakharov – Moscow 1961, Moscow Championship

105B

Independence of thought is a most valuable quality in a chess-player, both at the board and when preparing for a game.

White's tenth move, N–KN1, does not fall within the bounds of what we consider to be 'common sense'. Do the rules about the speediest possible development of pieces really no longer hold? And the rule that one should bring a new piece into play with every move? And why does the knight need to retreat to the back rank anyway? There was no point in playing 2 N–KB3 in that case.

The order to free KB3 issued from the HQ of General Command – from the white queen. Observe how freshly, originally and unashamedly the white queen solved its own problems. The task was not an easy one: the route from Q1 to KR5 was blocked, but the queen wanted to get to KR5, so the knight got the order: clear the way.

This explanation is meant by way of a joke. To be serious, White wants to control KB5 in good time, to make . . . P–KB4 as difficult as possible. The queen goes to KR5, the KN to KN3. So much fuss for a single pawn!

My game with Zakharov took place in the last round. It was adjourned and resumed the next morning. Black probably missed an easy win by 45 . . . Q–QN8, but when he realised his mistake, he decided not to take any more risks and . . . to play a match with Shamkovich for the title of champion of the capital.

1 P–K4 P–K4	13 N–N3 R–B2	25 P×P QP×P	37 Q–K2 B–Q3
2 N–KB3 N–QB3	14 P–N3 B–B1	26 R–B3 R/2–N2	38 R–QR1
3 B–N5 P–QR3	15 0–0 B–Q2	27 Q–R4 B–K1	38 . . . Q–QB4
4 B–R4 P–Q3	16 N/B3–K2 P–R4	28 N–B5 P–B5	39 R–R4 R–QB1
5 B×N+ P×B	17 B–Q2 Q–B1	29 P–QN4 B–N3	40 R–R5 Q–N3
6 P–Q4 P–B3	18 P–KR3 P–R5	30 Q–K1 B×N	41 R–R4 B–B1
7 P–B4 N–K2	19 QR–N1 P×P	31 R×B B×P	42 P–R4 R–N8
8 N–B3 P–QB4	20 P×P P–B3	32 R–QB1 B–R6	43 P–R5 R–QB8
9 P–Q5 R–QN1	21 N–B3 P×P	33 R–Q1 B–N7	44 P–R6 P–N4
10 N–KN1 N–N3	22 N×P N–K2	34 R–B3 B–Q5+	45 B–K1 B×P
11 Q–R5 (*105*)	23 P–B4 N×N	35 K–R2 R–N6	46 R–B1
11 . . . B–K2	24 BP×N B–N4	36 B–B3 B–B4	Draw agreed.
12 KN–K2 0–0			

THE OBSTINATE WHITE PAWN

White: I. Boleslavsky – Moscow 1945, USSR Championship

Who does not know that pawns, be they white or black, ought always to capture in the direction of the centre of the board?

And suddenly, such an experienced player as Boleslavsky captures with a pawn towards the side of the board: 13 BP ×B?

However, when the reader begins playing the game on further, he will undoubtedly feel a spark of sympathy . . . for the KRP, in fact, which obstinately refused to move towards the centre; he felt fine staying on the KR-file!

It emerges that not all chess rules are absolute, and that there are quite a few exceptions amongst them. How many?

There is no answer to that. I will say only that in chess there are thirty-two white and black fighting units, excluding the players, and if one was to make only one rule for each piece, there would already be a whole host of exceptions.

But the lives of chess pieces are more complex and rich, and cannot be squeezed into a framework of exceptions, or even rules.

All the same, why not 13 RP ×B? Mainly because the White KRP wanted to retain for itself the right to play P–KR3, to free the knight on KB3 from a pin in the event of . . . B–N5.

And with a solid knight on KB3 the QP is considerably strengthened.

It might be said then that the KRP *is* a 'central' pawn! So that sometimes such moves 'towards the edge' as BP ×B work nevertheless in favour of the central squares!

It is now up to the reader to split the hairs and decide whether 13 BP ×B followed the rules or broke them.

1 P–K4 P–K4	10 R–K1 B–N4	18 Q×B R–N1	27 P–Q7 R–Q1
2 N–KB3 N–QB3	11 N–B1 B–B5	19 P–Q5 Q–Q2	28 B–K5 R–N3
3 B–N5 P–QR3	12 N–N3 B×N	20 B–R7 R–R1	29 KR–Q1
4 B–R4 P–Q3	13 BP×B (106)	21 Q×P KR–B1	29 . . . N/3–K2
5 P–B3 B–Q2	13 . . . 0–0	22 B–Q4 Q–R5	30 B–B7 R–N2
6 0–0 KN–K2	14 P–KR3 P×P	23 B–B3 QR–N1	31 Q×R Q×Q
7 P–Q4 N–N3	15 P×P N/B3–K2	24 Q–R7 P–QB4	32 B×R Q×QP
8 B–K3 B–K2	16 B–N3 B–K3	25 P–K5 N×QP	Draw agreed.
9 QN–Q2 P–R3	17 R–QB1 B×B	26 P×P Q–N4	

'THE GAME IS NOT WORTH THE CANDLE'

Black: B. Sliwa – Moscow 1956, Alekhine Memorial Tournament

The failing of the Rubinstein system chosen by Black is its extreme passiveness, but it would be very unjust to blame the author of the system for this; all the critical arrows should be directed at one target: the person who plays it!

In those rare cases where White has not a single weak point in his camp, his attention, quite understandably, is switched entirely to looking for weak points in his opponent's.

The distinctive Q-side attacking plan in the Ruy Lopez – P–QR3, P–QN4, QN–Q2–N3 did not have time to move into its second stage of P–QB4–B5 before Black rashly played ... B–KN4?.

Possibly the Polish master was counting on blocking this diagonal by the manoeuvre ... B–K3–KB2, but was unable to carry out his plan.

To chess-players who collect rare chess ideas I can recommend the variation 17 ... P×N 18 B–N3+ P–B5 19 B×BP+ K–B1 20 P×P B–N4 21 B–R2 B×R 22 P×P B–N4 23 Q–R7 P×P 24 Q–R6 mate or Q–B7 mate!

Always remember: Q–R5 is a move that can never be taken lightly!

In conclusion, a piece of information: Rubinstein himself played the opening differently. He first went into the attack with ... P–KR3 and ... P–KN4. And if there was a threat to his KB2, he was not averse to spending a tempo on the move ... R–KR2.

1 P–K4 P–K4	9 QN–Q2 0–0	16 ... N/B3–K2
2 N–KB3 N–QB3	10 P–QR3 N–N3	17 N–B5 B–B3
3 B–N5 P–QR3	11 P–QN4 R–K1	18 B–N3+ P–Q4
4 B–R4 P–Q3	12 B–B2 P–R3	19 QR–Q1 P–N3
5 P–B3 B–Q2	13 N–N3 B–N4	20 N–Q3 KP×P
6 P–Q4 B–K2	14 N×B P×N	21 B/K3×P K–B2
7 0–0 B–B3	15 P–N3 P–B3	22 P–KB4 R–R1
8 B–K3 KN–K2	16 Q–R5 (*107*)	23 Q–K2 NP×P

24 N×P N×N	
25 R×N Q–QB1	
26 P×P B×P	
27 B×BP P×B	
28 R×B N×R	
29 B×N+	
Black resigns.	

THE MERCURIAL PAWN

Black: V. Simagin – Moscow 1947, Match for the title of Champion of Moscow

108W

This is one of my most successful attempts at the difficult art of positional play. Simagin could not fathom the meaning of P–KR4, and his king fell victim to a pawn breakthrough.

The subtlety of 29 P–K6 comes out in the variation 29 ... P×B 30 P–K7 R–K1 31 R–Q8 P×P 32 R×R+ K–R2 33 R–KR8+ K×R 34 P–K8=Q+ K–R2 35 Q–K1 N–Q4 36 Q–R1 N–N5, where Black is a queen down, but in exchange has a strong pawn on QR7. White is saved by his own pawn on QB5, which prevents the black knight from getting pawn support: by the march K–B2–K2–Q3–B3 the white king will tip the balance in his favour. There is also a simpler solution: 33 R–Q8! P–R8=Q+ 34 K–R2 Q–K8 35 P–K8=Q Q×P+ 36 K–N1.

There are probably many other complicated variations hidden in the position after 24 P–B4. I should like to draw the reader's attention to the importance of the open file for the rook, be it either the KB-file or the Q-file.

It should be added finally that this combination is nothing more than a technique; the pawn run P(K5)–K6–K7 was first met in the game Euwe-Keres in the 1938 AVRO tournament. But we should not be too hasty in drawing conclusions; it would be better to wait and see what Keres would say. But the most impatient ones can skip some pages and play through the game with the title: 'A Queen? Or a Knight with check?' (p. 204).

1 P–K4 P–K4	10 N–B1 N–R5	19 QR×B	27 P–B4 P–R4
2 N–KB3 N–QB3	11 N×N B×N	19 ... QR–Q1	28 P–B5 P–R5
3 B–N5 P–QR3	12 P×P P×P	20 QR–Q1 N–B1	(*108*)
4 B–R4 P–Q3	13 N–K3 B–K3	21 B–N3 Q–KN3	29 P–K6 N–B1
5 P–B3 B–Q2	14 Q–B3 Q–B3	22 Q×Q RP×Q	30 P×P+ K–R1
6 0–0 KN–K2	15 Q–K2 N–K2	23 P–KR4 R–Q3	31 B–B4 P–QN4
7 P–Q4 N–N3	16 R–B1 B–N4	24 P–KB4 P×P	32 B–K6 P–N4
8 QN–Q2 B–K2	17 N–N4 B×N	25 P–K5 R×R	33 R–Q7
9 R–K1 0–0	18 Q×B B×B	26 R×R N–N3	Black resigns.

THEORY AND PRACTICE

Black: P. Keres – Moscow 1948, USSR Championship

109B

The opening variation chosen by Keres had shortly before this game brought him a beautiful victory over Euwe. I had subjected this variation to a detailed analysis in one of the magazines, and Keres of course knew about this.

A new move-order proved of no tangible benefit to Black, and White gradually brought his forces back into active positions and was poised to launch an attack.

At this point Keres made an extremely clever pawn sacrifice and took over the initiative.

In order to weaken the pressure exerted by Black's pieces I had to allow the exchange of queens and fight on in a complex ending which held equal chances of a draw, a loss or a win.

The picture was a curious one: whilst Keres improved the position of his pieces, caring little about the loss of this or that fated pawn, I greedily grabbed third-rate pawns, mistakenly supposing that 'the pawns themselves will have the decisive word'. . . .

1 P–K4 P–K4	18 P–KN3 Q–R6	35 R×R N×R	50 K–B5 K–B2
2 N–KB3 N–QB3	19 P–KB4 P×BP	36 N–B3 N×P	51 N–B5
3 B–N5 P–QR3	20 P×P P–KB4	37 K–K3 N–N7+	51 ... R–KB3+
4 B–R4 P–Q3	21 R–B3 Q–R4	38 K–Q3 B×P	52 K–K4 P–N3
5 P–B3 B–Q2	22 P×P N–R5	39 P–Q5 R–B6+	53 N×P K–K2
6 P–Q4 KN–K2	23 R–B1 Q×Q	40 K–K4 R–B7	54 N–B7 N–B1
7 B–N3 P–R3	24 R×Q P–B4	41 R–Q1 (109)	55 N–N5 P–N4
8 QN–Q2 N–N3	25 K–B2 B–K2	41 ... K–N1	56 P–Q6+ K–Q2
9 N–B4 B–K2	26 B–N3+ K–R1	42 N–R4 N–R5	57 K–K3 N–K3
10 N–K3 0–0	27 B–K6 B×B	43 B–K3 R–N7	58 R–QN4 N–N2
11 0–0 R–K1	28 P×B P×P	44 N–B5 R×P	59 N–Q4 R×P
12 R–K1 B–KB1	29 P×P P–Q4	45 R–Q2 R–N5+	60 R–R4 K–K2
13 B–B2 N–R5	30 N×P B–Q3	46 R–Q4 R–N3	61 R–R6 K–B3
14 N×N Q×N	31 B–Q2 R×P	47 N–K6 B–Q3	62 P–R4 N–B4+
15 N–Q5 QR–B1	32 QR–B1 R–B1	48 B–B4 N–N3	63 N×N K×N
16 R–B1 N–K2	33 R–K1 R–N3	49 B×B R×B	White resigns.
17 N–K3 N–N3	34 R–KN1 R–B4		

FIVE AGAINST TWO

Black: V. Lyublinsky – Moscow 1945, Semi-Finals USSR Championship

110W

At the moment when Black completed his plan of development and strengthened the main point K4 as much as possible, the correlation of the forces of attack and defence was as follows: two against five!

The complete triumph of the prophylactic principles of A. Nimzowitsch meant over-protecting by 250 per cent.

Black rejected the tempting variation 5 ... B–N5 6 P–KR3 P–KR4!, and the reasonable 8 ... KN–K2, and the right to castle – all in favour of strengthening K4!

Such an original strategy by Black demanded, naturally, heroic efforts on the part of White to avoid following in the other's footsteps but to remain within the bounds of classical chess science.

I could not think up anything better than the usual pawn advance on the Q-side and the conventional manoeuvre QN–Q2–KB1–K3–Q5.

However, since the black bishops were quietly dozing behind their fence of pawns, even this plain plan of White's brought him victory, after, of course, several small piece skirmishes and mutual pawn clashes.

And I am led involuntarily to ask: was Black right in advancing his KP to the completely unprotected K4 square in the first place, and then, without there being any need for it, in bolstering this pawn by three-fold defensive measures?

1 P–K4 P–K4	11 B×N+ K×B	21 P–B4 N–N2	31 B–Q4 R–R5
2 N–KB3 N–QB3	12 Q–N3+ K–K1	22 QR–Q1 P×P	32 B×N NP×B
3 B–N5 P–QR3	13 QN–Q2	23 N×P N–B4	33 P–N6 P–B3
4 B–R4 P–Q3	13 ... R–KB1	24 N–Q5 B–K3	34 N–B7 Q–K4
5 0–0 B–Q2	14 B–N2 R–B2	25 N×B Q×N	35 Q×Q BP×Q
6 P–B3 P–KN3	15 P–QR4 K–B1	26 P–R3 R–R5	36 P–N7 R–N5
7 P–Q4 B–N2	16 P–N5 RP×P	27 Q–B3 R–R7	37 R–QN1 B–R3
8 R–K1 P–B3	17 RP×P N–R4	28 Q–B1 R–R1	38 R×R B–B5+
9 P–QN4 N–R3	18 Q–N4 P–N3	29 K–R2 K–B1	39 K–N1
10 B–N3 N–B2	19 N–B1 K–N1	30 Q–B4 R–R7	Black resigns.
(110)	20 N–K3 Q–K1		

A VIRTUOSO OF COMBINATIVE CHESS

Black: R. Nezhmetdinov – Moscow 1957, USSR Championship

The international master Rashid Nezhmet-dinov is a virtuoso of combinative chess.

Therefore each of us, before the start of a game with Nezhmetdinov, decides on a definite plan to limit strategy; that is, a plan whereby it will be easy for us to make combinations, but difficult for our opponent.

Everyone understands that one can in fact only realize such a plan in one's dreams; in the game everything is much more complex.

However, one fact is indisputable: when playing someone with as rare a gift for combinations as the master, Nezhmetdinov, each of us tries our utmost to heighten our state of readiness for action and subordinate our efforts to the main task, that of guessing, anticipating and eliminating any combinative breakthrough. If you look at our game from this standpoint, then I had a little success: at least I foresaw ... P–KB4, and replied immediately with the counter-thrust P–KB4!

I shall say nothing about what happened after that, as that would be an impossible task; the reader will understand it all himself.

Clearly 20 ... N–Q5 was meant to serve as the prelude to a crushing combination, and one might also surmise that the quiet Lopez move 23 B–B2 fell outside Black's field of vision.

1 P–K4 P–K4	11 B–N3 K–R1	*(111)*	29 B–N3+ K–B1
2 N–KB3 N–QB3	12 P×P P×P	21 P×N B×P+	30 QR–Q1 B×R
3 B–N5 P–QR3	13 N–R4 P–B3	22 K–R1 N–K6	31 R–Q8+ Q–K1
4 B–R4 P–Q3	14 P–N3 B–R6	23 B–B2 N–N5	32 R×Q+ K×R
5 P–B3 B–Q2	15 R–K1 R–Q1	24 N–KB3 Q–B3	33 B–B3 B×B
6 P–Q4 P–KN3	16 Q–K2 P–B4	25 B×R R×N	34 N×B K–K2
7 0–0 B–N2	17 P–KB4 KP×P	26 Q×R N–B7+	35 K–N1 P–B4
8 P–QR3 KN–K2	18 B×P P×P	27 Q×N B×Q	36 P–R4
9 B–K3 0–0	19 N×KP N–Q4	28 B–B6+ K–N1	Black resigns.
10 QN–Q2 Q–K1	20 B–N5 N–Q5		

A BORING EXISTENCE

White: D. Keller – Moscow Olympiad 1956

The reader has perhaps become bored with the same kinds of standard position, but if this is so, what about us, the masters and grandmasters!

You can easily get rid of your boredom by turning the page or picking up another book. *We* do not have such a possibility. In the auditorium people are waiting for moves, so whether we want to or not, we have to think and make a move.

There is, though, one sure way of getting away from a boring position, and that is to offer a draw in time!

And if your opponent says 'No', what then? Or if your team captain will not allow you to do it. There is nothing one can do about that. Work is work.

That is why chess-players try not to divide positions into boring ones and interesting ones: one must always work hard at a position, think hard. Even when the position has been well studied or is as boring as could be.

One can distinguish three stages in this curious game: Black builds a pawn wall; with the combinative move N–Q5 White finds a hole in Black's armour; the trappy manoeuvre ... Q–B6–B7–Q6–Q3 bewitched White and he quite simply left his rook en prise to Black's queen.

And that is all.

Of course, it caused no special joy, but I had fulfilled my job as captain.

1 P–K4 P–K4	12 B–B2 N–QR4	23 P×P RP×P	34 N×R Q×N
2 N–KB3 N–QB3	13 N–B1 N–B5	24 P–QB4 P–N5	35 R–R7 N–K7
3 B–N5 P–QR3	14 B–N3 N–N3	25 N–Q5 Q–Q3	36 Q–N5 Q–Q6
4 B–R4 P–Q3	15 N–K3 P–B3	26 N×P R–N1	37 R/7–R1 Q–Q3
5 P–B3 B–Q2	16 N–Q2 B–K3	27 N–B2 R×P	38 QR–Q1 Q×R
6 P–Q4 P–KN3	17 P–B3 N–R4	28 N–N1 N–N6	39 R×Q R×R+
7 B–KN5 B–K2	18 P–N3 0–0	29 R–R4 R–Q1	40 K–N2
8 B×B Q×B	19 0–0 QR–K1	30 N/1–R3 N–Q5	40 ... N/4–B5+
9 P×P P×P	20 Q–B2 N–Q2	31 P–B5 Q×P	*(112)*
10 QN–Q2 N–B3	21 B×B Q×B	32 K–R1 Q–B6	White resigns.
11 Q–K2 P–QN4	22 P–QR4 N–B4	33 Q–K3 R×N	

THE ADVANTAGE OF THE TWO KNIGHTS!

Black: V. Shiyanovsky – Odessa 1960, Semi-Finals USSR Championship

So much is written in books about the advantage of the two bishops that I feel compelled to say a few warm words about the chess cavalry.

This is not to say that the long-range bishops do not, in fact, in a large number of positions excel the quietly-moving knights; but does this mean that two bishops are always stronger than two knights?

When pawn chains are broken up and there are a lot of open diagonals on the board, then the long-range bishops are really good.

But one should not rush to any conclusions. There occur, and extremely often, situations where the outcome of the struggle is decided along a narrow section of the front. This is where the knights are irreplaceable.

And if the pawn chains are closed up, even temporarily, there is no greater aid than a knight.

Exploiting the weakness of Q5 and the lonely pawn on K4 in Black's camp, White brought both his knights imperceptibly closer to these points and they worked in conjunction, from KB3 and K3, to control the important section of the front.

In the final count both knights perished, but not in vain. And when the passed QBP set off to queen in the rook ending and Black capitulated, all those remaining alive – the king, the rook and several pawns – remembered the two white knights with gratitude.

1 P–K4 P–K4	13 N×N K–R1	24 N–B7 B×NP	36 R–K7 P–QR4
2 N–KB3 N–QB3	14 Q–Q2 P–QN4	25 N×R B×R	37 R–QR7
3 B–N5 P–QR3	15 B–N3 P–B4	26 Q×B R×N	37 ... R–K3+
4 B–R4 P–Q3	16 R–Q1 B–Q3	27 Q×P Q–K5	38 K–Q4 R–Q3+
5 P–B3 B–Q2	17 N–Q5 P×P	28 R–Q1 Q–KB5	39 K–K3 R–K3+
6 P–Q4 P–KN3	18 N–N5 N–R4	29 R–K1 R–KB1	40 K–Q2 R–Q3+
7 P×P P×P	19 N×KP B–KB4	30 P–B3 Q–B3	41 K–B2 R–K3
8 B–KN5 B–K2	20 Q–K2 N×B	31 Q×Q+ R×Q	42 P–QB4
9 B–K3 N–B3	21 P×N (*113*)	32 R×P R–Q3	42 ... R–K7+
10 QN–Q2	21 ... Q–R5	33 K–B2 P–N5	43 K–Q3 R×P
10 ... N–KN5	22 N×B P×N	34 K–K3 P×P	44 P–B5
11 N–B1 0–0	23 0–0 B–K3	35 P×P P–R3	Black resigns.
12 P–KR3 N×B			

PROTECTING ENTRY SQUARES

White: R. Wade – Amsterdam Olympiad 1954

Exchanging pawns on K5 has the aim of limiting the sphere of action of Black's dark-squared bishop on KN2.

At the same time White gets rid of the constant threat of ... KP × P. The open Q-file which results from this exchange does not mean a quiet draw at all. On the contrary, after it the advantages of a superior pawn formation tell for White. The black pawns are to blame, but who suffers? The queen! She simply cannot find a safe hiding-place.

The reader should note the forlorn position of Black's knight on QB3.

The question arises as to whether Black has to capture on K4 with his pawn? If he were to capture with the knight, White could play knight takes knight and then the attacking blow P–KB4.

I do not know if my system of defence is stronger (... P–KR3 and ... N–QR4), but the endgame that resulted proved to be not unfavourable to Black.

1 P–K4 P–K4	19 N–KB2	37 B–B1 R–Q1	56 R–B5 + K–K1
2 N–KB3 N–QB3	19 ... KR–Q1	38 R–Q2 R–KN1	57 N–Q5 N × P
3 B–N5 P–QR3	20 QR–K1 N–B3	39 P–QR3 B–K2	58 R–R5 N × P
4 B–R4 P–Q3	21 R–K2 N–R4	40 R–B2 N–N4	59 N–B3 R–B1
5 P–B3 B–Q2	22 B–B1 P–B5	41 N–N1 K–B2	60 K–B2 N–B7
6 P–Q4 P–KN3	23 R–Q1 N/3–B5	42 B–N2 R–Q1	61 N × P N–Q5
7 P × P P × P	24 N × N R × R +	43 K–K2 P–B4	62 R–K5 + K–Q2
8 0–0 B–N2	25 N × R N × N	44 P–N5 N–K3	63 R–Q5 + K–K3
9 B–KN5 KN–K2	26 K–B1 P–QR4	45 R–Q2 R–KN1	64 K–N2 N × BP
10 Q–Q2 P–R3	27 P–QN3 N–Q3	46 K–B2 N–Q5	65 N × BP + P × N
11 B–K3 N–R4	28 N–N2 P–R4	47 R–Q1 K–K3	66 R × P N–K4
12 B × B + Q × B	29 R–Q2 P–KN4	48 R–Q3 B–R5 +	67 R–B8 R–N1 +
13 Q × Q + K × Q	30 N–R4 P–N5	49 K–B1 N–N6	68 K–B1 K–Q2
14 N–R3 K–K3	31 P–B4 N–B2	50 N–K2 P × P	69 R–B5 R–K1
(*114*)	32 N–B3 P–B3	51 P × P N–R4	70 K–N2 B–N3
15 QR–Q1 P–N3	33 B–R3 B–B3	52 B × P K × B	71 R–Q5 + K–K3
16 N–K1 P–KB4	34 N–K2 P–QR5	53 R–Q5 + K–K3	72 P–R4 R–N1 +
17 P–B3 N–N2	35 P–N4 N–Q3	54 R × RP B–Q1	White resigns.
18 N–Q3 N–Q3	36 R–B2 N–B2	55 N × P + K–B2	

THE STRUGGLE FOR A DRAW

White: L. Aronin – Moscow 1957, USSR Championship

The move P×B consolidated for White a definite positional advantage. All the same Black ventured to offer a draw... and suffered a refusal. There was nothing else for me to do but to grit my teeth and pin my hopes on my favourite, the dark-squared bishop on KN2: would you be so kind as to prove that even with pawns on black squares you can demonstrate maximum activeness?

The struggle for a draw had an unexpected outcome.

Overestimating the strength of his position, my opponent wrongly transposed into the ending, where the role of first violin was played by... the dark-square bishop on KN2.

We will be fair, for the bishop itself, although it moved around the board a great deal, could not have ensured a breakthrough in the defence, it was not strong enough, but from observing the bishop, Black's two dormant knights became inspired. All of them together were able to develop their proper potential and by co-operating they infiltrated White's pawn position. And when the road was free, the king himself came along to enjoy the sweet fruits of success.

But the hero of the game was still the black bishop!

1 P–K4 P–K4	17 Q–K2 R×R	32 K–Q3 N–R2	46 K–Q3 N–N2
2 N–KB3 N–QB3	18 R×R B×B	33 N–R3 B–B1	47 N–Q2
3 B–N5 P–QR3	19 P×B Q–K3	34 P–B4 B–B4	47 ... N/2–B4+
4 B–R4 P–Q3	(115)	35 K–K2 P–N4	48 K–B2 N–R4
5 P–B3 B–Q2	20 P–QN4 P–B4	36 N–QN1 N–B1	49 B–R1 N–R5
6 P–Q4 P–KN3	21 B–B1 P–B5	37 B–N2 K–K3	50 K–Q3 P–N6
7 0–0 B–N2	22 K–R2 P–QR4	38 N/3–Q2	51 B–B3 N×B
8 P×P P×P	23 P–N5 N–Q1	38 ... N/1–Q3	52 K×N K–B4
9 B–KN5 KN–K2	24 N/1–Q2 N–B2	39 P–B3 N–N2	53 N×P+ N×N
10 Q–Q3 P–R3	25 Q–B4 Q×Q	40 N–R3 B–N5	54 K×N K–Q5
11 B–K3 P–N3	26 N×Q K–B1	41 N–B2 N–B4	55 K–N4 K–Q6
12 R–Q1 Q–B1	27 K–N1 K–K1	42 N×B P×N	56 K–N3 K–Q7
13 B–N3 B–N5	28 K–B1 R–Q1	43 B–B1 K–Q3	57 K–N4 K–B7
14 QN–Q2 0–0	29 R×R+ K×R	44 N–N1 N×NP	58 P–B5 K–Q6
15 P–KR3 B–K3	30 K–K2 K–Q2	45 B–N2 N–Q1	White resigns.
16 N–B1 R–Q1	31 P–QN3 N–B1		

A CHALLENGE TO A DUEL

White: L. Evans – Moscow 1955, USSR v USA

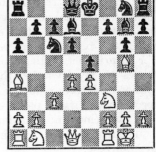

116B

The reader will, of course, have noticed that in many variations of the Ruy Lopez White's dark-squared bishop strives to get to KN5. We have the same picture here.

Nowadays it is somehow not the done thing, or at least it is considered inelegant, to give check to the king or to say 'en garde' to the queen; but if we decipher the meaning of B–KN5, we get the following:

'I, the dark-squared bishop, ask you, your highness the black queen, if you are prepared to engage with me in open and noble combat according to all the rules of the knightly duel. I am well aware, of course, that on a chess board you are far more highly valued than any bishop, but, be that as it may, I say to you: "defend yourself!" '

The bishop's address to the queen sounds rather polite, but what is the bishop actually thinking? He is thinking: 'Of course, the queen will not want to enter into single combat with me and, most probably, will hide itself in cowardly fashion on QB1. And then, perhaps, Black's KRP will want to show its metal and will play to KR3? Then I shall retreat to K3 – I'm not proud – but will Black's KRP be able to retreat? Cunning, isn't it? Or will the Black KN come out to KB3? Then I shall ask my QN to go to Q2, defending the KP, and then ask his colleague the light-squared bishop, to take Black's QN on QB3. The light-squared bishop will give the order for the QP to take on K5, but then – the irony of fate ... then the KN on KB3 will reap my laurels. Of course! The KN always comes out best!'

The dark-squared bishop's hopes were not realized in this game.

Black chose the move ... KN–K2 and by such a straightforward means both kept his queen where it was and retained control over his pawn on K4.

Was B–KN5 a blank shot then? Oh no! The bishop had set out for KN5 not only on its own wishes, but also on the order of the white queen.

When the bishop informed the queen in a hurt tone that Black had not complied with his secret thoughts and had played differently, the queen said: There is no need to get excited! This move had also been planned by me. I was calculating this possibility and now I will punish Black for the thoughtless weakening of his KB3 and KR3 squares.

You and I together will seize the QB1–KR6 diagonal, then we shall exchange off Black's KB and call to our assistance the QN, which, along the path Q2–QB4–K3–Q5, will thread its way closer to the black king and deal it a deadly check from KB6!

Observe carefully. If Black's KB leaves the board and I can penetrate to KR6 and our knight check from KB6, then the black king will only have one square to flee to: KR1. No, the king will not be jumping from K1 to KR1, but by the time I am talking about he will be on KN1. He will not really know of our plans and will surely not refuse to castle!

And then, when you will already be resting, I will call you forth, and have you lifted in a helicopter a little above the board so that you will be able to share with me the joy of our common victory after Q ×RP mate.'

So spoke the white queen, but whilst she was saying all this, the black king guessed his secret thoughts and decided not to allow the bishop onto his KR3! So this plan of White's was halted too. And he had to begin looking afresh for a means of breaking into his opponent's camp.

'Do not grieve, bishop!' the queen began again to console the other. 'You know me better than anyone else does, we are always together. Has there ever been a battle I was in danger of losing? Just wait, we will infuse some heat into it! We won't go for the K-side, we'll take the Q-side. And how the black king can intend castling after a silly move like . . . P–KR3, I don't know.'

I too, the author, did not know. And then suddenly . . . a draw!

But if we return from the world of fantasy to the tournament hall, the reason for all Black's troubles will become clear: the move 10 . . . P–KR3?. Black was wrong to listen to the white pieces' whisperings; he should have boldly castled – 10 . . . 0–0! and on 11 R–Q1 replied equally coolly, 11 . . . Q–K1!

1 P–K4 P–K4	8 B–KN5 (116)	14 QN–Q2 N–Q3	20 B–Q5 B × B
2 N–KB3 N–QB3	8 . . . KN–K2	15 P–QN4	21 R × B P–QB3
3 B–N5 P–QR3	9 P ×P P ×P	15 . . . N/4–N2	22 R–Q1 KR–Q1
4 B–R4 P–Q3	10 Q–B1 P–R3	16 P–QR4 0–0	23 N–Q2 N ×N
5 0–0 B–Q2	11 B–K3 N–R4	17 N–N3 K–R2	24 B ×N Q–K3
6 P–B3 P–KN3	12 R–Q1 P–QN4	18 N–B5 B–QB3	Draw agreed.
7 P–Q4 B–N2	13 B–B2 N–B1	19 B–N3 Q–K2	

THE DANGEROUS QUEEN VOYAGE

White: G. Ravinsky – Moscow 1944, USSR Championship

The Moscow Championship of 1947 was played in a sharp, uncompromising, competitive spirit. The leaders altered from round to round, and when the tournament came to its end, no clear winner emerged: places 1–3 were shared by the future grandmaster, Simagin, the master, Ravinsky, and myself.

There was nothing that could be done; a 're-run', as fencing fans say, was arranged for us.

The extra match-tournament was like a thriller story. To begin with Ravinsky lost both his games to Simagin, and I won a game off each of them and had two draws.

But in the third and fourth rounds everything changed.

Ravinsky overcame a psychological barrier and beat Simagin for the first time in his life, both in the first game and then in the second as well. I drew twice with Ravinsky and lost twice to Simagin.

Simagin won the tournament and already demonstrated at that time an enviable number of the most varied tactical and strategical ideas.

It was three years before this championship that I had had my début in the USSR Championship and my first meeting with Ravinsky. He and I achieved our master titles on the same day.

People are right when they say I am unlucky. How else could I have failed to win this game?

The daring attack by the pawns, then the mysterious manoeuvrings of the knights and the sudden rook sacrifice on a central square!

When the first clouds of smoke had disappeared from the battle-field, the black king made the enigmatic step from KN1 to KB1, the point of which only became clear after the fantastical leap . . . N–KB4!

A grandiose idea! At least that is how it struck me at the time of the game.

I had pinned all my hopes on this blow from my cavalry. Indeed, White's queen is in a trap and the tempting check on K7 is no longer possible; it is difficult to see what White can do.

In addition there is the threat of a terrible bishop check from Q5, and this blow, along the Q5–KN8 diagonal, would be aimed right at White's heart!

Alas, youth sees everything in rainbow colours! The prosaic variation, P×N, was interpreted by me as White capitulating and I gleefully played a confident check . . . only with the wrong piece. After . . . B–Q5 + and . . . R–R1 the white queen would have been trapped. I could have

achieved the same result with the quiet move ... R–R1, and then
... B–Q5 + !

But as my main efforts had been directed towards checking the mating
variation after 36 N–N6 Q–B4 + !, I picked up the wrong piece in the
time-scramble.

Whom has it not happened to ... ?

So many great feats by the pieces and then nothing. Only half a point.
I hope meanwhile that my opponent, master Ravinsky, does not come
across these words. He may get angry and start trying to show that all my
play was nothing more than bluff, that he had been wrong to agree to a
draw; he may say that he had even read in some foreign magazine about
his kindness and spinelessness, since both black pawns were not worth a
farthing.

No, Ravinsky will not say this – about the pawns. He was rather afraid
of them then and he is still afraid of them now. But some annotator or
other did in fact find an easy win for White, something like 41 R–Q5 B–K6
42 P–B6 P–Q7 43 R–QN1 P–B6 44 R–N7 Q–N6 45 R ×BP + K ×R
46 R–Q7 + !; but this variation is built on sand. One need only forget
about the queen and play 44 ... P–B7 for the picture to brighten up
immediately.

I had to content myself, then, willy-nilly with White's QNP and rely
on my connected passed pawns.

Of course, it would have been somewhat more gratifying to win White's
queen; but this is immaterial to the reader – he will already have spotted
a dozen other interesting moves.

1 P–K4 P–K4	12 B–N3 P–QN4	23 N–Q3 B–K3	34 Q–B2 K–B1
2 N–KB3 N–QB3	13 P ×P RP ×P	24 N ×N R ×N	35 Q–R7 N–B4
3 B–N5 P–QR3	14 P–QR4 P–N5	25 B–QB4 P–N6	(117)
4 B–R4 P–Q3	15 N–K2 N–B3	26 Q–B3 R–Q5	36 P ×N Q ×N
5 P–B3 B–Q2	16 Q–B2 N–N2	27 B ×B Q ×B	37 Q–R6 Q–B4 +
6 P–Q4 P–KN3	17 P–R3 0–0	28 P–R5 Q–R3	38 K–R1 B ×P
7 0–0 B–N2	18 N–Q2 P–B4	29 B ×R KP ×B	39 QR–N1 B–Q5
8 P ×P P ×P	19 N–B1 KR–B1	30 Q ×NP P–B5	40 R–N5 Q–B2
9 B–K3 Q–K2	20 N–B4 R–R3	31 Q–B2 N–Q3	41 R–Q5
10 P–B4 N–Q1	21 P–B3 N–K1	32 N–N4 Q–N4	Draw agreed.
11 N–B3 P–QB3	22 R–Q1 N/1–Q3	33 N–Q5 P–Q6	

A STUDY THEME

Black: B. De Greiff – Portoroz 1958, Interzonal Tournament

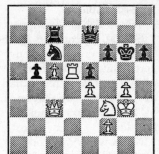

In itself the white rook's move to Q5 gives us no cause for objection, but would it not have been better to ensconce it on Q6? Particularly since the combination Black has in mind – 45 . . . N–Q5 46 N × N Q × R – would meet an equally elegant refutation, quite in the style of the old studies of the Platov brothers, – 47 P × Q! R × Q + 48 P–B3 P × N 49 P–Q7! and the white pawn cannot be stopped from queening!

Alas, these are mere dreams. Black has only to decline the sacrifice and play his king to KB2 or his rook to Q6 and White is left no better off.

This is all very well, the shrewd sceptic will say, but there is no need for the rook to go deep down the Q-file at all; why does it not try its strength in the region of the KR-file?

I cannot remember why I did not play such a move. I probably overestimated in my preliminary calculations the strength of 46 . . . N–Q5 (45 R–KR1 K–R2 46 N–R4 N–Q5, when White's attack is halted, whilst at the same time Black's passed QNP becomes strong).

But R–KR1 was the move I should have played all the same.

1 P–K4 P–K4	16 QN–Q2 R–Q1	31 P × P R × P	45 R–Q5 (*118*)
2 N–KB3 N–QB3	17 P–QN4 Q–K3	32 P–QN4	45 . . . K–R2
3 B–N5 P–QR3	18 R–R3 N–B1	32 . . . R–R8 +	46 Q–Q2 Q–N2
4 B–R4 P–Q3	19 R/1–R1 N–N1	33 K–R2 R–R2	47 R–Q6 N–K2
5 P–B3 B–Q2	20 P–B4 P–QB3	34 Q–B3 P–B3	48 Q–R5 R × P
6 0–0 P–KN3	21 P–R3 B–B1	35 Q–Q2 K–R2	49 Q–Q8 R–B1
7 P–Q4 B–N2	22 B × B K × B	36 Q–B3 R–B2	50 Q–Q7 R–B6
8 P × P P × P	23 P × P BP × P	37 P–N3 R–R2	51 K–N2 R–B3
9 B–KN5 KN–K2	24 N–N3 N–K2	38 P–N4 R–B2	52 R × R N × R
10 Q–Q3 P–R3	25 N–B5 Q–KB3	39 P–R4 P–N4	53 Q–B5 + K–R1
11 B–K3 B–K3	26 R–Q1 N/2–B3	40 K–N3 R–R2	54 Q–B8 + K–R2
12 Q–K2 0–0	27 R × R + Q × R	41 R–Q1 N–Q2	55 Q–B5 + K–R1
13 B–B5 P–QN4	28 R–Q3 Q–K2	42 P × P N × P	56 Q–B8 + K–R2
14 B–N3 B × B	29 Q–Q2 K–N2	43 P–N6 + K × P	Draw agreed.
15 P × B Q–B1	30 R–Q5 P–QR4	44 P × N R–B2	

SKILFUL DEFENCE

White: A. Suetin – Moscow 1952, USSR Championship

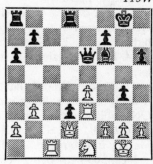

The black bishop was master of the board.

When Black's knight penetrated to Q5, White hoped to lure him away by cunning: he proposed an exchange on KB3. But the important knight knew his own value and would not agree to the variation 17 Q–Q2 N×N+ 18 P×N. Then White decided to give up his bishop for the knight, although he realized that it would be difficult for a lone white knight to effectively direct the operations of the pawns in both the centre and the wings. That is how Black's bishop came to be the master of the board.

And as ill luck would have it, all the white pieces were also deployed on black squares.

In such difficult conditions it was not easy to forestall the threat of . . . B–N4!. Nevertheless, my inventive opponent found a very sharp defence and, whilst balancing on a knife's edge, still managed to bring the game to a draw.

But perhaps instead of 23 . . . B–B3 it would have been better to move a pawn? Let us say 23 . . . P–KR4, when 24 P–KR4 would then be pointless.

Unfortunately the threat then of . . . B–R3 would be an illusory one, since after 24 R×P B–R3 25 R×R+ Black would simply be a rook down.

Possibly after a thorough analysis of the position some reader will find a win for Black.

1 P–K4 P–K4	11 B–K3 N–Q5	19 . . . KR–Q1	27 R×P R×R
2 N–KB3 N–QB3	12 B×B+ Q×B	20 QR–B1 Q–K3	28 N×R R–Q1
3 B–N5 P–QR3	13 N–B3 0–0	21 P–QN3 P–Q6	29 Q–K3 P–N3
4 B–R4 P–Q3	14 N–Q5 N/2×N	22 R–K3 P–N5	30 K–B1 P–KR4
5 P–B3 B–Q2	15 BP×N P–QB4	23 N–K1 B–B3	31 N–B2 P–B4
6 P–Q4 P–KN3	16 P×Pep Q×P	(*119*)	32 R–Q1 R×R+
7 0–0 B–N2	17 Q–Q2 P–KN4	24 P–KR4 B×P	33 N×R B–B4
8 P×P P×P	18 B×N P×B	25 P–B4 B–B3	34 Q–Q3 K–B2
9 B–KN5 KN–K2	19 KR–K1	26 P–K5 B–K2	35 Q×RP Q–Q4.
10 P–B4 P–R3			

Draw agreed in view of the variation 36 N–B3 Q–Q5 37 Q–N7+, and the black king cannot escape perpetual check.

CLIMBING THE BOLSHOE SEDLO

Black: Yu. Kaem – Dniepropetrovsk 1939, Ukrainian Championship

120W

There is a definite idea behind moving the QBP forward two squares: once White's light-squared bishop has got onto the QR4–K8 diagonal, let it stay there a little longer!

This is the direct benefit of P–QB4, but it achieves other things indirectly. White's QN, which usually takes the tiring route via Q2, KB1 and K3 to Q5, can now do this journey in two moves, not four!

I cannot help being reminded of Aeroflot's slogan: 'Save time! Use the air roads!'

And although chess was invented many centuries ago it begins to appear that this slogan applies to it too, or, to be more precise, to the chess knight, since he alone can fly through the air, he alone does not have to take roundabout routes, but can flit about like a butterfly.

Seen in this light it will not seem strange now that White chose to exchange pawns on K5 rather than play his pawn to Q5. It would have been a pity to take Q5 away from the knight!

The exchange of pawns has other positive sides too: the dark-squared bishop was able to move onto the QR3–KB8 diagonal, whilst the white queen immediately gained in strength, its X-rays penetrating now as far as Q8, which was probably not very pleasant for the black queen.

In the end the white knight achieved its life-long dream and invaded Q5. Its joy can only be compared with the excitement of the cardiac patients who at the end of a course of treatment in Kislovodsk do an audacious 20 kilometre walk up to the summit of Bolshoe Sedlo.

Under the cover of the cavalry outpost all three of White's major pieces, the queen and both rooks, were able to form up comfortably; and then the main heroine, the QBP, led the attack. Its run from B2 to B6 played an important role.

However, there was never any serious fighting. Black decided to copy White's manoeuvre: he played his rook to the Q-file, which was correct from a strategical point of view, but fundamentally mistaken from a tactical point of view. With the four-move combination 22 N ×BP R ×R + 23 Q ×R R ×N 24 Q–Q8 + and 25 Q ×R, White won the very important QBP, and although Black did not take the knight, the road was opened for White's QBP – the road to promotion! So there you have the modest 5 P–QB4. Its aim: P–B8 =Q!!.

Some years ago I happened to see in the press a game Fischer-Bisguier from the USA Championship. In one of the variations I came across the strong and beautiful move for White, B–QN6. And all because of the improvident weakening of Black's QN3 by 3 ... P–QR3?.

The beauty of chess ideas is often found behind the scenes, beyond the chess-board. I liked this game of Fischer's precisely because of the inconspicuous variation with B(K3)–QN6, which suddenly turned a drawn position into a won one.

Is one equally justified in this old game in putting White's win down to Black's ... P–QR3?

It was difficult later for Black to drive White's knight on Q5 away with a pawn, since the knight would have gone to QN6 and given direct help to the white rooks which were aimed at Q7.

Why is Duras's attack, 1 P–K4 P–K4 2 N–KB3 N–QB3 3 B–N5 P–QR3 4 B–R4 P–Q3 5 P–B4, so rarely used nowadays?

Because of the reply 5 ... B–N5!.

By ... N–KB3–Q2–B4–K3 and ... B–K2–B3 Black takes complete control of White's Q4 and renders White's pawn on Q3 helpless: it will not be able to advance to Q5 or Q4!

Of course, even here all is not lost. Lovers of old games can find the encounter Keres-Reshevsky from the match-tournament for the 1948 World Championship, in which White did not allow Black's knight onto its QB4, but played P–QN4 and concentrated his fire on the important black QB4 square.

Nevertheless the basic idea of this variation, to seize Q5, is not lost even after 5 ... B–N5; it is only that N–QB3–Q5 has to be played with a closed Q-file (and it will sometimes even be possible to get P–Q4 in). White should not grieve over this, since with a closed centre it is easier to get a flank attack going with P–KB4–KB5.

1 P–K4 P–K4	9 P×P P×P	16 Q×N Q–Q3	22 N×BP R×R+
2 N–KB3 N–QB3	10 0–0 0–0	17 P–B5 Q–QB3	23 Q×R Q–K2
3 B–N5 P–QR3	11 B–B5 R–K1	18 KR–Q1	24 N–Q5 Q–Q3
4 B–R4 P–Q3	12 Q–Q3 N–Q5	18 ... QR–B1	25 P–B7 B–B1
5 P–B4 B–Q2	13 B×B Q×B	19 QR–B1 Q–K3	26 Q–K2 P–B4
6 N–B3 P–KN3	14 B×N/7 Q×B	20 P–B6 P–N3	27 Q×P K–B2
7 P–Q4 B–N2	15 N–Q5 N×N+	21 P–QN4	28 N×P
8 B–K3 KN–K2	(120)	21 ... KR–Q1	Black resigns.

A RARE DRAW

White: B. Larsen – Portoroz 1958, Interzonal Tournament

Why such a quick draw? During the 1958 Interzonal the Dane seemed to tire of nothing: at that time he was still only learning. Learning to win, learning to lose and learning to draw.

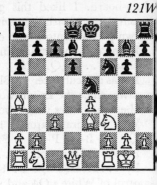

Nowadays one has to admit that Bent Larsen is a terrible pupil: out of the three subjects he has mastered only one, playing to win! As for losing, he does not want to do that. The same goes for everyone. It happens though; a man is not a machine after all.

On the other hand Larsen simply has not learnt to draw. No, no matter what other chess writers might say, the Dane has not become a 'super-class' grandmaster. What sets the 'super class' apart from the normal grandmaster is the ability to fashion draws: as many as are needed and in as many minutes as are given. This game, then, is a rarity.

Larsen does not like such banalities; he is a devotee of everything extraordinary.

During the Lugano Olympiad in the autumn of 1968 Larsen asked me to say a few words for the Danish fans, and I challenged their idol to a one-day contest of four games, with all the games to be played simultaneously, two with White and two with Black!

Larsen greeted this idea of a mutual simultaneous display with delight. To make sure I said to him:

'Bent, if you want only to play a match with me in Copenhagen with just one game an evening, I won't refuse even this banal creative activity.'

Since then all I have been able to do is wait.

1 P–K4 P–K4	5 P–B3 B–Q2	9 P×P QN×P	12 Q×Q+ N×Q
2 N–KB3 N–QB3	6 P–Q4 P–KN3	(*121*)	13 N–Q2 0–0–0
3 B–N5 P–QR3	7 0–0 B–N2	10 N×N P×N	Draw agreed.
4 B–R4 P–Q3	8 B–K3 N–B3	11 B×B+ Q×B	

APPRENTICE GRANDMASTER

White: A. Lutikov – Moscow 1959, International Tournament

122B

The International Chess Federation has not yet created the rank of apprentice-grandmaster, but if this were to happen one of the first to qualify would be our master, A. Lutikov. His successes seem to grow like mushrooms after rain and it is only the strict rules of FIDE that have prevented him from jumping over the title of international master.

Moreover the same formal ruling has prevented another master, I. Nei, from becoming a grandmaster. Both of them 'suffered' at Beverwijk: the former in 1964, the latter in 1965.

Even, however, without high-sounding titles the 'apprentice-grandmasters' are always dangerous. The present game characterizes the best side of Lutikov's creativeness. He seized the centre with simple moves and hoisted his knight onto the white K4 square, from where it could comfortably both observe and direct affairs. The dark-squared bishop had no direct way of combatting the knight.

It was necessary to resort to cunning: with the help of my KNP I nailed White's KBP to the spot and by building up pressure along the files I distracted White's pieces from any thoughts of attacking the Q-side.

Then, just when all the pieces had prepared themselves for a violent fight, there followed an unexpected agreement on a draw! In fact, neither White nor Black had a logical plan for playing for a win.

1 P–K4 P–K4	10 P–B4 KN–B3	18 N–B3 P–B5	25 P–N3 R–B3
2 N–KB3 N–QB3	11 N–B3 0–0	19 N–K4 N–B3	26 K–R2
3 B–N5 P–QR3	12 N–K1 Q–K2	20 Q–K2 N×N	26 ... R/1–KB1
4 B–R4 P–Q3	13 B–N5 P–B4	21 Q×N P–N5	27 QR–K1 P–R4
5 P–B3 B–Q2	14 P–QR4 P–R3	22 N–Q3 P×P	28 R–K2 Q–KB2
6 P–Q4 P–KN3	15 B–R4 P–KN4	23 RP×P Q–Q2	29 R–KR1 R–B4
7 0–0 B–N2	16 B–N3 N×KP	24 QR–N1	30 K–N1 (122)
8 P–Q5 N–N1	17 N×N P–B4	24 ... P–QR4	Draw agreed.
9 B×B+ N×B			

A CHAIN OF BLACK PAWNS

White: Ya. Klyavin – Moscow 1960, USSR Team Championship

123B

A knight, according to the standard scale of values, is equal to three pawns. Did Black really not know this?

Or did he forget? Neither, in fact: Black had no way of weakening the pressure of White's pawns other than by sacrificing his knight. For the well-fortified chain of white pawns from K4 to QB6 had split Black's position in two and threatened his whole Q-side with physical annihilation.

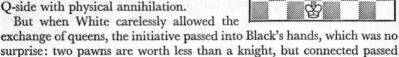

But when White carelessly allowed the exchange of queens, the initiative passed into Black's hands, which was no surprise: two pawns are worth less than a knight, but connected passed pawns.... They are often priceless!

Black rushed things in the endgame and allowed White to weaken his pawn ranks. The situation was very much simplified, the conflict subsided, and peace was concluded.

Just as in a good fairy-tale, everything turned out happily in the end.

Which of Black's pieces should be thanked for saving the half-point? I think the queen most of all: she commanded the battle, and her move 21 ... Q–QB5!! deserves two exclamation marks.

1 P–K4 P–K4	15 P–B6 Q–N5	27 R–R1 P–N6	41 R/B5 ×R
2 N–KB3 N–QB3	16 Q–B2 Q–R4	28 B–R5 P–K5	41 ... R ×R
3 B–N5 P–QR3	17 N–K2 Q–N5	29 N–Q2 B ×P	42 R ×P R–N5
4 B–R4 P–Q3	18 N–N3	30 R–N1 B–K4	43 K–K1 P–Q5
5 P–B3 B–Q2	18 ... N/2 ×QP	31 N ×NP N–B6	44 P–N4 B–B6
6 P–Q4 P–KN3	19 P ×N N ×P	32 B ×N B ×B	45 K–Q1 (*123*)
7 0–0 B–N2	20 B–N5 R–K1	33 R–R2 R–N3	45 ... B ×N
8 P–Q5 N/3–K2	21 KR–K1	34 N–Q2 R/1–N1	46 K ×B R–N7 +
9 B ×B+ Q ×B	21 ... Q–QB5	35 R–QB1 B–N7	47 K–K1 R–N8 +
10 P–B4 N–KB3	22 QR–B1 Q ×Q	36 R–B2 P–Q4	48 K–Q2 R–N7 +
11 N–B3 0–0	23 R ×Q N–N5	37 K–B1 K–B2	49 K–K1 R–N8 +
12 P–B5 KR–Q1	24 R/2–K2 P–B4	38 R–B5 K–K3	50 K–Q2 R–N7 +
13 Q–N3 QR–N1	25 R–Q1 N ×RP	39 N–K2 K–Q3	Draw agreed.
14 B–K3 P–QN4	26 B–Q2 P–N5	40 R/2–R5 R–N4	

REVENGE EIGHTEEN YEARS LATER

White: L. Shamkovich – Moscow 1961, match for the title of Champion of Moscow

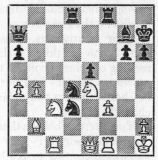

124W

This game is nowhere near as simple as it may seem. I would even say that it is not simple at all! A match is different from a tournament; one does not go in for odd openings in a match, which is why I decided to protect myself with well-tried armour: the Steinitz defence has served me faithfully and truthfully for many years.

The first complications arose after the moves P–QB4 and ... P–KR3. Who can create real threats first? Considering it theoretically, White's chances in such positions are always better: his king is safely defended. But chess is not an abstract debate, it is a fight, and in a fight things often get turned upside down.

I managed to create tension of various kinds in different areas of the board, which made it difficult for my opponent to calculate variations precisely, a field he is particularly strong in. His imprudent P–QR4 permitted the black pawn to make the daring journey from KB4 to K5, to KB6, disorganizing the defence. The black knight which had rushed forward to help seized the central Q5 square and set White's king very difficult problems.

Given these considerations, White's decision to freely give up the exchange cannot be criticized.

In Tiflis at the beginning of 1943 people had tried to hold a city championship. After six rounds the tournament folded up, but I had had time to lose a game to Shamkovich. So here, eighteen years later, was my revenge!

1 P–K4 P–K4	11 N–B3 P–KB4	19 ... Q–R2+	27 Q–Q2 N×BP
2 N–KB3 N–QB3	12 P–QN4 N–KB3	20 K–R1 P×P	28 Q–N2 N×R
3 B–N5 P–QR3	13 N–Q2 0–0	21 P×P N×P	29 R×N/1 Q–K6
4 B–R4 P–Q3	14 P–B3 P–B3	22 N×QP N–Q5	30 Q–K2 Q×Q
5 P–B3 B–Q2	15 Q–N3 K–R2	23 Q–Q1 QR–Q1	31 N×Q N–Q7
6 P–Q4 P–KN3	16 B–N2 P–QN4	24 N/6–K4 N–R4	32 N/2–N3 N×N
7 0–0 B–N2	17 P–QR4 P×BP	25 R–B1 N–B5	33 N×N R–B5
8 P–Q5 N/3–K2	18 N×P KBP×P	26 Q–K1 N–Q6	34 R–K1 R×N
9 B×B+ Q×B	19 QP×P	*(124)*	White resigns.
10 P–B4 P–R3			

THE TRIUMPH OF THE LOPEZ BISHOP

White: E. Gufeld – Leningrad 1963, USSR Championship

125B

There are some chess-players in the world, amongst them grandmasters too, who would consider it the greatest praise they could give to their creativeness to say: 'Honestly, I don't know a thing. Why should I go reading old chess books? I thought all these moves up myself – and not in the quiet of my home, but to the ticking sound of the chess-clock.'

If one were to believe that Gufeld thought up the manoeuvre P–KB5 followed by the knight penetrating to K6 himself and that he did not see it first in the famous Lasker-Capablanca (St Petersburg 1914) encounter, then one must confess that he played the whole of our game extremely logically and consistently.

Black pointlessly spent time on exchanging the dark-squared bishops, when it was the light-squared bishop that was a danger to him.

By the time I had realized my mistake and found the right plan it cost me too dearly to exchange White's bishop on QN3 and my QRP was catastrophically weakened.

Perhaps Black's sole chance of saving himself lay in immediately counter-attacking White's pawn on K4 by 34 ... Q–K3!.

1 P–K4 P–K4	17 P×N Q–K3	32 N×N R×N	46 R×P R×BP
2 N–KB3 N–QB3	18 N–Q5 QR–B1	33 R–B6 R/1–K1	47 R×P K–R2
3 B–N5 P–QR3	19 P×P N×P	34 P×P R×NP	48 R–B6 R–QN5
4 B–R4 P–Q3	20 Q–N3 P–KB3	35 R/1–QB1	49 P–N6 K–R3
5 0–0 N–B3	21 P–KB4 N–B3	35 ... R–K2	50 K–N3 K–N4
6 R–K1 B–N5	22 P–N4 KR–K1	36 R/1–B4	51 K–B3 R–N7
7 P–B3 N–Q2	23 K–R2 Q–B2	36 ... R/4–K4	52 P–R4+ K–R3
8 P–Q4 B–K2	24 Q–N4 QR–Q1	37 Q–KB3 P–N3	53 P–N4 R–N6+
9 P–KR3 B×N	25 R–QR1 N–N1	38 P×P P×P	54 K–K2 K–N2
10 Q×B B–N4	26 P–B5 (125)	39 Q–B3 R×P	55 R–B7+ K–B3
11 N–R3 B×B	26 ... R–K4	40 R×R R×R	56 P–N7 K–K4
12 QR×B 0–0	27 N–B4 R/1–K1	41 R×BP Q–K3	57 P–R5 P×P
13 QR–Q1 Q–K2	28 N–K6 R–K2	42 P–N5 R–K6	58 P×P K–B3
14 N–B2 P–QN4	29 P–QN3 R–K1	43 Q–B4 Q×Q	59 P–R6 K–N3
15 B–N3 N–R4	30 P–B4 N–B3	44 P×Q R–QN6	60 P–R7
16 N–K3 N×B	31 R×P N–Q1	45 R–Q7 R–N5	Black resigns.

MUTUAL ZUGZWANG

Black: G. Uusi – Tartu 1962, Training Tournament

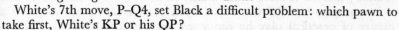

126B

White's queen attacked Black's king and knight alternately. And on each occasion the black pieces stepped out of the direct line of fire.

White had an advantage on the K-side and might have hoped in time to make use of his extra KP, but there was hardly any time for such an operation: Black's QBPs threatened to gradually queen.

Both sides in fact were pinned down by mutual threats; one might say there was mutual zugzwang on the board. Thus a draw.

White's 7th move, P–Q4, set Black a difficult problem: which pawn to take first, White's KP or his QP?

My opponent came up with a clever solution: he rejected the variation 7 ... P ×P 8 N ×P P–B4 9 N–B6 Q–Q2 10 N–R5, and the variation 7 ... N ×P 8 R–K1 P–KB4 9 P ×P P–Q4 10 N–B3.

His move 7 ... B–K2 was probably strongest in that position. Now, in the event of 8 P ×P N ×P 9 R–K1, Black can reply not 9 ... P–KB4, but 9 ... P–Q4, and White does not have 10 N ×P, since K5 is occupied by a white pawn.

Probably the best reply to 7 ... B–K2 was 8 R–K1!, retaining the possibility of the manoeuvre N–QR3–QB4–QR5 – but one can only try out one line in any game. . . .

1 P–K4 P–K4	11 N–B4 0–0	20 QR–Q1 N–K3	29 Q ×R N ×P
2 N–KB3 N–QB3	12 P–QN3 B–N5	21 P–KN3 P–R3	30 Q ×RP N–K3
3 B–N5 P–QR3	13 N–R4 B–R3	22 P–B5 R ×R	31 Q–R8 + N–Q1
4 B–R4 N–B3	14 P–QB3 B ×N	23 R ×R R–N1	32 Q–B8 K–R2
5 0–0 P–Q3	15 NP ×B B–Q3	24 P–QR4 R–N6	33 Q–B5 + K–N1
6 B ×N+ P ×B	16 B–K3 Q–K2	25 K–B2 R ×P	34 Q–B8 K–R2
7 P–Q4 B–K2	17 Q–K2 B–B4	26 Q–N2 R–N5	35 Q–B5 + *(126)*
8 N–B3 N–Q2	18 N ×B N ×N	27 Q ×P R ×RP	35 ... K–N1
9 P ×P P ×P	19 P–B3 KR–Q1	28 R–QR1 R ×R	Draw agreed.
10 N–Q2 P–QR4			

THE GRANDMASTER OF THE SUBTLE STUDY

White: N. Kopaev – Baku 1944, Semi-Finals USSR Championship

127B

The master Kopaev rarely plays in tournaments these days. This is regrettable since he, more than anyone else, is capable of finding an original combinative move in the quietest of positions.

But Kopaev is a master only in practical play. When he appears in the capacity of author of rook studies, he is completely unsurpassable and even the title of grandmaster would not really be good enough for him. Generally it is beyond the power of ordinary mortals to solve these studies.

In our encounter he was called upon to perform in two roles. As a master of practical play he composed amazing combinations uninterruptedly over the first forty moves, so that I finally lost the thread of my attack and was forced to go onto the defensive. Whilst after the resumption he demonstrated his abilities as a grandmaster of the subtle study and lured the black king into a mating net with elegant piece manoeuvres. To those who are still unfamiliar with Kopaev's studies I can recommend the chapter on rook endings in the second volume of 'Chess Endings'.

1 P–K4 P–K4	15 QN–Q2 Q–B3	29 N–B3 R × P	43 R–K6+ K–N2
2 N–KB3 N–QB3	16 P–N4 R–Q2	30 B × P P–B3	44 P–K8 = Q (127)
3 B–N5 P–QR3	17 P–N5 N–N1	31 R/5–N1 B × P	44 ... N × Q
4 B–R4 N–B3	18 P × P N × RP	32 R–K3 N × RP	45 R × N B–N4
5 0–0 P–Q3	19 R–N1 R/1–Q1	33 K–N3 R–N7	46 K–B5 N–Q2
6 R–K1 B–Q2	20 P–R3 B–K3	34 R × R B × R	47 B–R2 N–B4
7 P–B3 P–KN3	21 N–B4 N × RP+	35 P–K5 K–Q2	48 R–KN8+
8 P–Q4 Q–K2	22 K–R2 B × N	36 B–N8 P–R3	48 ... K–R2
9 P × P P × P	23 Q × B N–B5	37 P–K6+ K–K2	49 R–KB8 P–N4
10 B–B2 B–N2	24 R–N5 Q–K3	38 N–R4 N–B2	50 R–B7+ K–N1
11 P–QN3 0–0–0	25 Q × Q N × Q	39 N × P+ K–B3	51 K–N6 P–N5
12 Q–K2 N–KR4	26 N × P R–Q7	40 N–B4 B–K4	52 B–B4
13 P–QR4 N–B5	27 B × R R × B	41 P–K7 N–N3	Black resigns.
14 Q–B1 B–N5	28 B–N3 N/K3–B4	42 K–N4 B × N	

RAUZER'S DRAWING CUL-DE-SAC

White: I. Boleslavsky – Moscow 1949, USSR Championship

128B

Any player who first deprives his own knight of the right to move (by . . . P–Q3) and who then hastily grasps the enemy KP (as if he could not have taken it a move earlier) warrants censure.

Theory shows that one can play it like that, but the idea that 5 . . . P–Q3 and 6 . . . N×P are to some degree contradictory is a sensible one.

I chose move 6 to take White's KP quite deliberately. A long time before the game, in the surroundings of my study at home, I had analysed in an unhurried, painstaking and detailed way all the most likely attacking lines in this sharp, almost impudent, variation.

Even if one takes into account the fact that I knew detailed analyses of this move (opening theory assured me that both players cannot help falling into the famous Rauzer's drawing cul-de-sac), even still the player of the black pieces reminds one of a goat which insists on not taking the normal track, but goes up a steep mountain path instead.

What is this drawing cul-de-sac of Rauzer's?

This is what one might call the variation 6 P–B3 N×P 7 P–Q4 B–Q2 8 R–K1 N–B3 9 B×N B×B 10 P×P P×P 11 Q×Q+ R×Q 12 N×P B–K5 13 N–Q2 B–K2 14 N×B N×N, with appreciable simplifications which almost guarantee Black a draw.

I say 'almost' because a year or two after our game Boleslavsky found the curious move 15 B–R6! and thereby infused a spark of life into this apparently infinitely dreary endgame.

1 P–K4 P–K4	6 . . . N×P	12 B–KN5 B×B	17 R/1–K1 B–Q3
2 N–KB3 N–QB3	7 P–Q4 B–Q2	13 Q×B+ Q–Q2	18 R×R+ R×R
3 B–N5 P–QR3	8 R–K1 N–B3	14 Q×Q+ K×Q	19 R×R+ N×R
4 B–R4 N–B3	9 P×P P×P	15 N–Q2 QR–K1	20 N–K4 B–B1
5 0–0 P–Q3	10 N×P N×N	16 R–Q1 K–B1	Draw agreed.
6 P–B3 (*128*)	11 R×N+ B–K2		

CRITICAL SPECTATORS

Black: V. Smyslov – Moscow 1959, International Tournament

129B

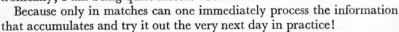

In the rapid pace of life today the most natural of tournaments between grandmasters, by which I mean matches, do not enjoy favour with either the spectators or organizers.

I was reminded of matches when I saw with what interest spectators were following my game with Smyslov, a game in which the play was in fact sharp and uncompromising, in the best match traditions.

And please do not think I mean this ironically; I am being quite sincere about it all!

Because only in matches can one immediately process the information that accumulates and try it out the very next day in practice!

It is said that matches are worse than tournaments because, although they involve two players of equal strength, victory only ever goes to one of them. My answer to that is that that means they are not of equal strength! Their strength has been measured according to un-reliable criteria: tournament criteria, whereas it should be . . . match criteria.

But matches, of course, should not be decided by who gets more points; rather by who is first to win a certain number of games, disregarding draws – exactly as it was one, two or three hundred years ago.

I know that everyone does not think the same way as me, but I definitely prefer match play. There is no problem of colour, one can revenge oneself for a loss, and there are other features, too, which argue in favour of matches. I believe that they will gradually come back into fashion again and be just as popular as all-play-all tournaments are today.

These thoughts came to me once more when I saw the interest the students of Moscow University were showing in my game with Smyslov.

The tournament controllers displayed laudable initiative in organizing a round away from the main centre. Faced with such critical spectators we felt a special responsibility, almost like being in a match!

We seemed not to disappoint the students' expectations: the game won the prize for the most hard-fought draw of the tournament.

In my efforts to win I overdid it somewhat and entered the forbidden zone with my king.

However, the black pieces, which had for a long time been intent on defence, could not regroup quickly for the attack.

The adjourned position looked won for White, but after long deliberation Smyslov found the brilliant defence, 41 . . . Q–R4!.

After the exchange of queens White again got the advantage, but I was too impatient in the endgame. So in the end a draw was a just reward for both players.

For lovers of combinations two moments can be singled out: the move 38 ... N–B4 +, which would have led to the win of the queen for rook and knight, and the move 45 K × R ?, which would have allowed the black queen to take the bishop on K4 with check and then also the rook on QR8.

Black did not check with the knight because he considered the variation drawing and Smyslov was wanting to win, and he overlooked 41 K–B3.

I for my part was not going to take the rook, because I did not want to lose.

Why then did I permit ... R–KN8 + ?

It was my fault, though not consciously: all night I had had to analyse masses of the most complicated variations, and in this heap of White and Black moves I did not see ... R–KN8 + at all.

In short, I, too, overlooked something.

The prize, then, for the hardest-fought, if not faultless, draw fell into worthy hands.

1 P–K4 P–K4	18 P–QR4 P × P	33 ... R × QBP	48 Q × Q N × Q
2 N–KB3 N–QB3	19 B × N Q × B	34 R × P R × R	49 R–R7 R–K8
3 B–N5 P–QR3	20 B × P P–B4	35 R × R R–B8 +	50 P–B3 K–B3
4 B–R4 N–B3	21 P × P B × P	36 K–N2 Q–B8 +	51 R × P + K–N2
5 0–0 B–K2	22 N–K3 B–N4	37 K–B3 Q–R8 +	52 R–R7 K–B3
6 R–K1 P–Q3	23 N × B B × N	38 K–K3 (129)	53 P–N4 R–K7
7 P–B3 N–Q2	24 Q × B R × N	38 ... Q–K8 +	54 K–N3 R–Q7
8 P–Q4 B–B3	25 P–R5 Q–B2	39 Q–K2 Q × NP	55 R–R6 + K–B2
9 B–K3 0–0	26 B–K4 R–B3	40 R–Q8 + N–N1	56 P–R4 R–Q2
10 QN–Q2 R–K1	27 R–K3	41 K–B3 Q–R4	57 P–N5 N–Q4
11 P–Q5 N–K2	27 ... R/1–KB1	42 R–R8 P–N3	58 R–R5 K–K3
12 P–QN4	28 R–KB1 N–K2	43 K–N2 K–N2	59 R–R6 + K–B2
12 ... N–KN3	29 R–Q3 P–QN3	44 Q–N2	60 B × N + R × B
13 P–N3 R–B1	30 P × P Q × NP	44 ... R–KN8 +	61 P–R5 P × P
14 N–B1 B–K2	31 Q–R2 Q–N4	45 K–R3 Q–B2	62 R–KB6 +
15 N/3–Q2 N–N3	32 R–Q2 R–B1	46 Q–R3 Q–Q2 +	62 ... K–N2
16 B–B2 P–QB3	33 R/1–Q1	47 K–R4 Q–K2 +	Draw agreed.
17 B–N3 K–R1			

Q-KR5 NEVERTHELESS!

Black: Yu. Averbakh - Baku 1961, USSR Championship

The attentive reader undoubtedly noticed that this book opened with a tale about the move Q-KR5.

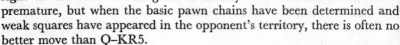

I did this deliberately, although I was also afraid that critical reviewers might suddenly take my recommendations to be a joke.

But I was not joking at all when I warned them against a carefree attitude towards the move Q-KR5.

Of course, this attack with the lone queen right at the start of the game is clearly premature, but when the basic pawn chains have been determined and weak squares have appeared in the opponent's territory, there is often no better move than Q-KR5.

My game with Averbakh is a successful example to illustrate such an occasion. Since Black's KN did not come out to KB3, KR5 is under White's control. All the more since . . . P-KN3 would be risky because Black is without his dark-squared bishop.

There is one further point in favour of the queen move to KR5. After White's KRP has moved from KR2 to KN3, White can, if time permits, play P-KN4, P-KN3, then bring his king to KN2 and put his rook on KR1. Black will find it difficult to defend his KRP since . . . P-KR3 would be out because of B × RP, with a winning attack.

Averbakh is a player with huge experience and knowledge. Seeing the queen on KR5 he immediately took prophylactic measures, and although in the end he lost the Q-file, he still drew the game.

Nevertheless, have a look at Q-KR5 from time to time (by Black as well)!

1 P-K4 P-K4	9 B-K3 B-B3	17 P × P B × N	24 B-N3 P-KN3
2 N-KB3 N-QB3	10 QN-Q2 N-K2	18 RP × B Q × P	25 Q-R6 B-K3
3 B-N5 P-QR3	11 B-N3 N-KN3	19 B-KB4 Q-K2	26 R/1-Q1 B × B
4 B-R4 N-B3	12 Q-K2 R-K1	20 B-Q5 N-N3	27 P × B QR-Q1
5 0-0 B-K2	13 QR-Q1 Q-K2	21 Q-R5 (130)	28 Q-Q2 R × R
6 R-K1 P-Q3	14 N-B1 N/2-B1	21 . . . N-K4	29 Q × R P-KR4
7 P-B3 0-0	15 N-N3 N-R5	22 B × N P × B	30 P-QN4
8 P-Q4 N-Q2	16 N × N B × N	23 R-Q3 P-QB3	Draw agreed.

THE SPARKLING QUEEN

Black: Ya. Estrin – Moscow 1953, Moscow Championship

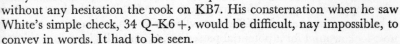

In this game I realized one of my favourite comic combinations.

It would have been easy to play my king away (32 K–R1) and create the unparryable threat of R ×N, but what of that would have stuck in my memory?

Seen in this light, the serene move 32 B ×P seemed to me the most attractive solution to the problem.

Estrin apparently could not believe his lucky stars: in a flash he took the bishop and without any hesitation the rook on KB7. His consternation when he saw White's simple check, 34 Q–K6 +, would be difficult, nay impossible, to convey in words. It had to be seen.

Black felt extremely grieved and he tried with all his might to restrain the swift advance of the two disconnected white pawns with his two rooks.

But therein lay the strength of the white pawns: they were disconnected! For as soon as the black rooks went after one of the pawns, that pawn immediately froze on the spot, whilst the other took its next step towards the 8th rank. The alternate steps of the pawns were controlled from far off by the white queen.

1 P–K4 P–K4	17 N–Q2 B ×N	31 ... Q–Q5 (*131*)	45 Q–KB7
2 N–KB3 N–QB3	18 B ×B Q–B3	32 B ×P N ×B	45 ... R–KN3
3 B–N5 P–QR3	19 Q–K4 N–N2	33 Q ×N R ×R	46 P–N4 R–N1
4 B–R4 N–B3	20 B–K3 0–0	34 Q–K6 +	47 K–N3 R–N3
5 0–0 P–QN4	21 Q–QB4 Q–B2	34 ... R–B2 +	48 Q–B8 + R–N2
6 B–N3 P–Q3	22 Q ×NP P–B4	35 K–R1 Q–B3	49 K–B3 K–N3
7 P–B3 B–K2	23 P–R5 N–Q1	36 R ×Q P ×R	50 Q–KB5 +
8 P–QR4 P–N5	24 P–KB4 P ×P	37 P–R6 R–QR6	50 ... K–R3
9 P–Q4 B–N5	25 B ×KBP Q–N3	38 P–N5 R–R8 +	51 Q–B6 + R–N3
10 P–Q5 N–QR4	26 Q–B4 N–B2	39 K–R2 K–N2	52 Q–B8 + R–N2
11 B–B2 P–N6	27 B–R2 QR–N1	40 Q–B8 P ×P	53 K–K4 K–N3
12 B–Q3 N ×KP	28 P–QN3 Q–B7	41 P–Q6 R–Q8	54 Q–KB5 +
13 B ×N P–KB4	29 Q ×RP R ×P	42 Q ×P K–R3	54 ... K–R3
14 P–R3 P ×B	30 R–B2 Q ×P	43 P–R7 R ×RP	55 Q–B6 +
15 P ×B P ×N	31 R/1–KB1	44 Q ×R R ×P	Black resigns.
16 Q ×BP B–N4			

THE DISTANT PASSED PAWN

Black: A. Ufimtsev – Leningrad 1947, USSR Championship

Whoever creates a distant passed pawn first usually also wins the game.

But it is hard work creating a distant passed pawn and a troublesome business. First one has to win a pawn and then by a joint effort of the pieces clear its path to the queening square.

And if one does not have an extra pawn, how should one proceed then?

Then the minor pieces will prove an invaluable aid. By seizing the squares in front of the opponent's pawns, they nail them down fatally to the board, when it becomes a matter of indifference whether you have an extra pawn or not; look around for a potential passed pawn, and I'll give you a 100 per cent guarantee you will find one.

In the game we shall be looking at there turned out to be such a 'nailed-down' pawn in Black's camp at Q3. Its passiveness even meant that White could organize a pawn advance on the Q-side, so that, in the event, it was like a fairy-tale come true.

There was an equal number of pawns on the board, but White's knight occupied the important Q5 square and a passed pawn appeared in White's camp. So how did things go on from there?

Alas, it was the usual story – time-trouble: we lose count of the moves, each of us hurries to try and make the moves before his flag falls and we lose the thread of our ideas.

White could have won by means of the 'skewer': 57 Q–R4 Q ×N 58 Q ×P + N–N2   59 Q–N8 + K–N3   60 Q ×Q, but, unable to keep track of his calculations, White was afraid to play a sacrifice he had not worked out in all its details and he overlooked that Black could play 57 ... N–B3.

White's 55 K–R2 also requires explanation. I had intended the variation 55 N–B7 R ×N 56 P ×R Q ×R   57 Q–N8 Q–R8 +   58 K–R2 and the white pawn queens unhindered.

Suddenly I saw the perpetual check 58 ... Q–QB8   59 P–B8 =Q Q–KB5 +   60 K–N1 Q–B8 +   61 K–R2 Q–KB5 + etc.

It is always useful to keep this idea in mind, but it is not always possible to put it into practice! In this case the black queen could not have gone to QB8: White would already have got in P–B8 =Q. But it isn't easy to see everything in time-trouble!

Probably the many young grandmasters of today are right when, having once decided upon some complicated variation, they do not check out all the nuances a second time, but execute their conception boldly and resolutely. And yet such a style of play is not to my own liking. I love to turn over the plan I have chosen in my mind and look at it from all angles. But I cannot do anything about that, such is the law of the competitive game: a move every four minutes! As they say, 'In the jungle, follow the law of the jungle, and woe betide anyone who does not!'.

I have always had the deepest respect for the original talent of the master, A. Ufimtsev. In fact, I was one of the first to start using his system of defence in serious practice.

This draw with him, however, remained long in my mind for a different reason: if I had won I would have had a good chance of taking third prize and obtaining a second score in the national championship towards my grandmaster title, . . . but that was not to be.

Still, there is a logic to everything: Ufimtsev had lost a won endgame to me by an inconceivable error in the semi-finals of the Moscow Championship in 1945 and had thereby failed to get amongst the winners. Thus we were now level, 1–1.

1 P–K4 P–K4	23 P–QR3 N–B5	44 Q–N3 R–N1	64 R–N2 K–B3
2 N–KB3 N–QB3	24 N–K2 N–K3	45 R–N1 Q–Q5	65 R–N4 Q–B4
3 B–N5 P–QR3	25 B–N3 R–B1	46 Q–B2 K–B2	66 Q–N2 Q–K6
4 B–R4 N–B3	26 P–B4 P×P	47 P–R3 R–N2	67 Q–N1 Q–B4
5 0–0 P–QN4	27 B×P B–R5	48 N–Q5 (132)	68 R–N3 Q–KB7
6 B–N3 B–K2	28 B–N3 B×B	48 . . . Q–B4	69 R–N2 Q–Q5
7 P–Q4 P–Q3	29 Q×B Q–N2	49 Q–R2 R–R2	70 K–R1 Q–K6
8 P–B3 0–0	30 N–B3 N–B4	50 Q–N3 K–B1	71 R–N4 Q–B7
9 P–Q5 N–N1	31 Q–N1 N–Q2	51 P–N6 R–QN2	72 R–N3 Q–Q5
10 Q–K2 QN–Q2	32 N–Q5 N–N3	52 R–R1 P–B4	73 Q–K1 R×P
11 B–B2 B–N2	33 N×N Q×N	53 P×P P×P	74 Q×RP+
12 R–Q1 P–B3	34 R–Q5 P–B3	54 R–R8 Q–B3	74 . . . K–N3
13 P×P B×P	35 N–K1 R–KB2	55 K–R2 K–N2	75 R×R Q×R
14 QN–Q2 N–B4	36 N–B2 R/2–B2	56 Q–N3+ K–B2	76 K–R2 Q–B2
15 N–B1 Q–B2	37 N–K3 R–B3	57 Q–KB3 N–B3	77 Q–N4+ K–B3
16 N–N3 Q–N2	38 P–QR4 Q–B2	58 R–R5 P–B5	78 Q–N8 Q–KN2
17 B–N5 N–K1	39 R/5–Q2 R–B8	59 Q–QN3 N×N	79 Q–Q8+ K–K3
18 B×B Q×B	40 Q–Q3 R×R+	60 R×N K–B3	80 K–N1
19 R–Q2 P–N3	41 R×R Q–B3	61 R–N5 P–R4	80 . . . Q–QR2+
20 R/1–Q1 R–N1	42 P–N5 P×P	62 P–B3 P–R5	81 K–R1 Q–KN2
21 P–N4 N–K3	43 P×P Q–B4	63 Q–N1 K–N2	Draw agreed.
22 Q–K3 K–N2			

RACING EACH OTHER

Black: L. Evans – Moscow 1955, USSR v USA

133W

I write about this game with mixed feelings. It is pleasant for me to show the readers one more model of a concerted attack, but I am aware at the same time that Black's defence in the opening was not of the highest order and bore a clearly visible experimental character.

Moreover, instead of 21 K–R1?, the move K–N2! won more quickly.

The concluding 15–20 moves were made in mutual time-trouble; the players did not even seem to have time to press their clocks, which were only altered 'wholesale', after a series of five to seven moves.

Nonetheless, I still find pleasure in playing through this curious game.

Black lingered over castling and played ... P–KN3 too early. This oversight allowed White to play 11 P–QN4! with advantage and develop an attack down the QB-file.

The black queen suspected something was amiss and rushed for cover on the K-file. But everything had already been prepared in White's camp for an exchange sacrifice, and the move 16 R×N duly came.

White's pieces received invaluable help from their pawns, which were rushing so quickly to the 8th rank that one had the impression that one was watching an athletics competition, not chess, with the pawns racing each other.

1 P–K4 P–K4	13 B–N2 B–KN2	25 P–KR4 N–B2	35 R×R B–K1
2 N–KB3 N–QB3	14 QR–B1 B–N2	26 Q–R1 N–K4	36 R–K7 Q–B8
3 B–N5 P–QR3	15 B–N3 Q–K2	27 P–N5 R–K1	37 R×B+ K×R
4 B–R4 N–B3	16 R×N B×R	28 Q–Q4 Q–N5	38 Q–K4+ K–Q1
5 0–0 P–QN4	17 P×P N–R4	29 P–B3 Q–Q2	39 Q–K7+ K–B1
6 B–N3 P–Q3	18 P–N4 N–B5	30 P×P N–B2	40 B–K6+ K–N1
7 P–B3 N–QR4	19 P×P Q–Q2	31 P–K5 P–N4	41 Q–B7+ Q×Q
8 B–B2 P–B4	20 N–K5 N–R6+	32 R–K1 P×P	42 P×Q+ K–N2
9 P–Q4 Q–B2	21 K–R1 B×N	33 P–K6 Q–B1	43 B×N R–KB1
10 QN–Q2 P–N3	22 B×B P–B3	(133)	44 B–Q5+
11 P–QN4 P×NP	23 B–N3 K–B1	34 Q×P R×P	Black resigns.
12 BP×P N–B3	24 K–N2 N–N4		

NIGHT AND DAY

Black: G. Borisenko – Riga 1958, USSR Championship

134W

The master Georgy Borisenko is one of our greatest theoretical experts. But there are different types of experts: some are so named because they have learnt everything, whilst others, like Borisenko, go beyond that and invent.

He looks for new variations night and day, and on every occasion his opponents are confronted with the latest move he has prepared at home.

My turn came too.

I drew out 11 . . . N–B3 in this lottery. A normal type of move, but the moment chosen for it is not the most suitable (so it seems to me, though my opponent may think differently).

On the other hand, when, three years later, I made an implicit proposal to my opponent to repeat this variation, he chose the Petroff Defence. So did he agree with me, or had he not yet finished his analysis of 11 . . . ˉˉˉ–B3?

It fell to the lot of the black QP to be the chief success of this game. It not only battled its way through alive to K7, but it also gave check to the white king – it is not every pawn that manages that!

1 P–K4 P–K4	15 N–B3 N×KP	29 B×B P×B	42 B–K3
2 N–KB3 N–QB3	16 N×N B×N	30 P–Q5 B–Q1	42 . . . Q–QB5+
3 B–N5 P–QR3	17 B–Q2 P–Q4	31 Q–N8 P–K6	43 K–Q1 K–B2
4 B–R4 N–B3	18 N×P R–B1	32 K–B1 P–K7+	44 Q–R8 K–K1
5 0–0 B–K2	19 R–QB1 R×R	(134)	45 Q–N7 P–N4
6 R–K1 P–QN4	20 Q×R N–Q6	33 K–K1 P–R3	46 B–B5 P–B4
7 B–N3 P–Q3	21 N×N B×N	34 Q–B8 P–N3	47 Q–B6+ K–B2
8 P–B3 0–0	22 Q–B6 B–B5	35 P–Q6 K–R2	48 Q–Q7+ K–N3
9 P–KR3 N–QR4	23 B–Q1 B–B3	36 B–B3 P–B3	49 Q–K8+ K–R2
10 B–B2 P–B4	24 P–QN3 B–Q6	37 P–QN4 K–N2	50 Q×B Q–Q6+
11 P–Q4 N–B3	25 B–QN4 Q–B1	38 Q–N7+ Q–B2	51 K–K1 Q–N8+
12 B–K3 BP×P	26 Q–N6 R–K1	39 Q×RP Q–Q4	52 K–K2 Q–K5+
13 P×P N–QN5	27 R×R+ Q×R	40 B–Q2 Q×NP	53 B–K3
14 B–N3 B–N2	28 B–KB3 B–K5	41 K×P Q–K5+	

Black overstepped the time limit.

TAL IN HIS ELEMENT

White: M. Tal – Tiflis 1959, USSR Championship

The chess goddess Caissa foresaw endless discussions about the infinite nature of chess and, in order to make it easier to find arguments, she invented the Ruy Lopez by way of proof!

The move 3 B–N5 is saying, as it were: 'I can see the square QB4, yes, and I can see Black's KBP, but first I shall concern myself with the general improvement of my health and later, if there is time, I shall come back to the QR2–KN8 diagonal and think a little too about Black's KBP.'

After such a preamble it is clear why the number of devotees of 3 B–N5 grows, not daily, but every second.

And when Tal undertook this sortie with the bishop, I decided to arrange a counter-attack on White's KBP (12 ... Q–N3).

Tal played his knight to KN5, but refused to take my bishop on K3. I was caught between two stools: I thought it would be a pity to change my plan, and yet there was nothing really to wait for.

All the same, I was rather optimistic about my position after the 27th move. And even today I do not think I would have lost in the event of 28 ... K×B   29 N×BP+ K–N2   30 N×R R×N   31 R–R7 K–N1 32 R–N7 B–B3 33 R×NP N×P   34 P×N B×P.

Alas, the variation 20 ... N–Q5? fails because of 21 P×N P×P 22 N–Q5 B×N   23 P×B P–Q6   24 Q×B P×B   25 B–K3 P×R=Q 26 B×Q Q–B4 27 N–K6 +!

1 P–K4 P–K4	13 P×BP P×P	24 Q×KP Q×Q	34 R–N7 R–K3
2 N–KB3 N–QB3	14 N–B1 B–K3	25 N×Q N×P	35 R×R K×R
3 B–N5 P–QR3	15 N–K3 QR–Q1	26 R–R1 N–N6	36 P–R4 R–KN1
4 B–R4 N–B3	16 Q–K2 P–N3	27 B×N P×B	37 P–KB4 B–B4 +
5 0–0 B–K2	17 N–N5 P–B5	(135)	38 K–B1 P×RP
6 R–K1 P–QN4	18 P–QR4 K–N2	28 B–R6+ K–N1	39 R–N5 R–QB1
7 B–N3 P–Q3	19 P×P P×P	29 N–B6 R–QB1	40 P–B5+ K–Q3
8 P–B3 0–0	20 R–N1 N–QR4	30 QR–Q1 R×N	41 P–QN4 P–R6
9 P–KR3 N–QR4	21 N–B3 Q–B2	31 R×N P–B3	42 R×B P–R7
10 B–B2 P–B4	22 N–Q5 B×N	32 R×P P–N4	43 B–B4 +
11 P–Q4 N–B3	23 P×B KR–K1	33 R×QNP K–B2	Black resigns.
12 QN–Q2 Q–N3			

A BLUNDER IN TIME-TROUBLE

Black: S. Reshevsky – Zurich 1953, Candidates' Tournament

136B

The name of Reshevsky has not been out of the pages of the press now for over fifty years, and he still has no intention of giving up chess.

But the title of world champion has always eluded him. This is understandable: there are many gifted players, but there is only one world champion. When this game was played we both still had secret hopes of reaching the abode of the saints, the chess throne, or of getting a little nearer to it.

An amusing episode occurred as the game was being adjourned. Having hurriedly made his 40th move, Reshevsky offered a draw!

This third offer of a draw that evening rather surprised me; I looked more carefully at the board and saw the reason for all the commotion. Black had no defence against 41 B–B5 with the threat of 42 B–B8 + K–N1 43 B–R6 mate. By winning this encounter I set something of a personal record: in the 1950 Candidates' Tournament I had managed to beat Najdorf 2–0, and now I had repeated this result against Reshevsky.

Which is to say that I was pleased – at that time they were both reckoned to be by right the strongest players in the West.

1 P–K4 P–K4	15 Q–K2 N–QR4	28 P×P Q×BP	41 B–B5 (*136*)
2 N–KB3 N–QB3	16 P–QR4 R–N1	29 Q×Q P×Q	41 ... B–K2
3 B–N5 P–QR3	17 P×P P×P	30 R–R4 N–Q2	42 B×R B×B
4 B–R4 N–B3	18 P–KN3 P–N3	31 R×P N–B4	43 P–B5 P–K6
5 0–0 B–K2	19 K–R2 B–K3	32 N–K4 N/1–K3	44 P–B6 N–K5
6 R–K1 P–QN4	20 N–K3 P–B5	33 N×N N×N	45 R–K8 P–B4
7 B–N3 P–Q3	21 R–Q1 R×R	34 R–QN4 N–Q6	46 B–B4 B–Q3
8 P–B3 0–0	22 Q×R R–Q1	35 R–N8+ K–N2	47 P–B7 B×NP+
9 P–KR3 N–QR4	23 Q–K2 Q–B1	36 B–K3 P–K5	48 K–N2 B×P
10 B–B2 P–B4	24 N–Q5 B×N	37 R–K8 B–B3	49 R–K7+ K–B3
11 P–Q4 Q–B2	25 P×B R×P	38 R–QB8 N×P	50 R×B P–B5
12 QN–Q2 N–B3	26 P–N3 N–B3	39 P–B4 R–QR4	51 K–B3
13 P×BP P×P	27 N–N5 N–Q1	40 B–N3 R–R6	Black resigns.
14 N–B1 R–Q1			

A COMBINATION SPOTTED

Black: Yu. Averbakh – Moscow 1968, Moscow Championship

The move 17 ... P–N3 was not unexpected for me. I had decided even during my preparation for the game to abandon the standard solution, 18 N–K3, and first play my bishop to KR6.

Black found a good plan of defence, beginning with 19 ... B–KB1. Averbakh assessed the position shrewdly; he felt intuitively that the dark squares in Black's camp could be protected even without the bishop on KB1. True, to do this he had to have recourse to another paradoxical manoeuvre, ... N(QB3)–Q1 –QN2!

I still managed to discover a weak point and to break through with my rook onto Q7. But unfortunately the lone rook ran up against a prickly hedgerow of black pieces and pawns.

I beg lovers of combinations to turn their attention to the minor episode from our game which took place off-stage – 28 ... R–Q1 29 N ×N R ×Q 30 N–K8 +, winning back the queen.

And although my combination was spotted by Averbakh, please do not be sceptical about it. In the first place, this idea – N ×N and N–K8 + – might do you a good turn in different circumstances, and secondly, it did help me to transpose into a favourable ending.

I did not manage to win, but I can honestly say that if I was offered this endgame to play as Black, I would refuse.

1 P–K4 P–K4	13 P ×BP P ×P	24 KR–Q1	33 R–QB7 N–Q3
2 N–KB3 N–QB3	14 P–QR4 R–N1	24 ... R ×R +	34 R–Q7 R–N3
3 B–N5 P–QR3	15 P ×P P ×P	25 R ×R N–Q1	35 K–K2 R–R3
4 B–R4 N–B3	16 N–B1 R–Q1	26 Q–Q2 N–N2	36 K–Q2 K–N4
5 0–0 B–K2	17 Q–K2 P–N3	27 N ×B+ P ×N	37 K–K3 K–B3
6 R–K1 P–QN4	18 B–R6 B–K3	28 N–N4 (*137*)	38 P–KN3 P–N4
7 B–N3 P–Q3	19 N–K3 B–KB1	28 ... N ×N	39 K–Q2 N–B2
8 P–B3 0–0	20 B–N5 B–K2	29 Q–Q7 + Q ×Q	40 R–N7 N–Q3
9 P–KR3 N–QR4	21 B–R6 B–KB1	30 R ×Q + K–B3	41 R–QB7 R–R7
10 B–B2 P–B4	22 B ×B K ×B	31 P ×N P–R3	42 R–Q7
11 P–Q4 Q–B2	23 N–N5 K–N2	32 K–B1 P–B5	Draw agreed.
12 QN–Q2 N–B3			

UNORIGINAL MOVES

Black: V. Alatortsev – Moscow 1948, USSR Championship

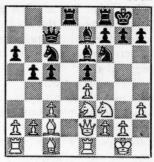

138B

There are numerous good defences for Black. Sometimes we choose the most fashionable system, but another time we search in the recesses of our memories for a long-forgotten, decrepit variation.

The variation 12 ... N–B3 is old, but has not gone out of fashion. For many years it was considered defensive: Black tried to keep White's knights out of KB4 and KN4, and he wasted time on the prophylactic moves ... P–KN3 and ... P–KR3.

Nowadays players know that 16 ... P–B5 should be played, and if 17 N–N5, then 17 ... P–R3 18 N ×B P ×N 19 P–QN4 N–Q5, and Black wins as in the game Fischer-Kholmov, 1965. But when our game was being played this idea was only going through the modelling stage.

Therefore the players chose a different game to imitate, the encounter Smyslov-Euwe from the tournament for the World Championship of 1948, and we were highly successful in our enterprise: our paths parted only on the 21st move.

The familiar manoeuvre, P–KN4, K–R1 and R–KN1, gave White attacking chances which I, unfortunately, did not take best advantage of.

And although White stood better even at the adjournment, we willingly agreed on a draw; clearly neither of us was an advocate of that very difficult task of home analysis.

1 P–K4 P–K4	13 P ×BP P ×P	22 ... R/1–Q1	33 B–K4 R/4–Q3
2 N–KB3 N–QB3	14 N–B1 B–K3	23 K–R1 N–KN1	34 P ×P N–Q5
3 B–N5 P–QR3	15 N–K3 QR–Q1	24 R–N1 K–R1	35 N ×N KP ×N
4 B–R4 N–B3	16 Q–K2 (*138*)	25 P–KR4 B–B1	36 P ×P Q ×P
5 0–0 B–K2	16 ... P–N3	26 P–N5 P–KR4	37 P–N4 Q–N3
6 R–K1 P–QN4	17 N–N5 B–B1	27 N–R2 N–R4	38 R/N1–K1
7 B–N3 P–Q3	18 B–Q2 K–N2	28 P–N3 N–QB3	38 ... R–K3
8 P–B3 0–0	19 QR–Q1 P–R3	29 N–B3 Q–B1	39 Q–B4 B–Q3 +
9 P–KR3 N–QR4	20 N–B3 B–K3	30 K–R2 P–N5	40 K–N2 N–K2
10 B–B2 P–B4	21 B–N1 R–Q2	31 N–Q5 B ×N	41 B–Q3 B–K4
11 P–Q4 Q–B2	22 P–KN4	32 P ×B R ×P	Draw.
12 QN–Q2 N–B3			

ORIGINAL WORK OR PLAGIARY?

Black: S. Zhukhovitsky – Kiev 1940, Ukrainian Championship

The author has so often picked fault with young players in this book that he may have created the false impression that he himself never used to use other people's ideas or suggestions.

Please do not believe him!

I played all sorts of variations, my own and other people's, but since initially few of my own were good ones, willy-nilly I played other people's (good ones!). The reader can see one such opening variation on this page.

If I am to be honest, I do not even know when the opening variation ends and when what I created begins. I probably started to use my own brain somewhere around move 25, when I resolutely played P–KB4.

Do I reprehend myself for such shameless plagiary? No, I do not. The Ruy Lopez is that kind of opening; we all play it the same when we are playing well. On the other hand, when we make mistakes and play badly, then no two games will be alike.

I, for example, go straight to the bottom (i.e. to the last move of a known variation) without even hesitating; I am the poorest 'floater' of all the Lopez grandmasters.

This is because there are such a large quantity of Lopez stamps impressed on my aged memory; it always seems to me that I have seen the position somewhere before and that it is lost for Black. . . .

For those who want to check White's final conception, I give the sharp variation 29 . . . R–R2 30 N–R6 N×N 31 Q–R5 B–N6 32 Q×N+ K–N1 33 Q×BP!.

1 P–K4 P–K4	10 B–B2 P–B4	18 P–N5 P×P	26 P–K5 P–N4
2 N–KB3 N–QB3	11 P–Q4 Q–B2	19 N×NP N–K2	27 B×P P×B
3 B–N5 P–QR3	(*139*)	20 N×B P×N	28 B×N B–R5
4 B–R4 N–B3	12 QN–Q2 N–B3	21 N–N4 N–R2	29 B–K4 B–N6
5 0–0 B–K2	13 P×BP P×P	22 K–R1 K–R1	30 B×R R×B
6 R–K1 P–QN4	14 N–B1 R–Q1	23 R–KN1 N–N1	31 N–B6 Q–B2
7 B–N3 P–Q3	15 Q–K2 B–K3	24 R–N2 B–K2	32 Q–R5+
8 P–B3 0–0	16 N–K3 P–R3	25 P–KB4 P×P	Black resigns.
9 P–KR3 N–QR4	17 P–KN4 B–KB1		

TWO EXAMS

White: A. Konstantinopolsky – Moscow 1945, USSR Championship

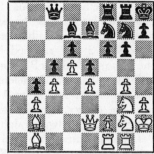

140B

In the autumn of 1936 I had a stroke of luck: I was accepted into a children's chess club.

The rules of entry were strict: each novice had to answer a whole series of questions. But I drew a lucky ticket.

Looking at me severely, the examiner asked: 'What books have you read?'

I guessed that he meant chess books and I smartly retorted: 'Sozin's *What Everyone Should Know About The Endgame.*'

'Well, that's excellent! Here, then, you have a king and I'll have a king and a pawn. Now keep your eyes on them both – I shall attack and you defend!'

I tried very, very hard. I even held my breath, and the spectators surrounding us in a thick ring seemed to do the same. A move, a cunning move, careful, a reply, a move, a reply, a move, don't hurry, think, a reply.

The examiner smiled:

'Well done, come to the lessons tomorrow – only make sure you're not late.'

I breathed a sigh of relief.

And here we are ten years later – a second exam, this time in a complex variation of the Ruy Lopez. Looking through this manoeuvring game now I can see that I satisfied Aleksandr Markovich Konstantinopolsky in this exam too.

1 P-K4 P-K4	12 QN-Q2 N-B3	23 Q-K2 B-Q2	32 K-N1
2 N-KB3 N-QB3	13 P-Q5 N-Q1	24 B-N2 R-R1	32 ... R/N1-B1
3 B-N5 P-QR3	14 N-B1 N-K1	25 QR-KB1	33 K-B1 N-R3
4 B-R4 N-B3	15 P-QR4 R-N1	25 ... R-KN1	34 K-K1 N-B2
5 0-0 B-K2	16 P×P P×P	26 B-N1 QR-KB1	35 K-Q1 R-N1
6 R-K1 P-QN4	17 P-B4 P-N5	27 N-K1 Q-B1	36 R/1-N1 N-N4
7 B-N3 0-0	18 P-N4 P-N3	28 N-N2 (*140*)	37 R-R1 N-B2
8 P-B3 P-Q3	19 N-N3 N-KN2	28 ... R-K1	38 P-B3 R/K1-B1
9 P-KR3 N-QR4	20 K-R2 P-B3	29 N-K3 B-Q1	39 P-R4 N-R3
10 B-B2 P-B4	21 R-KN1 K-R1	30 R-N2 Q-B2	40 B-B1 N-B2
11 P-Q4 Q-B2	22 P-N3 N-B2	31 R-R1 B-B1	Draw.

A TRANSPARENT THREAT

Black: V. Panov – Baku 1944, Semi-Finals USSR Championship

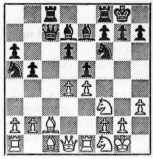

Black was extremely bold in accepting the pawn sacrifice, but his boldness, as it emerged later, was based on a sober assessment of the possibilities of the position.

White's attack reached its climax with the rich move 28 B×P+, but it was at that point too that Black's defensive relay came into action: his king moved hurriedly away into the corner, the tension fell, and the game became drawn straight away.

It was an interesting duel nonetheless!

The knight move from K5 to KN4 contained the transparent trap: 26 ... N×N 27 B×B Q×B(7) 28 B×P+ K×B 29 Q-Q5+ K-N3 30 P×N with unavoidable mate. But the black king, as we have said, was not tempted by the apparently defenceless bishop and sensibly moved into the corner.

Chess positions, however, are often so complex that one can almost always find something new in them. We have only to look at the board 'from a different angle' and numerous secret combinations will then be revealed to us.

The reader could therefore analyse this game again and put the experience he accumulates from it, together with the combinations he finds, into practice.

There are probably those who would criticize 20 P-QN3 and give preference to 20 P-Q5.

It is easy to talk about this now, when we know how the game went, but at the time I was playing the game it was a much more difficult decision to take. And I had not had much experience by then either. It was perfectly natural that I should want to open the QB-file and the QR2–KN8 diagonal.

1 P–K4 P–K4	9 P–KR3 N–QR4	16 N×N P×N	24 R×R R×R
2 N–KB3 N–QB3	10 B–B2 P–B4	17 B–Q2 KR–K1	25 N×P B–Q4
3 B–N5 P–QR3	11 P–Q4 Q–B2	18 B–B3 B–B1	26 N–N4 N×N
4 B–R4 N–B3	12 QN–Q2 B–Q2	19 R–QB1 B–B3	27 B×B Q×B/7
5 0–0 B–K2	13 N–B1 BP×P	20 P–QN3 BP×P	28 B×P+ K–R1
6 R–K1 P–QN4	14 P×P QR–B1	21 B×P B×P	29 Q×N R–B2
7 B–N3 P–Q3	(*141*)	22 P×P P×P	Draw agreed.
8 P–B3 0–0	15 N–K3 N–B5	23 B–N2 Q–N2	

MATCHES, WHERE ARE YOU?

Black: V. Panov – Moscow 1946, Moscow Championship

Nowadays individual matches are not in fashion, but I can remember many very interesting duels. One such took place in Moscow in 1936. L. Steiner and that true knight of the attack, V. Panov, were playing. It was from then onwards that I was struck by how masterfully Panov plays the Ruy Lopez as White or Black.

We followed the game Verlinsky-Panov, from the Moscow Championship of the previous year, up to move 16, and then my attention was attracted by the manoeuvre 16 QP ×P N ×P 17 N–N3 P–B4 18 P ×Pep N ×P/B3 19 N–N5 infiltrating with the knight to K6. But why should Panov lead his opponent into this position a second time? Of course, because he had no need to capture the KBP with the knight! With the gambit move 18 ... B ×P Black can get rich counter-play.

To my amazement, instead of 17 ... P–B4! Black played 17 ... KR–Q1?. In answer to my question after the game: 'Why not ... P–B4?' Panov replied that he did not like the variation 18 P ×Pep N ×P/B3 19 N–N5, which the reader already knows about.

'Yes, of course,' I said, 'but you could have sacrificed a pawn'. Afterwards this variation was firmly established for a long time in master practice.

And a year later Panov himself routed Ravinsky in brilliant style – in this very variation and, I should like to believe, not without the help of the trenchant 18 ... B ×P!

1 P–K4 P–K4	12 QN–Q2 B–N2	22 Q–N4 B–B1	31 R–K1 Q–B3
2 N–KB3 N–QB3	13 N–B1 BP ×P	23 QR–B1	32 B–K7 B–B1
3 B–N5 P–QR3	14 P ×P QR–B1	23 ... Q–QN3	33 B/5 ×Q Q ×B
4 B–R4 N–B3	(142)	24 N–R5 R ×R	34 B ×B Q ×B
5 0–0 B–K2	15 B–Q3 P–Q4	25 R ×R Q–K3	35 Q–K7 K–N1
6 R–K1 P–QN4	16 QP ×P N ×P	26 B–B5 Q ×P	36 Q–Q7 Q–B4 +
7 B–N3 P–Q3	17 N–N3 KR–Q1	27 N–B6 + K–R1	37 K–R2 N–B5
8 P–B3 0–0	18 Q–K2 B–N5	28 P–B4 Q–K7	38 R–K8 + K–R2
9 P–KR3 N–QR4	19 R–B1 Q–B3	29 N ×R Q ×N	39 Q–B5 +
10 B–B2 P–B4	20 N–N5 N ×N	30 Q–R4 P–R3	Black resigns.
11 P–Q4 Q–B2	21 B ×N R–K1		

LOPEZ OR KERES?

Black: P. Keres – Moscow 1951, USSR Championship

Why does Black first put his queen on the Q-file and then himself turn this closed file into an open one, as if urging the White pieces to rush into an attack on the queen?

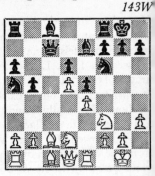

It is impossible to answer this question in one word, and I do not even know if there is an answer at all.

Black's idea, ... BP × P and ... B–N2, is only one of the many openings experiments that P. Keres has so often made in serious tournaments. And although subsequently he did not persist with this particular order of moves, it is perfectly possible that the practical testing he gave ... B–N2 stimulated him to elaborate further fruitful ideas.

It has always been like that in chess: the moves seem to be the same, but the ideas are always fresher. Take, for example, the games Em. Lasker-Ed. Lasker and Maroczy-Reti from the 1924 New York tournament. In these a similar variation was played: 12 ... B–Q2 13 N–B1 BP × P 14 P × P KR–B1, though today we no longer put the KR on QB1, but the QR. At that time, however, grandmasters were not unanimously agreed as to what was White's best reply. Em. Lasker replied 15 R–K2, Maroczy 15 B–Q3.

If one of the sitting committees of FIDE were suddenly to think of renaming some openings and variations, then the Ruy Lopez ought to be one of the first to be renamed, as the Keres opening, so great a contribution has the Estonian grandmaster made to the theory of this opening.

1 P–K4 P–K4	12 QN–Q2 BP × P	21 P–R3 Q–R2	32 B–Q2 B–Q2
2 N–KB3 N–QB3	13 P × P B–N2	22 N–N3 B–Q1	33 B × B N × B
3 B–N5 P–QR3	14 P–Q5 B–B1	23 B–B1 B–R4	34 Q–Q3 B–Q5
4 B–R4 N–B3	(143)	24 Q–B3 Q–N3	35 B–K3 N–B4
5 0–0 B–K2	15 N–B1 B–Q2	25 N–N4 N × N	36 Q–B2 B × B
6 R–K1 P–QN4	16 N/3–R2	26 P × N P–N3	37 R × B R × R +
7 B–N3 P–Q3	16 ... KR–B1	27 QR–N1 Q–Q1	38 Q × R Q–Q1
8 P–B3 0–0	17 B–Q3 N–N2	28 Q–K3 Q–R5	39 N–B1 R–N1
9 P–KR3 N–QR4	18 P–QN4 P–QR4	29 B–K2 B × P	40 Q–B2 R–R1
10 B–B2 P–B4	19 B–Q2 P × P	30 B × P B–N3	41 N–Q2
11 P–Q4 Q–B2	20 B/2 × P N–B4	31 B–B6 R/R1–N1	Draw agreed.

AN INNOVATION?

Black: E. Geller – Moscow 1951, USSR Championship

144B

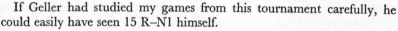

I happened to read in an openings book that 15 R–N1 was an innovation specially prepared by Bronstein for his decisive game with Geller.

This is not true.

Several days before that I had played P–QN4 against Keres, but I had not been able to hold the pawn on QN4 as I had nothing prepared to parry Black's ... P–QR4.

It was natural that I should correct my mistake this time.

If Geller had studied my games from this tournament carefully, he could easily have seen 15 R–N1 himself.

But the game was indeed of great importance for the distribution of the gold, silver and bronze medals: it was taking place in the penultimate round.

True, I was not taking part in this struggle, but alongside me on the stage of the October Hall in the House of Unions a fierce, uncompromising battle was going on between Petrosian, Keres and Geller, who were all on the same number of points.

Considering the purely chess content of the game, the fate of the encounter was decided by the exchange of Black's pawn on QN4 for White's on KB2, for although one was white and the other black, their disappearance from the board favoured only White!

1 P–K4 P–K4	15 R–N1 (*144*)	27 N×NP Q–N3	39 P×B R×BP
2 N–KB3 N–QB3	15 ... B–Q2	28 Q–K2 B–N6	40 Q–N5 P–Q4
3 B–N5 P–QR3	16 B–Q3 KR–B1	29 B–K3 Q–Q1	41 R–KB1 P–R3
4 B–R4 N–B3	17 N–B1 B–Q1	30 N–R7 R–B6	42 Q–N3 N–K1
5 0–0 B–K2	18 N–N3 Q–R2	31 Q–Q2 R–R6	43 Q–K5 R–Q1
6 R–K1 P–QN4	19 R–B1 N–K1	32 N–B6 Q–B3	44 Q–R5 N–B3
7 B–N3 0–0	20 K–R1 N–N2	33 N/3×P	45 B×N R×B
8 P–B3 P–Q3	21 P–N4 P–QR4	33 ... B/N6×N	46 R×R P×R
9 P–KR3 N–QR4	22 P–R3 P×P	34 R×Q B×R	47 Q–B3 R–Q3
10 B–B2 P–B4	23 P×P B–K2	35 B–QB4 R–B6	48 Q–N4+ K–R2
11 P–Q4 Q–B2	24 N–K2 B–Q1	36 P–K5 R×B/B5	49 Q–B8 R–N3
12 QN–Q2 BP×P	25 B–Q2 B–N3	37 P×B N×P	50 Q–B7
13 P×P B–N2	26 N–B3 B×P	38 B–Q4 B×N	Black resigns.
14 P–Q5 B–B1			

Ruy Lopez's Opening 157

AN EXPERIMENTAL POINT

White: A. Khasin – Baku 1961, USSR Championship

145W

'The truth will out' – I somewhat prefer being White in the Ruy Lopez to being Black. Nevertheless, I have at times had to change my spots and agree, in the interests of the further perfecting of White's attack, to play current variations with the unloved Black pieces. In such experimental games I have rarely managed to win; I often drew, but more often I lost.

In short, the experiment to some degree is at the cost of one tournament point.

Well, one has to pay for knowledge.

The idea of the variation I chose against Khasin is to gain a tempo by leaving out ... Q–B2. Black's rook on QB1 and his bishop on QN2 forced White to play his pawn to Q5, but is this all that beneficial to Black? Could it not be that he has suggested to White the right attacking plan? What is more, the queen was forced to go from Q1 to QB2, and Black, it is obvious, achieved nothing by his sly ... QR–B1.

I should be thankful, then, that the game ended in a draw and that a half of the sacrificed experimental point came back to me.

Perhaps White played his temporary exchange sacrifice on QN7 too early? After all, did he not have to return the pawn he won? However, after Black's ... B–Q1 the dangerous bishop was threatening to take an active role, and Khasin wisely decided that he should wait no longer.

1 P–K4 P–K4	11 P–Q4 BP×P	20 P–QR4 P×P	29 B×P R/1–N1
2 N–KB3 N–QB3	12 P×P B–N2	21 R×P Q–N4	30 B×R Q×B
3 B–N5 P–QR3	13 QN–Q2 R–B1	22 R–R3 R–B2	31 R–K2 N–Q2
4 B–R4 N–B3	(145)	23 R–N3 Q–Q2	32 B–K3 B–N3
5 0–0 B–K2	14 P–Q5 Q–B2	24 Q–Q2 R–R1	33 K–N2 B×B
6 R–K1 P–QN4	15 B–N1 N–R4	25 P–N4 N–B3	34 Q×B Q–N6
7 B–N3 P–Q3	16 N–B1 P–N3	26 N–R2	35 Q×Q R×Q
8 P–B3 0–0	17 B–R6 KR–K1	26 ... R/1–QB1	Draw agreed.
9 P–KR3 N–QR4	18 N–K3 N–QB5	27 B–Q3 B–Q1	
10 B–B2 P–B4	19 N×N Q×N	28 R×B R×R	

THE BITTER FATE OF THE IMPROVISER

White: W. Unzicker – Krems 1967, International Tournament

Unzicker had played a match of eight games with Keres, and without any prior agreement all eight had been Lopez's! I also wanted to try my strength. And although I knew I was undertaking a fruitless task (three-quarters of the pages of any openings manual are filled with the Ruy Lopez) I still secretly hoped that I would suddenly find some move of great genius at the board! But, however much I racked my brains, I could not think up anything whilst the clock ticked beside me. And with a sigh, I played the next book move.

I do not know how long my creative sufferings would have dragged on, but suddenly, after about a couple of dozen moves, my opponent deviated from studied recommendations and with Q–K2 began a direct attack on my Q-side pawns.

It is possible that had I not had such a rich 'Lopez' experience, I would not have been able to hold this game.

. . . You should have been there in the tournament hall to see Unzicker's amazement when, in answer to the stereotyped knight invasion via KN3–KB1–K3–Q5, Black lazily, almost nonchalantly, carried out the mirror-like manoeuvre . . . N(Q2)–KB3–KR4–B5.

Why did Black spend time on the moves . . . P–QR4 and . . . P–QN5? Because these very moves cemented his Q-side and K-side into one!

Moreover, by seizing control of the important QB6 square, Black could put aside any fear of the position being opened up any more. If . . . P–QN5! had not been played, 30 . . . P–B3! would not have been possible.

1 P–K4 P–K4	10 B–B2 P–B4	18 B–N2 P–N3	25 P×P P×P
2 N–KB3 N–QB3	11 P–Q4 Q–B2	19 Q–Q2 B–N2	26 N–K3 N–R4
3 B–N5 P–QR3	12 QN–Q2 BP×P	20 B–Q3 N–Q2	27 N–Q5 N–B5
4 B–R4 N–B3	13 P×P B–N2	21 QR–Q1	28 N×N P×N
5 0–0 B–K2	14 N–B1 QR–B1	21 . . . R/K1–Q1	29 B×B K×B
6 R–K1 P–QN4	15 B–N1 KR–K1	22 B–N1 P–QR4	30 Q–N2 + P–B3
7 B–N3 P–Q3	(146)	23 N–B1 N–B3	31 R–QB1 Q–Q3
8 P–B3 0–0	16 N–N3 B–B1	24 Q–K2 P–N5	Draw.
9 P–KR3 N–QR4	17 P–N3 N–B3		

THE KNIGHT'S DUEL WITH THE PAWN

White: L. Shamkovich – Moscow 1967, Grandmasters and Masters Tournament

147B

Is the outcome of the duel obvious? Is the knight stronger than the pawn?

How can I put it? A mobile knight is stronger than a passive pawn, but then a mobile pawn is stronger than a passive knight!

Now if anyone doubts the strength of a pawn, let him set up the following position: a white pawn on QR2 and a black knight on White's KR1. White to move. I play 1 P–R4, and you try and catch up with my pawn!

In my encounter with Shamkovich the knight and pawn duel was a twofold one: I had to keep an eye on both so as not to overlook the quiet P–QN3!.

If Black had not opened the QB-file, he would have had little cause to worry: any attack on his pawn on QN4 would have been met by . . . P–QB5; but now, with the black QBP gone, the only defender of the NP would be the knight itself. Was White's king move to KR2 necessary? Of course there was as yet no imminent threat of a sacrifice on KR3, but the king's intention was by no means just to defend the pawn! He was taking into account a knight check from K2 in the variation 19 . . . Q ×B! 20 Q ×Q R ×Q 21 R ×R N–K7 + and so sensibly stepped aside.

Whatever advocates of the Ruy Lopez may say, I prefer to play it as White: then you have the attack, then you have the initiative. Whilst as Black. . . .

1 P–K4 P–K4	13 P ×P B–N2	24 B–K3 N–B3	35 P–B4 K–N2
2 N–KB3 N–QB3	14 N–B1 QR–B1	25 N–Q2 N–Q2	36 K–N2 P–B4
3 B–N5 P–QR3	15 B–N1 (*147*)	26 R–QB1 Q–R4	37 KP ×P B–N2
4 B–R4 N–B3	15 . . . N–R4	27 P–R3 R ×R	38 N–Q2 B ×P+
5 0–0 B–K2	16 N–K3 KR–K1	28 Q ×R R–B1	39 K–B2 KP ×P
6 R–K1 P–QN4	17 N–B5 B–B1	29 Q–N1 B–K2	40 B ×BP N–K4
7 B–N3 0–0	18 P–Q5 N–KB5	30 R–QB1 Q–Q1	41 B ×N P ×B
8 P–B3 P–Q3	19 K–R2 P–N3	31 P–QN4 R ×R	42 P ×P P ×P
9 P–KR3 N–QR4	20 N–K3 N–B5	32 Q ×R Q–QB1	43 B–K4 B–K3
10 B–B2 P–B4	21 N ×N Q ×N	33 Q ×Q+ B ×Q	44 B–N7
11 P–Q4 Q–B2	22 P–KN3 N–R4	34 N–N3 B–Q1	Draw.
12 QN–Q2 BP ×P	23 B–Q3 Q–B2		

WHERE WAS THE KEY?

Black: P. Keres – Amsterdam 1965, Candidates' Tournament

Working on a book reminds one of the work of archaeologists.

In the strata that form over many years one has to search not only for the games one wants, but also for the motives for which one move or another was made.

I spent two hours on this particular position, silently contemplating White's moves and Black's pawns: P–QN4, and . . . P–QR5.

It is strange, very strange, that I let the black pawn past so willingly and . . . then began marking time. Then I suddenly remembered.

36 P–QN4 was correct, but after 36 . . . P–R5 I suddenly got scared about the variation 37 R–B6 B×R 38 P×B N–Q1 39 P–N5 N×P 40 P×N R×P, when there could be no question of my winning.

The key to the combination was the quiet move 40 N–N6 (instead of 40 P×N), forcing the reply 40 . . . R/1–B2; then White sharply changes the course of the attack by 41 N–Q5, and wherever the queen retreats, there follows the triumphant advance of the pawn, 42 P–N6.

It was a pity. It is not so much so today; but in 1956 I was chagrined. Counting two games adjourned in won positions (against Panno and Filip) I had excellent chances of going a point ahead, and who can know what might have happened then. . . .

1 P–K4 P–K4	15 B–N5 P–R3	29 N–B1 Q–N4
2 N–KB3 N–QB3	16 B–R4 N–KR4	30 R–KN3 Q–K2
3 B–N5 P–QR3	17 P–Q5 N–Q1	31 N–K2 N×N+
4 B–R4 N–B3	18 B×B Q×B/K2	32 Q×N R–Q1
5 0–0 B–K2	19 KN–Q4 N–B5	33 R–R3 B–Q2
6 R–K1 P–QN4	20 N–KB5 Q–B3	34 Q–K3 R–QB1
7 B–N3 P–Q3	21 R–K3 K–R2	35 B–Q3 B–K1
8 P–B3 0–0	22 P–QR4 P×P	36 P–QN4 P–R5
9 P–KR3 N–QR4	23 R×P B–B1	*(148)*
10 B–B2 P–B4	24 R–N4 N–N2	37 K–R2 R/2–R1
11 P–Q4 Q–B2	25 R–QB3 P–N3	38 B–K2 R–B2
12 QN–Q2 BP×P	26 N–K3 P–QR4	39 P–N5 Q–Q1
13 P×P N–B3	27 R–N6 Q–Q1	40 R–R2 K–N2
14 N–N3 B–N2	28 N–B4 R–R2	41 R–B6 R–N1
42 R–Q2 P–R4		
43 R–Q1 K–N1		
44 K–N1 K–R2		
45 Q–R3 Q–K2		
46 Q×RP N–B4		
47 Q–B2 B×R		
48 QP×B R×NP		
49 N×QP R–N3		
50 B–N5 N–K3		
51 B–R4 N–Q5		
52 Q–B5 R/3×P		
53 B×R R×B		
White resigns.		

THE BRAVE BLACK KING

Black: V. Zagorovsky – Leningrad 1947, Semi-Finals USSR Championship

149W

The ex-world correspondence champion, V. Zagorovsky, was still trying to make a place for himself in chess in those far-off days.

Our game was a quick one, but a sharp one, so we are not to blame for the result of a draw.

White's attempt to bring his queen to KN5 met with a resounding rebuff and he had then to turn the wheel sharply to the left, to QR5.

Since my collection does not contain the defence 3 . . . P–QR3 4 B–R4 P–B4!, it is timely for me to mention the great work my opponent has done on rehabilitating this long-forgotten page of chess history.

Because of his analyses of the defence 3 . . . P–QR3 and 4 . . . P–B4 and the practical successes he has had with it, it can justifiably be given Zagorovsky's name.

The main point of his defence is the move 7 . . . P–QB4 after 5 P–Q4 N×P 6 N×N P×N 7 Q×P, since the endgame after 8 Q–K5+ Q–K2 9 Q×Q+ K×Q is no worse for Black at all.

This example shows that, given the desire, one can plainly dig up something new in almost any book variation. And with the appearance of something new in one position problems inevitably arise in hundreds and thousands of similar positions.

Thus in the defence 1 P–K4 P–K4 2 N–KB3 N–QB3 3 B–N5 P–QR3 4 B–R4 P–B4 nobody hopes any longer for an advantage in the variation 5 P–Q4 KP×P 6 N×P; they have believed Zagorovsky. But everyone to a man is conducting excavations in the gambit variation 6 P–K5 B–B4 7 P–B3 P×P 8 N×P, where Black does not have it too easy.

1 P–K4 P–K4	8 P–B3 0–0	14 N–N3 KR–B1	19 B–N2 R–K1
2 N–KB3 N–QB3	9 P–KR3 N–QR4	*(149)*	20 Q–Q2 P×P
3 B–N5 P–QR3	10 B–B2 P–B4	15 P×KP P×P	21 P×P P–B5
4 B–R4 N–B3	11 P–Q4 Q–B2	16 N–B5 B–B1	22 Q–R5 Q–B4
5 0–0 B–K2	12 QN–Q2 B–Q2	17 P–QN3 N–N3	23 Q×Q B×Q
6 R–K1 P–QN4	13 N–B1 N–B5	18 P–B4 P×P	Draw agreed.
7 B–N3 P–Q3			

THE FIELD OF ACCURATE ASSESSMENTS

Black: P. Keres – Moscow 1949, USSR Championship

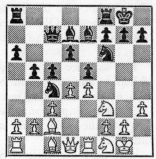

The most surprising thing about this hectic game is that I played it after a run of seven peaceful draws.

Obviously all my pent-up energy was expended in this one evening. Was the result of the game a fair one?

One rarely finds games, tournaments or matches where one can answer such a question in the affirmative without having to hesitate. In a game between players of equal strength the outcome always depends on a hundred minute factors whose existence we often do not even suspect.

All the critic (and I am speaking now as a critic) is capable of doing is to point out the final mistake which led to catastrophe. All the more so, as Black's mistake here is obvious: it was the move 31 ... R×R?.

And had it not been that mistake, what guarantee is there that Black would not have made another? Or White? Or Black again?

For example, White could have played, instead of 30 B–B5, 30 R×R R×R 31 Q–Q5 K×B 32 Q–R5+!, but who can say with certainty what the most correct way of continuing the attack would be?

The moves P(K5)–K6–K7 were impudence, but impudence which came off: the position went outside the field of accurate assessments, and Keres does not like this; he has faith in his ability to calculate any number of variations, but there are often so many of them!

And where, in which department of the brain, can the ones that have already been calculated be kept?

1 P–K4 P–K4	11 P–Q4 Q–B2	20 Q–K2 P–N5	28 Q–Q1 N–K6
2 N–KB3 N–QB3	12 QN–Q2 B–Q2	21 P–K5 P×P	29 B×N P×B
3 B–N5 P–QR3	13 N–B1 N–B5	22 P×P B–N4	30 B–B5 P–K7
4 B–R4 N–B3	(150)	23 B–N5 N–K1	31 Q–Q4 R×R
5 0–0 B–K2	14 N–N3 KR–B1	24 QR–B1 Q–R2	32 Q–R4+ K–N1
6 R–K1 P–QN4	15 B–Q3 N–N3	25 P–K6 P–B3	33 Q–R7+ K–B2
7 B–N3 0–0	16 N–R4 B–B1	26 P–K7 Q×P	34 Q–R5+ K–N1
8 P–B3 P–Q3	17 P–KB4 BP×P	27 B×RP+	35 B–R7+
9 P–KR3 N–QR4	18 P×QP P×QP	27 ... K–R1	Black resigns.
10 B–B2 P–B4	19 N–B3 N–B5		

POLARIZED EMOTIONS

Black: G. Uusi – Moscow 1956, Moscow Championship

Black's plan – for his QN to break through onto the enemy's QB3 square – is interesting, but White managed to organize his forces to repel it.

The sacrifice of a pawn, a knight, a bishop, or any piece, confers on the initiator of such an action a small measure of transient joy, and an unpleasant sensation is experienced by the leader of the army that has to suffer it.

Why do I say 'suffer'? Surely not every sacrifice wins immediately? No, but the fact remains that the person sacrificing feels spiritually uplifted, his emotions are clearly positive ones, whilst the person forced to accept a sacrifice is invariably upset, if even only slightly.

Here, however, I am talking about short-lived bursts of emotion, for when the unfavourable score of the game is chalked upon the results table, then a bad, negative feeling can settle in one's heart for a long time.

Therefore, when you are undertaking a dubious sacrifice, remember the long-lasting emotions, and follow the example of Petrosian: his emotions are more stable, since they often feed on the sacrifice-offerings of others. I too do not like sacrificing on the off-chance.

It is said that Vladimir Pavlovich Simagin once said of me: 'What a combinative player he is! Show me just one of his sacrifices which you could accept with impunity!'

1 P–K4 P–K4	10 B–B2 P–B4	19 R–QB1 Q–N1	28 Q–Q7 K–B2
2 N–KB3 N–QB3	11 P–Q4 Q–B2	20 Q–Q2 N–N4	29 P×B Q–N4
3 B–N5 P–QR3	12 QN–Q2 B–Q2	21 B–QB4 N–R6	30 R–B6 R×P
4 B–R4 N–B3	13 N–B1 KR–K1	22 B–Q5 N×B	31 R×BP+
5 0–0 B–K2	14 N–N3 P–N3	23 P×N P–B3	31 ...K×R
6 R–K1 P–QN4	15 B–R6 N–B5	24 P×P QP×P	32 B–N5+ K×B
7 B–N3 P–Q3	16 P–N3 N–R6	25 N–K4 B–KB4	(151)
8 P–B3 0–0	17 B–Q3 BP×P	26 P–Q6 B×N	33 Q×R+
9 P–KR3 N–QR4	18 P×P P–N5	27 P×B B×N	Black resigns.

A DRAW IN HAND

Black: B. Ivkov – Moscow Olympiad 1956

152W

The variation ... B–Q2 and ... KR–K1 bears the provisional title in my openings file of 'The Yugoslav Wall'.

And it seems to be commonly accepted that this solid defence was invented by Smyslov but worked out in all its details by Yugoslav players.

What did this game show?

White succeeded in exchanging the dark-squared bishops, in smothering Black's piece initiative on the Q-side and even in preparing P–KB4.

However, when the game opened up and the right moment came for the P–KB4–KB5 advance, White dragged his feet and accepted the draw offered him.

Why? Because we were approaching the end of the Olympiad, the match score was +1–0 = 2, and I could not afford to take any risks – and what kind of attack can one have without risks?

There is truth in the saying that one is repaid a hundredfold for one's good deeds. Eight years later, in Belgrade, I played the opening of my game recklessly, got into a difficult position, and Bora Ivkov ... without hesitation offered me a draw.

In an article devoted to assessing the tournament, grandmaster Korchnoi tried at length to establish by analysis the reasons for such an unexpected decision. His conclusion, that Ivkov's character was extremely peace-loving, was intuitively right, but could Korchnoi have known that after shaking hands with me Ivkov said:

'Do you remember, it was I who asked you for a draw in Moscow?'

1 P–K4 P–K4	9 P–KR3 N–QR4	15 B–R6 B–KB1	22 N–B3 B–K3
2 N–KB3 N–QB3	10 B–B2 P–B4	16 B × B K × B	23 N–R2 B–B5
3 B–N5 P–QR3	11 P–Q4 Q–B2	17 Q–Q2 K–N2	24 KR–K1 B–B2
4 B–R4 N–B3	12 QN–Q2 B–Q2	18 QR–Q1 B–K3	25 N–N4 N–B5
5 0–0 B–K2	13 N–B1 KR–K1	19 B–N1 N–N1	26 Q–K2 KP × P
6 R–K1 P–QN4	(152)	20 N–N5 B–B1	27 P × P P × P
7 B–N3 P–Q3	14 N–N3 P–N3	21 R–KB1 P–B3	Draw agreed.
8 P–B3 0–0			

LARGE-SCALE MANOEUVRES

Black: S. Gligoric – Leningrad 1957, USSR v Yugoslavia

This is a perfect model for Black's play in this difficult defensive system. As a result of long years of trial and testing of this opening Gligoric has a very deep and keen appreciation of Black's varied defensive resources in the Ruy Lopez.

See how quietly the bishop on K2 floats across to the more dependable KN2 square and with what dignity the QN completes the unexpected manoeuvre from QB3 to Q1–K3–KB1–KR2.

Homage must also be paid to the other bishop, whose unhurried movements could calm the most fiery temperament: first ... B–Q2, and then move after move: to B1–Q2–K1–Q2–KN5.

Gligoric thought longest over his secret 41st move. He apparently felt sorry for the bishop, but there is no escaping fate. One cannot, either, pass over his rook's moves in silence: they seemed to sense the weak points in the position and rushed to occupy one, and then another, advantageous firing position!

Only the black queen on QB2 remained motionless. All praise to her! Who will say now that QB2 is not the ideal position for the queen!....

But White's queen just could not make up her mind which was the best square for her. From the 19th move onwards she was tormented by doubt and periodically, every nine moves, she changed position. Whatever one might say, there were large-scale manoeuvres!

1 P–K4 P–K4	12 QN–Q2 B–Q2	22 P–Q5 N–B1	32 P–QR4 N–N3
2 N–KB3 N–QB3	13 N–B1 KR–K1	23 B–N5 P–KR4	33 P–QN3 B–Q2
3 B–N5 P–QR3	14 N–N3 P–N3	24 P–B4 N/1–R2	34 N–N5 N×N
4 B–R4 N–B3	15 B–Q3 B–KB1	25 B–K3 P–N5	35 B×N R–KB1
5 0–0 B–K2	16 B–N5 B–N2	26 B–B2 B–Q2	36 P–R4 B–N5
6 R–K1 P–QN4	17 R–QB1 N–B3	27 R–R1 P–R4	37 Q–Q2 QR–K1
7 B–N3 P–Q3	18 B–N1 N–Q1	28 Q–Q1 R–R1	38 N–N3 N–B1
8 P–B3 0–0	19 Q–Q2 N–K3	29 P–R3	39 R–KB1 N–K2
9 P–KR3 N–QR4	20 B–K3 QR–Q1	29 ... R/K1–N1	40 QR–K1 K–R2
10 B–B2 P–B4	21 QR–Q1 B–QB1	30 B–Q2 B–K1	41 B–Q1 B×B
11 P–Q4 Q–B2	(153)	31 N–B1 N–Q2	Draw agreed.

THE DEATH OF THE KP

Black: S. Gligoric – Moscow 1956, Alekhine Memorial Tournament

154W

The book you are reading covers only a tiny part of the varied possible types of chess positions, even when one is thinking only of those types arising after the opening moves 1 P–K4 P–K4.

But leaving aside the great variety that exists in openings and considering in concrete terms openings whose first move is 1 P–K4 P–K4, then in these by far the most important of the pawns are the two KPs.

Sometimes these two pawns offer themselves for sacrifice in the interests of an attack. But it can also happen that the central pawn perishes in vain, just like that, not even for a pinch of snuff. Then things are bad. This is exactly what happened in this game when, to my opponent's surprise, I took his KP with my knight. The rest was technique.

1 P–K4 P–K4	22 B–N3 R–R3	41 K–K3 P–N4	61 N–B1 K–Q4
2 N–KB3 N–QB3	23 Q–Q3 Q ×P	42 R–Q4 R–R6+	62 N–Q3 N–R4
3 B–N5 P–QR3	24 P ×P P ×P	43 R–Q3 R–R4	63 N–N4+ K–K4
4 B–R4 N–B3	(154)	44 K–Q4 N–Q2	64 N–Q3+ K–Q4
5 0–0 B–K2	25 N ×P B–K3	45 R–Q2 K–B3	65 N–N2 K–B4
6 R–K1 P–QN4	26 N–B4 Q–N5	46 N–K2 N–K4	66 K–Q3 K–Q4
7 B–N3 P–Q3	27 QR–B1 R–B3	47 N–B3 K–B4	67 K–K3 N–B3
8 P–B3 0–0	28 R ×P R/1–B1	48 R–N2 P–R5	68 N–Q3 N–R4
9 P–KR3 N–QR4	29 R/1–QB1	49 R–N3 N–B3+	69 P–B4 P–N5
10 B–B2 P–B4	29 ... N–Q2	50 K–K3 R–K4+	70 N–K5 P–N6
11 P–Q4 Q–B2	30 R/3–B2 N–B4	51 N–K4 R–R4	71 K–Q3 N–N6
12 QN–Q2 B–Q2	31 Q–QB3 Q ×Q	52 R–N5+ R ×R	72 N–B3 N–B4+
13 N–B1 KR–K1	32 R ×Q N ×P	53 N–Q6+ K–K4	73 K–K3 N ×P
14 N–K3 P–N3	33 R/3–B2 R–N1	54 N ×R N–N5	74 N–Q4 N–N7
15 P–QN4 P ×NP	34 N–R5 R ×R	55 N–B3 P–B4	75 N ×P N–B5+
16 BP ×P N–B5	35 R ×R B ×B	56 P–R4 N–B7+	76 K–B3 N–Q7+
17 N ×N P ×N	36 N ×B R–R1	57 K–Q2 N–Q5	77 K–N4 K–K5
18 B–Q2 P–B6	37 P–B3 N–B3	58 N–K2 N–B3	78 N ×RP N–B8
19 B–R6 P–R4	38 R–Q2 P–R4	59 K–Q3 K–Q4	79 N–B5
20 NP ×P B–KB1	39 K–B2 R–R5	60 K–B3 K–B4	Black resigns.
21 B ×B R ×B	40 N–B1 K–N2		

CRAMPED SPACE

Black: T. Van Scheltinga – Beverwijk 1963, International Tournament

Black's attempt to rid himself of his dark-squared bishop, so as not to have to worry about its future fate should a position arise where pawn chains are interlocked, will be of some interest to those readers who like to classify variations.

155B

As many hundreds and thousands of Ruy Lopez games have shown, White's pawn chains are for the greater part deployed on squares of a different colour to Black's KB, and this powerful piece ends up cramped for space, hemmed in by its own pawns.

To avoid so bitter a fate, the experienced Dutch master arranged to exchange the dark-squared bishops, being content to spend three tempi on doing it – the normal value of a clear piece in positions of an open type.

Sometimes it is possible to delay one's development. But this is what happened here: whilst Black was preparing for trench warfare, the game suddenly came alive. Because of the threat of B ×N and P–Q5, winning Black's pawn on QB5, Black was forced to liquidate White's QP; the centre opened up and a gaping hole appeared in Black's position on Q3.

But the square Q3 is a black one, and since the black bishop had left the board, there was no one left to defend it.

A certain amount of responsibility for the course of events lies with White too: I saw that the black bishop would be exchanged, so why then should I block up the centre?

1 P–K4 P–K4	9 P–KR3 N–QR4	17 B–N3 *(155)*	24 Q–N3 KR–Q1
2 N–KB3 N–QB3	10 B–B2 P–B4	17 ... KP × P	25 N × RP +
3 B–N5 P–QR3	11 P–Q4 Q–B2	18 P × P P × P	25 ... K–R2
4 B–R4 N–B3	12 QN–Q2 P–R3	19 B × B N × B	26 N–B5 Q × NP
5 0–0 B–K2	13 N–B1 N–B5	20 B × N P × B	27 Q–R4 + K–N1
6 R–K1 P–QN4	14 N–N3 R–K1	21 Q × P B × N	28 N–K7 +
7 B–N3 P–Q3	15 N–R4 N–R2	22 N × B N–K3	Black resigns.
8 P–B3 0–0	16 N/4–B5 B–N4	23 Q × QP Q–N2	

THE PROGRAMMED PAWN

White: L. Shamkovich – Moscow 1962, International Tournament

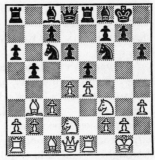

It is said you never get two identical games anywhere in the world. And this assertion is true. Because the game of chess is not only moves, but also people who make moves, and they, the people, are always different. Even if two masters play identical games on the same day, something will inevitably distinguish them: the time, their ages, the psychological pressure of the previous game and so on.

But if we were only to consider the moves, then there is one which can be seen in almost every Ruy Lopez. I am talking about P–QR4 by White, which seems to be programmed before the game starts. This move is often made out of considerations of fashion and routine, but Shamkovich knew how to extract from it every conceivable advantage. Observe the magnificent itinerary of the rook from QR1 to QB7.

From the point of view of opening theory, Black's move, 12 . . . B–N2, deserves attention. And not because it is good, but because it is . . . inappropriate. A more solid reputation is enjoyed by the quick manoeuvre . . . N–QR4–B5–N3, so that the knight does not get stuck for ages on QR4 and QN2, as happened in this game.

But if you insist on moving the bishop, then 12 . . . B–Q2 would be better.

1 P–K4 P–K4	12 N–B1 B–N2	24 Q–B3 N–K2	36 R/1–QR1
2 N–KB3 N–QB3	13 N–N3 N–QR4	25 N–N4 B×N	36 . . . R–KR1
3 B–N5 P–QR3	14 B–B2 P–B4	26 Q×B Q×Q	37 R–B6 K–B1
4 B–R4 N–B3	15 P–Q5 B–B1	27 P×Q K–R2	38 P–B4 P–B3
5 0–0 B–K2	16 P–N3 K–R1	28 N–K2 B–B3	39 N–N1 K–K1
6 R–K1 P–QN4	17 B–Q2 N–N1	29 P–N3 K–N2	40 N–B3 P–N4
7 B–N3 0–0	18 R–KB1 P–N3	30 K–N2 N–N1	41 P–B5 N–B1
8 P–KR3 P–Q3	19 N–R2 B–KN2	31 R–R3 QR–N1	42 R–R7 R–R2
9 P–B3 P–R3	20 N–N4 Q–R5	32 P×P P×P	43 N–Q2 N–Q2
10 P–Q4 R–K1	21 N–K3 N–N2	33 R–R6 B–Q1	44 N–N1 B–K2
11 QN–Q2 B–B1	22 P–N4 P–B5	34 B–K3 N–B3	45 R–B7
(156)	23 P–R4 B–Q2	35 P–B3 N–Q2	Black resigns.

A MOVE OF ANOTHER'S CREATION

White: A. Zakharov – Leningrad 1963, USSR Championship

It is a remarkable feature of the Ruy Lopez that, for all the similarity of the opening moves, it is very rare for two games to copy each other.

And yet with each tournament it proves more difficult to find new, untrodden paths. One must consider Keres's discovery, which I risked using, one such find.

I say 'risked', because to use an opening with confidence one must know it thoroughly; and what did I know then about ... N–Q2?

Only that at the great international tournament of 1924 in New York the Czech grandmaster Richard Reti once tried this move against Edward Lasker.

It was played then, though, on move 12, whilst Keres proposed trying the knight move with the black queen on Q1 and before White's obligatory QN–Q2.

That the situation was exactly as I relate it can easily be seen from an analysis of the game. I not only failed to seize the initiative, but in addition I came under a strong attack from the young Rostov master. True, the adjourned position looked more hopeful for Black, but I spoiled that too.

What a good thing it is that I play other people's variations so rarely!

1 P–K4 P–K4	12 QN–Q2 BP×P	24 QR–KB1	35 P×P BP×P
2 N–KB3 N–QB3	13 P×P B–B3	24 ... B–K1	36 R–R4 B×B
3 B–N5 P–QR3	14 P–Q5 N–N3	25 K–N2 N/3–Q2	37 R/1×B R–K4
4 B–R4 N–B3	15 N–B1 B–Q2	26 P–KR4 N–B3	38 R–B6 Q–K2
5 0–0 B–K2	16 P–QN3 N–N2	27 N–R2 Q–B1	39 B–B3 N–Q2
6 R–K1 P–QN4	17 P–KN4 R–B1	28 P–N5 N–N5	40 R–K6 R×R
7 B–N3 0–0	18 B–Q2 P–N3	29 N×N Q×N	41 P×R Q×KP
8 P–B3 P–Q3	19 N–N3 R–B2	30 B–Q1 Q–B1	42 B–N4 Q–K4
9 P–KR3 N–QR4	20 K–R2 B–N2	31 P–B4 P×P	43 R–R1 N–B4
10 B–B2 P–B4	21 R–KN1 K–R1	32 B×P Q–Q1	44 R–Q1 B–B2
11 P–Q4 N–Q2	22 B–K3 N–B4	33 P–R5 R–K2	45 Q×P
(157)	23 Q–Q2 R–N1	34 R–R1 B–K4	Draw.

ALL CHOICE MOVES

Black: V. Alatortsev – Moscow 1944, USSR Championship

158B

Playing against Alatortsev was very much like fighting a windmill.

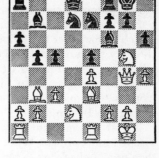

In themselves all White's moves were strong. Who could object to such solid manoeuvres as N–KN5, Q–KN4, P–KR4, R–KB1, QR–K1 and P–KB4?

On the surface everything was correct; the only thing was that each of these moves was made at the wrong time and was irrelevant.

So many choice moves. There was enthusiasm, but as yet no mastery.

Moreover, White began sounding the retreat too early. Since the knight had decided to go to KN5, then it should stay there: ... P × N would not have been that good for Black, even if his bishop could escape from KB3 to Q1. The KR-file would become open and White, whose pieces were deployed close to Black's king, could in favourable circumstances have penetrated to KR8. I am saying all this to justify the bold manoeuvre 18 N(Q2)–KB1–N3–R5!, and in criticism of the timid retreat 18 N–R3?.

Most probably White would have lost even if he had adopted that plan, but at least there would have been something of a fight, instead of his waiting passively to capitulate.

As I look through this game more carefully now, I can see that White was wanting to avoid at all costs the systematic, strategical type of game in which my opponent is still today reputed to be a great authority.

1 P–K4 P–K4	12 QN–Q2 N–K2	21 Q–R5 N–KN1	32 R–B1 P–B4
2 N–KB3 N–QB3	13 N–N5 P–R3	22 Q–N4 N–B4	33 P–K5 P–B5
3 B–N5 P–QR3	14 P–KR4 P–B4	23 Q–N3 N–Q6	34 Q–B3 N–KB4
4 B–R4 N–B3	15 P × BP P × P	24 R–K2 N × NP	35 B × N P × B
5 0–0 B–K2	16 Q–N4 (*158*)	25 P–B4 B × N	36 R/2–B2 N–K6
6 R–K1 P–QN4	16 ... P–B5	26 Q × B P × P	37 R–K1 Q × KP
7 B–N3 P–Q3	17 B–B2 Q–B2	27 B × P B–K4	38 N–B1 Q × BP
8 P–B3 0–0	18 N–R3 K–R1	28 B × B Q × B	39 R–N1 P–Q7
9 P–KR3 N–Q2	19 R–KB1	29 R–B5 Q–K3	White lost on
10 P–Q4 B–B3	19 ... QR–Q1	30 Q–N3 N–Q6	time.
11 B–K3 B–N2	20 QR–K1 B–B1	31 P–R5 N–K2	

CARDOSO THE CONQUEROR

White: R. Fischer – Portoroz 1958, Interzonal Tournament

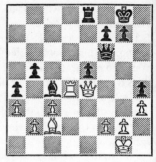

At the time of the Portoroz Interzonal Robert James Fischer was only 15 years old.

His greatest achievement had been a match victory over the Filipino R. Cardoso, the very same outsider of Portoroz 1958 to whom in the final round I contrived to lose a point, my pass into the Candidates' Tournament and my last chance to take revenge on Botvinnik.

But at the moment I want to consider Fischer, not Cardoso. What struck me even then was Fischer's art in playing simple endgames.

He conducted the defence irreproachably: 43 P–KN3! and 58 B–Q1! – one cannot fault him here; but what also had to be seen was what finesses he demonstrated as we analysed together when the game was over.

Why is so little attention paid in our time to the endgame?

Can it really be because of the brilliant attacks of Torre and Spielmann?

Perhaps it is because that whilst the great Capablanca was alive, few people could boast about their endgame!

1 P–K4 P–K4	18 N–R2 Q×P	33 R/1–Q1 R×R	48 K–B2 B–B5
2 N–KB3 N–QB3	19 N–N4 B–K2	34 R×R P–R4	49 K–K3 K–K3
3 B–N5 P–QR3	20 N–K3 B–K3	35 Q–K3 Q–B5	50 R–B2 K–Q3
4 B–R4 N–B3	21 Q–K2 KR–Q1	36 Q–K1 P–R5	51 R–Q2+ K–K2
5 0–0 B–K2	22 R–Q1 N×N	37 R–Q4 Q–B3	52 R–B2 K–K3
6 R–K1 P–QN4	23 B×N P–QR4	38 Q–K4 (*159*)	53 R–Q2 P–N4
7 B–N3 P–Q3	24 B–Q3 P–R5	38 ... P–N3	54 P×P R–R6
8 P–B3 0–0	25 P–R3 B–B3	39 R–Q2 Q–B5	55 K–B2 R–R7+
9 P–KR3 N–Q2	26 B–B2 P–Q4	40 R–Q1 Q×Q	56 K–K1 R–R8+
10 P–Q4 N–N3	27 P×P B×QP	41 B×Q K–B1	57 K–B2 P–K5
11 B–K3 R–N1	28 Q–N4 B–K3	42 R–Q7 R–N1	58 B–Q1 R–B8+
12 QN–Q2 B–B3	29 Q–N3 B–B5	43 P–KN3 P×P	59 K–K3 R–K8+
13 P–Q5 N–R4	30 B–N5 R–K1	44 P×P B–K3	60 K–B2 R–B8+
14 B–B2 N/4–B5	31 B×B Q×B	45 R–Q2 K–K2	61 K–K3 R–K8+
15 N×N N×N	32 R–Q2	46 P–R4 P–B4	62 K–B2
16 B–B1 P–B3	32 ... R/N1–Q1	47 B–B2 R–KR1	Draw.
17 P×P Q–B2			

THE KNIGHT SHIELDS THE QUEEN

Black: S. Furman – Moscow 1949, USSR Championship

In this game I had had enough of copying other people's play, so I tried to avoid well-known variations.

But the capture on Q4 with the pawn instead of the knight can hardly be considered an innovation.

Readers will undoubtedly be interested in the astute plan devised by Furman, who is one of our most profound players. The title, however, of 'positional player' does not mean at all that a grandmaster is not gifted with amazing combinative vision.

Black was not afraid to put his knight on Q4, although that square would only seem to be defended by the lone queen.

Nonetheless, however much you might try to find a way of winning this knight, I can assure you that nothing will come of it.

Having suffered a fiasco in the opening, White tried to aim for Black's KN2 and, to make the bishop's blow the more powerful . . . White hid his bishop on the most distant square, QR1!

Interesting, too, was the endgame, where both sides concentrated their main attention on Black's passed pawn on QB4.

1 P–K4 P–K4	17 Q–K2 N/3–Q4	31 R–B1 Q–N3	47 P–R4 P×P
2 N–KB3 N–QB3	18 R–Q1 N×N	32 Q–QB4 Q–QB3	48 P×P R–K3+
3 B–N5 P–QR3	19 P×N N–Q4	33 R–Q1 R–Q2	49 K–B3 K–N3
4 B–R4 N–B3	(*160*)	34 R–N1 N–B5	50 R–B7 B×P
5 0–0 P–Q3	20 B–N2 Q–Q2	35 Q–K4 Q×Q	51 R×P B–B3
6 R–K1 P–QN4	21 P–B4 P×P	36 N×Q N–K3	52 B–Q2 B–N4
7 B–N3 B–K2	22 Q×P KR–Q1	37 P–N3 B–K2	53 B–K3 B×B
8 P–B3 0–0	23 QR–B1 Q–K3	38 B–B3 N–N4	54 P×B K–B3
9 P–KR3 B–K3	24 P–R3 N–B2	39 N×N P×N	55 P–R5 R–K4
10 P–Q4 B×B	25 N–Q2 R–Q4	40 P–QR4 R–Q6	56 R–B6+ R–K3
11 Q×B P×P	26 Q–QR4	41 R–QB1 P–B4	57 R–N6 K–K4
12 P×P N–QR4	26 ... R/1–Q1	42 P×Pep P×P	58 R×R+ K×R
13 Q–B2 P–B4	27 N–B1 Q–QN3	43 K–B1 K–B2	59 K–B4 K–B3
14 N–B3 N–B3	28 R×R N×R	44 K–K2 R–Q3	60 P–K4 P×P
15 P×P P×P	29 B–R1 P–R3	45 R–QN1 P–B4	61 K×P K–K3
16 P–K5 N–QN5	30 N–N3 B–N4	46 R–N7 R–QB3	Draw agreed.

THE MOVE IN THE ENVELOPE

Black: M. Botvinnik – Moscow 1944, USSR Championship

This was my first encounter with Botvinnik and I was, of course, pleased to win.

It was a long and difficult struggle, with many phases to it.

In the opening Botvinnik set me an exam on theory: Chigorin's 9 ... B–K3 was not used in tournaments in those days.

It goes without saying that as soon as the opportunity to attack Black's KN2 arose, I took it (moves 15 to 17).

But first a cold shower awaited me in the form of ... R–K1, and then the combinative breakthrough ... B×P+ ... and White was already forced back onto the defensive.

The key to Botvinnik's combination was the move ... P–B4 in the variation 20 K–B1 P–B4 21 Q×KBP R–KB1 22 Q×N B–Q5+!

The forced play led to an endgame where Black's active rooks compensated for his slight material deficit.

In addition White's Q-side pieces had clearly missed the beginning of the show. It was too late to bring them into the fight via the centre, so I took the decision to open up the natural highway, the QR-file.

By the clever use of all my pieces I succeeded in exchanging off one of the two dangerous rooks, and the game could have been agreed drawn after thirty moves. A lot of the merit for this goes to White's QB, which, by the deeply thought out moves B–Q2–B1–K3–B1–K3, held the heterogeneous forces of White's QNP and QN and Black's pawn on Q6 firmly together.

Not wishing to retreat, Botvinnik renewed his efforts, and into the attack came Black's KRP.

This action was mistaken, as the white king suddenly found an ideal place freed for it at K4. This factor was undoubtedly not taken into account by Black in time.

The initiative passed into White's hands, but he (as was subsequently the case in many games between the same players) in time-trouble and coming up to the adjournment, wrongly declined to go in for a forced line and played the waiting move 40 K–K4.

This allowed Black to strengthen his position. Then came anxious days of waiting. What move had my opponent sealed in the envelope?

Home analysis showed that after 41 ... R–B6! 42 N–K4 R–B7 43 K×P P–N6 44 N–Q2 Black's QNP is lost, but after the black rook goes from QB7 to QB4, White's KRP also falls.

A draw!

But what if a different move had been written down?

Although even then no win could be seen for White, any chances – and not bad ones here – were only on his side.

The position aroused great interest amongst the tournament participants, but I made evasive replies to any questions: 'I haven't analysed it yet, I don't know'.

But to myself I thought: 'Ask my opponent what his move is, and I will tell you the likely result. . . .'

At the resumption it turned out that Black had not chosen the strongest move, and he also, perhaps, did not play the ending the best way.

After covering great distances, White's knight was able to penetrate to KB8 and force the capitulation of the black forces.

Had Black not allowed the combinative stroke 62 N–Q4+ K–K5? 63 N–K6 K–B4 64 N–B8! R–Q1 65 B–Q6 R×B 66 P–R7, then if the game had taken its logical course it could have come down to a duel between the lone black rook and White's bishop, knight and pawns.

Can White's minor pieces ensure the promotion of a pawn on KN8? They can, but it will still require no little work.

1 P–K4 P–K4	18 R–Q1 B–R5	35 K–B2 R–B7+	51 N–K4 K–N3
2 N–KB3 N–QB3	19 Q–N4 B×P+	36 N–Q2 R×P	52 N–B2
3 B–N5 P–QR3	20 K×B N×P	37 B–B4 R–R7	52 ... R–QN8+
4 B–R4 N–B3	21 R×Q N×Q+	38 K–K3 R–R6	53 K–B2 R–QR8
5 0–0 B–K2	22 P×N QR×R	39 K–Q4 K–B2	54 K–N2 R–R6
6 R–K1 P–QN4	23 P×P P×P	40 K–K4 P–N5	55 N×P R–QB6
7 B–N3 P–Q3	24 B–Q2 R–Q6	41 K–Q4 (161)	56 N–K3 R–Q6
8 P–B3 0–0	25 R–R5 R–QN6	41 ... R–R4	57 N–B2 R–Q1
9 P–KR3 B–K3	26 B–B1 P–B3	42 P–R6 R–QN4	58 N×P K–B4
10 P–Q4 B×B	27 R–R3 R–Q6	43 K–B4 R–N3	59 N–B6 R–Q2
11 Q×B P×P	28 R×R P×R	44 K–B5 R–N2	60 K–B3 K–K5
12 N×P N×N	29 B–K3 R–K5	45 N–N3 K–N3	61 K–B4 K–B4
13 P×N P–B4	30 K–B3 R–N5	46 K–B4 R–N3	62 N–Q4+ K–K5
14 P×P P×P	31 B–B1 P–N4	47 N–B5 K–R2	63 N–K6 K–B4
15 P–K5 N–Q2	32 P–KN3 R–QB5	48 K–N3 P–Q7	64 N–B8
16 P–QR4 P–B5	33 B–K3 P–R4	49 B×P R–Q3	Black resigns.
17 Q–N3 R–K1	34 P×P P–KN5+	50 B–B4 R–Q8	

A SECOND POINT

Black: A. Liliental – Moscow 1944, USSR Championship

162B

The way of playing the opening which the reader can see in this game is very characteristic of the style of modern grandmasters.

But in those days opening theory had not yet proliferated to the point where one was forced to copy another person's play. However, I can understand Liliental: Botvinnik's prestige was very great at that time, and still is, moreover, today, and which of us would refuse to repeat the variation of a famous theoretician?

Liliental must be given his due: he did not simply repeat Botvinnik's variation – he prepared his own improvement on it for our game. Only, is it an improvement to retreat the knight right back to K1?

Possibly Black reasoned thus: of course, it would be good to play the knight to Q2, but then Black's Q3 would be weak.

All this is logical, but . . . N–K1 has its failings too: Black gets a weak central square, Q4. White's QN set out for it straight away, and whilst Black was defending himself against N–Q5, White gained time and created the conditions necessary for the knight's infiltration on Q6.

1 P–K4 P–K4	11 N×P N×N	21 Q–K7 N–K3	30 K–R2 N–Q5
2 N–KB3 N–QB3	12 P×N B×B	22 N–Q6 (162)	31 N–Q6 N–K3
3 B–N5 P–QR3	13 Q×B P–B4	22 ... K–N1	32 N×R R×N
4 B–R4 N–B3	14 P×P P×P	23 QR–Q1 Q–B3	33 P–B5 N–B1
5 0–0 B–K2	15 P–K5 N–K1	24 Q–R4 P–N5	34 R–Q6 Q–K1
6 R–K1 P–QN4	16 Q–N3 Q–N3	25 Q–QB4 R–Q2	35 R–K1 P–QR4
7 B–N3 P–Q3	17 N–B3 R–Q1	26 P–B4 R–B2	36 P–K6 P×P
8 P–B3 0–0	18 B–N5 B×B	27 R–QB1 N–Q5	37 P×P
9 P–KR3 B–K3	19 Q×B N–B2	28 KR–Q1 N–N4	Black resigns.
10 P–Q4 P×P	20 N–K4 K–R1	29 N–K4 R/1–B1	

I took an even greater liking to the Lopez attack after this memorable game.

I do not know if it was luck or what, but only six rounds had gone by in this, my first, USSR Championship and from three Ruy Lopez's I had already taken two points: an undoubted success for someone making his debut!

A GLIMMER OF A COMBINATION

White: A. Koblencs – Leningrad 1946, Semi-Finals USSR Championship

163W

This game might be called the contest of unrealized hopes.

Simply because, first, I had hoped to catch Koblencs with the combination 16 P–QR4 P–B5 17 Q–N3 R–K1 18 R–Q1 B–R5 19 Q–N4 B × P +!, which is good for Black. But nothing came of it.

Then Koblencs wanted to mate me on my KN2. Nothing came of that either.

And then later still Black hoped to win the endgame, where his pawns were more compact and he had a more active king. But White's defensive resources proved sufficient for the draw.

Even this modest game, however, has some significance for opening theory. The reader knows what effort has to be put into searching for new lines and how seldom one succeeds in finding them. And yet year by year, tournament by tournament, move by move, chess-players do find new ideas.

Who is not familiar, for example, with R. Kholmov's numerous convincing victories in the variation 10 . . . B × B 11 Q × B Q–Q2, or 11 P × B P × P 12 P × P – victories as Black, not as White!

And now quite recently a new idea has appeared: 10 . . . B × B 11 Q × B P–Q4 with full equality.

1 P–K4 P–K4	15 P–K5 N–Q2	27 K–R2 Q–Q6	41 R–KB2 R–Q1
2 N–KB3 N–QB3	16 Q–N3 R–K1	28 Q–K3 R–QB3	42 R–K2 B–B1
3 B–N5 P–QR3	(163)	29 P–KN3 Q × Q	43 R–KN2 B–K2
4 B–R4 N–B3	17 B–R6 B–B1	30 P × Q P–B6	44 R–K2 R–Q4
5 0–0 B–K2	18 B–B4 P–B5	31 P × P R × BP	45 R–KN2 P–N5
6 R–K1 P–QN4	19 N–B3 N–B4	32 R–Q1 B–K2	46 R–R2 R–Q1
7 B–N3 P–Q3	20 N–K4 N × N	33 R–Q7 P–R3	47 R–K2
8 P–B3 0–0	21 R × N Q–Q4	34 P–R5 K–B2	47 . . . R/1–QB1
9 P–KR3 B–K3	22 R/1–K1 P–B4	35 R–R7 R–B3	48 R–Q2 R/1–B2
10 P–Q4 B × B	23 R/4–K2 B–N5	36 K–R3 K–K3	49 R–R8 R–B1
11 Q × B P × P	24 R–KB1 R–K3	37 P–K4 P × P	50 R–R7 R/1–B2
12 N × P N × N	25 P–KR4	38 R × KP R–Q1	51 R–R8 R–B1
13 P × N P–B4	25 . . . R–KN3	39 K–N4 R–Q6	52 R–R7 R/1–B2
14 P × P P × P	26 Q–KR3 R–K1	40 R–K2 R–Q5	Draw agreed.

DIVIDING THE POINT INTO FOUR

White: A. Suetin – Leningrad 1960, USSR Championship

The variation where Black sacrifices his KP on K5 is very tempting.

Who could refuse the possibility of getting an easy game, rich in combinations, at the small price of the loss of a pawn? They used to play gambits in the olden days, so why not now?

But the idea of trying this variation on Suetin in particular came to me, I think, quite by chance.

When you are playing a theoretician, you tend to see things in a gloomy light. I did not know which defence to choose, and then I suddenly remembered this abandoned variation.

Why is it that this variation is not used by grandmasters?

Books on the Ruy Lopez recommend the line Suetin chose, but more to my taste is Boleslavsky's idea: 17 R ×P B ×R 18 B ×B – in return for the exchange White has ample opportunity for combinations.

It is said that Suetin found a stronger line for White somewhere in the region of moves 20 to 30. I certainly allow that that was possible.

I, too, on move 21 improved on the continuation Flohr chose against Levenfish: instead of 21 . . . N–Q3?, which was met by 22 B–R3, I played the more active 21 . . . Q–B4.

So far I have been talking about the opening and middlegame. In the endgame I tried to perform a miracle, and, alas . . . suffered a setback when I was almost at my goal. Even today, though, I am reluctant to believe that a king, rook and knight are incapable of overcoming a king and rook.

But that evening Suetin kept finding amazing saving moves.

Now if one could automatically have an extra quarter of a point for an extra knight, a chess-player's life would be sweet indeed! I would immediately, and quite willingly, without having to be forced into it, have exchanged rooks and I would have carried my extra charger on my shoulders to the tournament controller. But these happy days, which even such a virtuoso as Emanuel Lasker used to dream about, have not as yet dawned.

When will they be?

I should like to live until such times, although it is hardly likely that tournament organizers and judges will ever want to put kindness in place of their anger and heed the just complaints of experienced players who are skilful at their jobs too.

Organizers and foreign patrons never have the time to discuss seriously with grandmasters, who are forced by the threat of death by a draw to go in for various insufficiently well-founded, or rather, adventurous, combinations. One has only to look at Tal's play in his Copenhagen match with Larsen. And it is always with only a single aim in mind: that no-one should accuse us of avoiding a struggle or of trying to end the game with the division of the point into two equal parts. . . .

So why not arrange things so that we do not get this 'equal division'?

One needs only an inkling of common sense to realize that playing with White and playing with Black are not the same thing. The former is much easier than the latter.

There would be nothing dreadful, therefore, in the suggestion that for a draw Black should get a certain bonus in the form of 0.1 point, whilst White would have to have 0.1 point taken away. . . .

Even such a minimal change in the scoring of draws could considerably increase White's interest in winning and Black's in drawing. The main thing would be that the peaceful division of the point into two equal parts would disappear.

1 P–K4 P–K4	22 Q–B2 N–N3	42 B–K3 P–N5	62 R×P N×P
2 N–KB3 N–QB3	23 P–Q6 QR–Q1	43 R×KRP R–B6	63 R–R4 R–N1
3 B–N5 P–QR3	24 R–QB4 Q×Q	44 P–N5 R–B3	64 R–KB4 N–Q6
4 B–R4 N–B3	25 R×Q P–B5	45 R–R7 P–N6	65 R–Q4 N–B7
5 0–0 B–K2	26 B–K3 P×P	46 R–R5+ K–K3	66 R–R4 R–N3
6 R–K1 P–QN4	27 P×P R×P	47 B–Q4 R–B5	67 R–QN4 K–R3
7 B–N3 P–Q3	28 R/1–QB1	48 B–R8 P–N7	68 R–KB4
8 P–B3 0–0	28 . . . R/1–Q1	49 R–R6+ K–B4	68 . . . N–N5+
9 P–KR3 B–N2	29 B–B4 R–Q8+	50 B×P N×B	69 K–R3 N–B3
10 P–Q4 P×P	30 K–R2 R×R	51 P–N6 R–B1	70 R–B5 N–K5
11 P×P P–Q4	31 R×R R–Q6	52 P–R4 K–N5	71 P–R5 R–K3
12 P–K5 N–K5	32 R–B6 N–Q4	53 P–N7 R–KN1	72 K–R4 N–B3
13 N–B3 N–R4	33 B–Q6 P–QR4	54 R–QN6 N–Q6	73 R–R5 R–K6
14 B–B2 P–KB4	34 R–R6 N–N5	55 R–QR6 N–N7	74 R–R6 K–KB6
15 P×Pep B×P	35 R–R8+ K–B2	56 R–KN6+	75 R–R5 R–B8
16 N×N P×N	36 N–K5+ B×N	56 . . . K–R4	76 R–QN5
17 B×P B×B	37 B×B R×NP	57 R–N6 N–Q6	76 . . . R–KR8+
18 R×B P–B4	38 R–R7+ K–K3	58 R–QR6 N–N7	77 K–N3 N×P+
19 P–Q5 N–B5	39 B×P P–R5	59 R–QN6 N–Q8	(164)
20 R–N1 Q–Q2	40 P–N4 N–Q6	60 R–N4 P–R6	78 K–N4.
21 P–QN3 Q–B4	41 B–Q4 K–Q4	61 R–R4 R×P	

With these pieces the result is a draw. The author tried for fifty moves, in all good faith, but in vain, to disprove this. The game ended in a draw on move 128.

BREYER'S MOVE

Black: S. Gligoric – Amsterdam 1964, Interzonal Tournament

Probably each of you has had occasion to observe that sometimes masters play the opening very quickly, but sometimes they spend a long time thinking over each move. And the most surprising thing is that, despite this, both games develop completely identically over the first 10–12 moves.

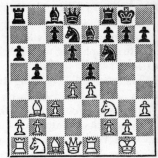

This happens because the players interpret the problem facing them differently. Some see the opening as a necessary evil and hurry as fast as possible to make all the studied moves, even if they are not confident about some of them. Others try mentally to substantiate each of their moves.

Of course, there is not always a clear-cut distinction. If one were to consider those whose play combines both tendencies, the first prize would have to go to Svetozar Gligoric.

Breyer's idea of taking back the move ... N–QB3 and making way for the QBP has proved exceptionally opportune and viable. The attack 11 N–R4! forces Black to go in for the sharp variation 11 ... N×P 12 N–B5 N/2–B3 13 N×B+ Q×N 14 R–K2 P–B4 15 Q–K1, when the knight, stranded in foreign territory, is in danger, though it can always be sacrificed to advantage. For example, 15 ... B–N2 16 B–B2 KP×P 17 P–B3 P–Q4 18 P×N QP×P.

Do any of you like the look of these menacing black pawns? Whose game would you choose to play, White's or Black's?

I do not know the answer to this question myself, so I deferred in favour of 14 P–QR4.

1 P–K4 P–K4	8 P–B3 0–0	14 P–QR4 B–N2	21 B×N N×B
2 N–KB3 N–QB3	9 P–KR3 N–N1	15 RP×P BP×P	22 R×P B–R7+
3 B–N5 P–QR3	10 P–Q4 QN–Q2	16 N–B3 P×P	23 K–R1 B–B5
4 B–R4 N–B3	(165)	17 N×QP N–B4	24 K–N1 B–R7+
5 0–0 B–K2	11 P–B4 P–B3	18 N–Q5 B×N	25 K–R1 B–B5
6 R–K1 P–QN4	12 P–B5 Q–B2	19 B×B QR–K1	26 K–N1 B–R7+
7 B–N3 P–Q3	13 BP×P B×P	20 B–K3 N/4×P	Draw.

THE PROFESSOR OF PSYCHOLOGY

Black: N. Krogius – Kiev 1965, USSR Championship

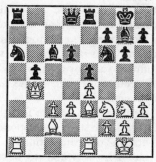

Grandmaster Krogius is a singularly strong opponent. He has decided to set down his most varied experience of the game in a book, which he has given the extremely original title of 'Man in Chess'.

Why that, and not, say, 'The Mastery of Attack' or 'The Art of Defence'? The fact is that Krogius is a psychology candidate; he is working on the psychology of chess and he is, of course, a professor in this field.

What can be said about our game?

The retreat of the knight to QN1, which was fashionable that year, the slow advance of the white pawns, the sudden breakthrough in the centre, the numerous piece exchanges which inevitably followed from it and, finally, White's greatest achievement, the black pawn on QN4 cut off from the general mass.

If one analyses this rather cheerless game thoroughly, one can also discover a psychological element: Black's 22 ... N–R3!.

It was as if Krogius was asking: 'Is 22 Q–N4 playing for a draw or a win?'. And I replied: 'For a win! Otherwise I would have played 23 Q–N2 N–B4 24 Q–N4, with repetition of moves.'

I was unable to win the rook ending of four pawns against three.

P–K4 P–K4	13 B–B2 R–K1	24 P–Q4 N × P	36 B × N R × B
N–KB3 N–QB3	14 P–QN4 N–K3	25 N × N P × N	37 R × P R–B7
B–N5 P–QR3	15 P–QR4 B–KB1	26 N × P B × N	38 K–B1 K–B1
B–R4 N–B3	16 N–N3 P–N3	27 P × B N–B2	39 P–N3 K–K2
0–0 B–K2	17 B–K3 B–N2	28 R × R Q × R	40 K–N2 K–K3
R–K1 P–QN4	18 Q–B1 P–B4	29 B–Q4 N–K3	41 K–B3 R–R7
B–N3 0–0	19 NP × P N × BP	30 B × P B × B	42 K–K3 P–R5
P–B3 P–Q3	20 P × P P × P	31 Q × B Q × Q	43 P × P R–R5
P–KR3 N–N1	21 Q–N2 B–B3	32 R × Q R–QB1	44 K–B3 R × P
10 P–Q3 QN–Q2	22 Q–N4 N–R3	33 B–K3 R × P	45 K–N3 R–R5
11 QN–Q2 B–N2	(166)	34 R–QN4 N–B2	46 P–R4 R–QB5
12 N–B1 N–B4	23 Q–N1 P–Q4	35 B–N6 P–R4	Draw agreed.

IT HAPPENS IN REAL LIFE TOO

Black: R. Wade – Moscow Olympiad 1956

When things are peaceful grandmasters usually look for new lines of development, which means opening innovations; but when times are tougher, with only four minutes a move, they try to prove the correctness of their home findings to their opponent.

But such tactics are fraught with distinct dangers: what if your opponent were to find a hole in your calculations there and then, or what if he was able to beat off an attack which you had estimated in your home analysis as being stronger?

Masters, therefore, often avoid fashionable lines in the opening and prefer a quiet development of pieces, without any pretensions to a lightning victory.

So it is here.

Declining any of the ambitious attempts to refute 9 . . . N–N1, White set about gradually building up his forces on the K-side.

Suddenly some hitherto unstudied law of chess mechanics came into action, and my opponent began a daring attack.

If the end goal of the attack, Black's taking control of Q4 with his knight, is worth the pawn that is lost, then one might approve of 13 . . . P–Q4. But I am not certain that anyone will want to repeat Black's experience.

Nonetheless it was an extremely dour struggle: but the black king's fate was decided all of a sudden by the check from White's knight which had been dozing on K5. Just like people. Does it not happen like that in real life? A check – and that's it!

1 P–K4 P–K4	13 N–N3 P–Q4	23 R–QB1 B–R2	33 N–B5 + P × N
2 N–KB3 N–QB3	14 P × P N × P	24 K–R2 R × R	34 Q–KN3 +
3 B–N5 P–QR3	15 N × P B–Q3	25 R × R K–B1	34 . . . N–N5 +
4 B–R4 N–B3	16 P–Q4 R–K1	26 R–K1 P–N3	35 P × N
5 0–0 B–K2	17 P–KB4 P × P	27 N–N3 Q–N3	35 . . . Q–KR3 +
6 R–K1 P–QN4	18 P × P N/2–B3	28 B × N B × B	36 K–N1 Q–KN3
7 B–N3 0–0	19 Q–Q3 B–B2	29 N–Q7 + (167)	37 B–K3 P–R4
8 P–B3 P–Q3	20 B–Q2 B–N3	29 . . . N × N	38 R–K5 B–K5
9 P–KR3 N–N1	21 QR–Q1	30 B–N4 + K–N2	39 P–N5 Q–QB3
10 P–Q3 QN–Q2	21 . . . R–QB1	31 R × R P–QR4	40 R–K7
11 QN–Q2 B–N2	22 N–B5 R–B2	32 B–Q2 N–B3	Black resigns.
12 N–B1 P–B4			

WHOSE MOVE?

White: A. Tolush – Riga 1958, USSR Championship

Two white queens on one diagram!

The property pawns have of queening is almost never realized, and even more rarely whilst the 'main' queen is still alive on the board. Here, however, a pawn did become a queen.

But at the end of the game it is written: 'White resigns'.

How can that be? He had two queens and lost? The queens must be black, then, surely?

All I have forgotten to say is whose move it is.

The most powerful weapon in chess is to have the next move!

Tolush revealed his trump-card, the attack along the KN-file, too soon and allowed Black to arm his fortress: ... P–KN3 and ... B(K2)–B3–N2.

At the same time the hole that appeared on White's Q3 in the course of the fighting captivated the ubiquitous black knight's attention more and more.

All the later complications arose perfectly naturally, but the outcome of them was certain in advance: the white king's position was too shaky, and the black queen and that deadly black pawn on KB6 were too close at hand.

And yet the idea White had of transferring his knight to K3 via QR3 and QB2 is a highly attractive one: granted, the white knight would have spent three moves just the same if he had gone via Q2 and KB1, but how boring it would have been for him in comparison!

1 P–K4 P–K4	11 P×B N–QR4	21 R–KN3 B–N2	31 N–K7+ R×N
2 N–KB3 N–QB3	12 P–KB4 N×B	22 P–B5 RP×P	32 P×R P×R
3 B–N5 P–QR3	13 P×N N–Q2	23 N×P Q–B3	33 Q–Q8+ K–R2
4 B–R4 N–B3	14 N–R3 P×QP	24 N–B6 N–B4	34 P–K8=Q (168)
5 0–0 B–K2	15 P×P P–QB4	25 P×P RP×P	34 ... Q–R6+
6 R–K1 P–QN4	16 P–Q5 B–B3	26 R–KB3 Q–R5	35 K–K1 N–Q6+
7 B–N3 P–Q3	17 N–B2 R–K1	27 P–K5 B×P	36 K–Q2 Q–R3+
8 P–B3 0–0	18 P–N4 P–B5	28 R×B Q–N5+	37 K–B3 Q×B+
9 P–Q4 B–N5	19 Q–Q1 P–QR4	29 K–B1 P×R	White resigns.
10 Q–Q3 B×N	20 R–R3 P–N3	30 P–Q6 P–K5	

THE ROOTS OF TIME-TROUBLE

Black: A. Matanovic – Belgrade 1964, International Tournamen

It would be best to begin my commentary on this game with a few words about time-trouble. But I am not referring to that unique situation when a player has to reel off, come what may, the set number of moves – 32, 40 or 48, depending on when the time-control has been fixed for. That is to say, that time when you feel absolutely terrible or, more to the point, you never know whether to look at the board or at your menacingly raised flag.

Here I am referring to a different kind of time-trouble: when you hav sufficient time and a quiet position, but it is difficult to find the right move

My game with Matanovic is an excellent example of this. We had spen only seven minutes each on the first thirteen moves (it looked as if ther would be no question of time-trouble in this game). However, over move 16–21 we together consumed 2½ hours. And here it is interesting to not that we used an exactly equal amount of time each.

Where did the minutes go to? To reflecting on the fate of the piece Here is a quick tally: White – move 16, 24 minutes; 20, 20 mins; 21, 3 mins; 22, 1 min.; Black – move 16, 24 mins; 19, 22 mins; 20, 30 mins 21, 0 min.

But what were the players thinking about so intensely? White wa wanting to drive the black knight away from its QB5 and start an attac on Black's QP, whilst Black was desperately trying to prevent this. It i precisely in such tight phases of a game that we should look for the roo of the now fashionable time-troubles.

1 P–K4 P–K4	10 B–K3 P×P	19 R–N1 P–QR4	27 B–K3 R–B3
2 N–KB3 N–QB3	11 P×P N–QR4	20 B–N3 P–R3	28 QR–B1
3 B–N5 P–QR3	12 B–B2 N–B5	(169)	28 ... R/1–QB1
4 B–R4 N–B3	13 B–B1 P–B4	21 B×N B–K3	29 R×R R×R
5 0–0 B–K2	14 N–B3 P×P	22 Q–Q1 R×B	30 R–QB1
6 R–K1 P–QN4	15 Q×P R–B1	23 P–QN3 R–B3	30 ... R×R+
7 B–N3 P–Q3	16 B–Q1 P–N5	24 N–Q4 B×N	31 B×R P–Q4
8 P–B3 0–0	17 N–Q5 N×N	25 Q×B Q–N3	32 P×P B×P
9 P–Q4 B–N5	18 Q×N/Q5 B–B3	26 Q×Q R×Q	Draw.

A STROKE OF TOURNAMENT LUCK

Black: I. Zaitsev – Moscow 1967, Grandmasters and Masters Tournament.

170B

'He was incredibly lucky today!' I heard these words after I had played 36 Q–Q5+ and my opponent had stopped the clocks.

Next day Zaitsev met me with a smile: 'You know, I could have saved the game; instead of 35 ...B×N? I should simply have played my king into the corner. It would have been a certain draw then!'

I certainly was lucky that day, I won't argue about that. But does it not strike the reader that the words 'He was lucky' might equally appropriately be addressed to Zaitsev?

I had at my disposal the obvious and technically simple win by 35 Q–Q5+ K–R1 36 Q–B7!. But I think it was grandmaster Reti who said: 'In chess we value the exception, not the rule'. Quite so: the combinative blow 36 ...Q–R8+ 37 K–K2 R×N+ 38 P×R Q×P+! would have saved Black's day!

What could I do? Taking into account my opponent's time-trouble, I decided to choose the variation that was more difficult for him: where there was not one long continuation but several one-move continuations.

Zaitsev took fright at the sight of the greedy white rook on the 7th and, with no time left to think, wanted to shelve the problem for the moment and first wipe out his old enemy, the knight on K3.

... Which of us was lucky?

1 P–K4 P–K4	11 P–QB3 P–Q3	21 Q×N Q–N2	30 K–B1 Q–K4
2 N–KB3 N–QB3	12 Q–B3 B–K3	22 P–QN4 B–R2	31 P–QN3 Q–R7
3 B–N5 P–QR3	13 BP×P B×B	23 R–R3 P–B4	32 N–K3 B–B5
4 B–R4 N–B3	14 P×B P–QB4	24 P–R4 QR–K1	33 R–Q8 R/5–K1
5 0–0 B–K2	15 KP×P B×P	25 Q–B3 R–K5	34 R×R R×R
6 R–K1 P–QN4	16 P×P B×BP	26 P–R5 B–N1	35 R–Q7 *(170)*
7 B–N3 0–0	17 R–Q1 Q–B1	27 R–K3 Q–KB2	35 ...B×N
8 P–Q4 N×QP	18 N–B3 N–B2	28 P–R6 P×P	36 Q–Q5+
9 N×N P×N	19 B–B4 N–K3	29 R/K3–Q3	Black resigns.
10 P–K5 N–K1	20 N–Q5 N×B	29 ...Q–K3	

'WHEEL TO WHEEL'

Black: P. Keres – Budapest 1950, Candidates Tournament

Even in cycling races lasting many days a pair or more of riders often finish 'wheel to wheel'. And even a scrupulous examination of photographs does not help us in determining which of them was first.

On the eve of my game against Keres I was half a point behind the leader, but Boleslavsky drew quickly with Ståhlberg in the last round, thus kindly presenting me with the chance of catching him up. This I succeeded in doing.

The result of my game with Keres entitled me to play a 12-game match against Boleslavsky.

These twelve games ended in a draw, 6–6, and only a successful opening variation used at the close of the extra 2-game mini-match gave me the chance of challenging the world champion in 1951.

By an irony of fate, this match too ended in a draw: 12–12. 'Wheel to wheel'.

The gambit variation with the sacrifice of the important central pawn is, in my view, quite correct: White gets a mobile KP and KBP pair. Our game in some measure confirmed this view. The game was fairly even for a long time, but Keres had only to underestimate the strength of 29 Q–N5 and things suddenly deteriorated for his king. I could have gone in straight away for 30 R–B4 P×P 31 Q–R6 P×R=Q+ 32 K–R2, but winning this game meant too much to me, so I tried to play as simply and safely as possible.

1 P–K4 P–K4	10 P–KR3 B×N	19 K–R1 B–B1	28 P–B6+ K–R1
2 N–KB3 N–QB3	11 Q×B P×P	20 R–B1 B–N2	29 Q–N5 P–N6
3 B–N5 P–QR3	12 Q–Q1 P×P	21 B–Q2 P–QB4	30 P×P Q–N5
4 B–R4 N–B3	13 N×P N–QR4	22 B–R4 R–KB1	31 P×N Q×B
5 0–0 B–K2	14 B–B2 R–K1	23 QR–N1 Q–N3	32 R–B4 Q–B7
6 R–K1 P–QN4	15 P–B4 P–N5	24 P–B5 B–Q5	(*171*)
7 B–N3 0–0	16 N–Q5 N×N	25 Q–KN3 N–B5	33 Q–R6
8 P–Q4 P–Q3	17 Q×N P–QB3	26 B–R6 B–N2	Black resigns.
9 P–B3 B–N5	18 Q–Q3 P–N3	27 B×B K×B	

A PAWN OR THE ATTACK?

White: I. Boleslavsky – Moscow 1950, 6th Match Game

172W

The gambit idea of F. Marshall, the USA Champion for many years, first blazed in the chess firmament long ago, during the game Capablanca-Marshall, New York 1918.

White's anti-classical pawn move, P–QB3, seems itself almost to suggest what his opponent's course should be: to act as speedily as possible, whilst White's QR, QN and QB have not made a single move!

The alternative is knight to QR3. But what kind of a move is that? It would be better for the knight to knock and pass, as those 'dominoes' fans, Geller, Spassky, Stein, Korchnoi and Fischer often do in positions of stalemate.

Thus the bold idea of 8 . . . P–Q4 was born.

What was the point of White's 21 P–R3? It was to defend QN4; in certain variations after . . . BP×P, . . . B–QN5 could be unpleasant for White. But was there anything wrong with 21 N–B3?

It, too, would have been a good move, and would have led to much sharper play. Here are some of the most interesting variations:

a) 21 N–B3 N–B5? 22 Q–B2 N–Q6 23 N–R4 Q–K5 24 B–B3 N×R 25 B×Q.

b) 21 N–B3 B–B5! 22 N–R4 Q–N4 23 N–B3 Q–B4 24 N–R4 Q–N4 25 N–B3.

c) 21 N–B3 B–B5 22 N–R4 Q–B3 23 Q–B3 P×P 24 P×P N×B 25 Q×B Q×Q 26 P×Q N–B4, or 25 P×N B×KP+!

d) 21 N–B3 B–B5 22 Q–Q2 N×B 23 P×N B–R3 24 N–K5 P–B3 25 B–B2 Q–N4 26 N–B3 Q×KP+!

Lovers of the Marshall attack will know many similar combinations, but this is already a lot for one small page.

1 P–K4 P–K4	8 P–B3 P–Q4	15 Q–Q3 B–KB4	21 P–R3 P×P
2 N–KB3 N–QB3	9 P×P N×P	16 Q–B1 Q–R4	22 P×P B–B5
3 B–N5 P–QR3	10 N×P N×N	17 B–K3 B–KR6	23 Q–B3 B×B
4 B–R4 N–B3	11 R×N P–QB3	18 B–Q1 Q–B4	24 P×B Q×Q
5 0–0 B–K2	12 P–Q4 B–Q3	19 Q–K2 QR–K1	25 B×Q N×P
6 R–K1 P–QN4	13 R–K1 Q–R5	20 N–Q2 P–B4	Draw agreed.
7 B–N3 0–0	14 P–N3 Q–R6	(172)	

ON THE VERGE OF A DRAW

Black: B. Ivkov – Sochi 1968, USSR v Yugoslavia

When Ivkov, after White's 44th move, touched the black king's crown, I must confess I was expecting the move . . . K–K2 and I was already getting ready to celebrate victory. For, indeed, after 44 . . . K–K2? 45 N/2–K4! Black's pieces would be in a position of Zugzwang, the white king could march to Q3 unhindered, and with a bit of luck White might even execute a final mating combination: 45 . . . R–QB1 46 P–R4 P×P 47 P–N5 K–K1 48 P–N6

B×P? 49 N–Q6+ K–B1 50 N–K6+ K–N1 51 R×NP+ K–R1 52 N–KB7 mate!

However, by the single brilliant move, 44 . . . K–N1!, the Yugoslav grandmaster and ex-junior world champion destroyed all White's secret combinations, and the game, which had been on the verge of a draw for so long, was safely guided to a drawn finish. Which was all quite logical.

I do not know what theoretical value 9 P–QR3 has. Black refrained from the Marshall Attack, 8 . . . P–Q4, whilst I in turn did not want to play the conventional 9 P–KR3; so a new, or relatively new, variation arose via this cautious move of the QRP. And did you notice that my opponent did exactly the same thing and played . . . P–KR3?

1 P–K4 P–K4	14 P×P P×P	26 R/2–B2 R–Q1	39 R–B6 N–Q4
2 N–KB3 N–QB3	15 N–B3 R–N1	27 N–Q2 P–Q4	40 R–R6 N–N3
3 B–N5 P–QR3	16 P–R3 B–K3	28 B–B5 N–N4	41 N/1–Q2 R–B2
4 B–R4 N–B3	17 B×B P×B	29 P–KR4 N–B2	42 R×R+ B×R
5 0–0 B–K2	18 P–QN4 B–B1	30 N/3–N1 N–Q3	43 R–R7 N–Q4
6 R–K1 P–QN4	19 Q–N3 Q–Q2	31 B×N B×N	44 N–B5 (173)
7 B–N3 0–0	20 R–Q1 Q–KB2	32 N–QB3 B–K2	44 . . . K–N1
8 P–B3 P–Q3	21 B–K3 KR–Q1	33 P×P P×P	45 N–K6 R–QB1
9 P–QR3 P–R3	22 QR–B1 Q–K1	34 Q–B5 B–Q3	46 N–K4 K–B2
10 P–Q4 R–K1	23 R–Q2	35 N–N3 Q–Q2	47 N/6–B5 K–N1
11 P–Q5 N–QR2	23 . . . R/Q1–B1	36 Q×Q R×Q	48 N–K6 K–B2
12 P–B4 P–B3	24 Q–N1 N–Q1	37 N–N1 P–Q5	49 N/6–B5 K–N1
13 QP×P N×BP	25 Q–Q3 N–B2	38 P–B3 K–B2	50 N–K6

Draw by threefold repetition of moves.

ROOKS BURSTING ONTO THE SEVENTH

Black: E. Geller – Moscow 1952, USSR Championship

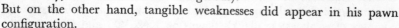

174B

Chess kings need pawn protection not only at the height of the middlegame storm but also in the endgame.

The distinctive pawn shelters come in various shapes, but the most reliable are considered to be those which defend the king from attack on two sides: along the rank and along the file.

By his bold pawn play Geller was able to beat off altogether White's attack (which, admittedly, was not all that dangerous). But on the other hand, tangible weaknesses did appear in his pawn configuration.

This comment might serve as a reminder to young chess-players: remember about the approaching endgame – do not weaken your pawn chains without having a serious reason for doing so!

Does that mean that the author recommends not moving one's pawns at all, but keeping them on the second rank to defend against possible enemy rook diversions? No, I didn't say that. Pawns, like pieces, must play their part in the chess battle, and if the king orders them forward, then forward they must go.

Geller assessed the possibilities of the position accurately, move for move, and was even first onto the attack, against White's pawn on QB3. But what if both white rooks penetrated to the seventh rank? White's king is protected, but how are things with Black's?

Away with fear! Black's king has not such a bad life either: let the white rooks penetrate to the seventh, let them attack Black's KR2; just one move, . . . N–KB3!, and all the threats are repelled.

The draw was agreed by the players because of the 'toothlessness' of the position.

1 P–K4 P–K4	10 B–B2 P–B4	19 N–Q5 B×B	28 P–KN3 P×NP
2 N–KB3 N–QB3	11 QN–Q2 N–B3	20 Q×B N×N	29 RP×P B×N
3 B–N5 P–QR3	12 N–B1 N–Q2	21 B×N N–K2	30 P×B N–K2
4 B–R4 N–B3	13 P–QR4 R–N1	22 B–N3 P–B4	31 P–Q4 N×P
5 0–0 B–K2	14 N–K3 N–N3	23 Q–N5 P–QB5	32 P×P P×P
6 R–K1 P–QN4	15 P×P P×P	24 B–B2 N–B3	33 R×P (174)
7 B–N3 0–0	16 B–N3 K–R1	25 Q×Q R×Q	33 . . . P–N5
8 P–Q3 P–Q3	17 N–Q2 B–N4	26 N–K3 P–B5	Draw.
9 P–B3 N–QR4	18 N/2–B1 P–N3	27 N–Q5 B–K3	

A BISHOP OFF-SIDE

Black: E. Gereben – Beverwijk 1963, International Tournament

175B

A queen and knight, in the opinion of many specialists, work together considerably more effectively than do a queen and bishop. What is the reason for this fact?

The queen and knight supplement each other's actions, whereas the queen and bishop often duplicate each other's work by creating excessive strength down a diagonal, whilst lacking striking power in other directions.

The final part of this game is a good illustration of this rule, in addition to which we see a whole instructive complex of weaknesses: Black's pawns on KN2, Q3 and QN4 and the indefensible points of entry, KB4 and Q4. The game is a model for anyone wanting to study a manoeuvring fight with mistakes on both sides.

The opening, too, is not without poison. The rarely met variation 7 . . . 0–0! 8 P–KR3! is, if you like, a vaccine against the Marshall Attack, since White's QN can go to QB3.

If you still want to play 8 . . . P–Q4?, please do! 9 P ×P N ×P 10 N ×P N ×N 11 R ×N B–N2 12 N–B3 N–B5 13 P–Q4 N ×NP 14 B–Q5 B ×B 15 R ×B.

1 P–K4 P–K4	17 N–N4 R–K1	32 P–R3 R–R3	48 N–B5 (*175*)
2 N–KB3 N–QB3	18 P–Q5 B–K2	33 R–N1 P ×P	48 . . . Q–Q1
3 B–N5 P–QR3	19 P ×P N–R4	34 RP ×P B–B2	49 N–K3 K–N1
4 B–R4 N–B3	20 N–K3 Q–B1	35 R–R1 R/1–R1	50 Q–N4 B–R2
5 0–0 B–K2	21 N–Q5 Q ×BP	36 R ×R R ×R	51 N–B5 Q–B3
6 R–K1 P–QN4	22 P–QN3 N–N2	37 K–N2 B–N1	52 Q–Q1 B–N1
7 B–N3 0–0	23 B–K3 N–B4	38 R–Q2 R–R6	53 Q–Q5 Q–Q1
8 P–KR3 B–N2	24 B ×N Q ×B	39 Q–N1 K–R2	54 Q ×NP K–R2
9 P–Q3 P–Q3	25 R–QB1 B–Q1	40 R–R2 Q–R3	55 Q–N7 B–B2
10 P–B3 N–Q2	26 Q–Q2 P–R3	41 R ×R Q ×R	56 N–K3 K–N1
11 QN–Q2 B–B3	27 KR–Q1	42 Q–Q3 Q–R3	57 N–Q5 B–N1
12 N–B1 N–B4	27 . . . P–QR4	43 P–R5 B–R2	58 N–K7+ K–R2
13 B–Q5 N–K2	28 P–N3 Q–B3	44 Q–K2 Q–N2	59 N–B6 Q–B2
14 B ×B N ×B	29 Q–Q3 N–B1	45 N–R4 N–B2	60 Q ×Q B ×Q
15 N–K3 N–N3	30 P–KR4 N–K3	46 N ×N Q ×N	61 N–K7
16 P–Q4 P–B3	31 P–QN4 Q–N2	47 Q–B3 B–N1	Black resigns.

THE BOLD KNIGHT MOVE

Black: V. Antoshin – Moscow 1956, Moscow Championship

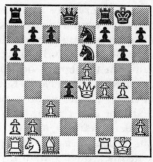

A short, boring draw, isn't it?

Yes it is.

However, the opening variation which occurred in this game is not that harmless. There were occasions when Black could be faced with imminent death, after 9 . . . N–B4 10 Q–N4 N–K3? 11 N×P N×N 12 B–R6!, or 9 . . . P–Q4! 10 B×N P×B 11 N×B+ Q×N 12 R–K1 P–B3 13 P–KB3 N–B4? 14 P–QN3! P×P 15 B–R3, but knowledge spreads very fast, and now even those readers who did not know this variation before will not make such a mistake.

But I was not counting on my opponent making a mistake; such tactics are in themselves mistaken. My plans were quite straightforward. I wanted to drive the black knight away from the centre and only then, if circumstances allowed, to begin a pawn-storm, using my extra pawn on the K-side.

All went as planned, except that at the critical moment for Black Antoshin forced the exchange of queens by the brilliant move 18 . . . N–QB4!, and my attack immediately evaporated.

I should, possibly, have found a more comfortable square for my queen than K4, but all the textbooks say that 'the strength of the queen is best demonstrated when it is in the centre of the board', and, as it turned out, it was not easy to break this precept.

One might address two further observations to White. First, if you keep two Q-side pieces, the rook and the knight, in cold storage for a whole twenty moves, then you should be glad that you were able to get an easy draw. And, second, would it not have been better to play 13 B–N5 instead of 13 B×B, so as to pin the black knight on K2, if only temporarily?

1 P–K4 P–K4	8 N×P 0–0	14 Q–B3 N–K2	19 Q×QP
2 N–KB3 N–QB3	9 N–B5 P–Q4	15 Q–K3 N–K3	19 . . . Q×Q+
3 B–N5 P–QR3	10 N×B+ N×N	16 P–KB4 P–KN3	20 P×Q N–K3
4 B–R4 N–B3	11 P–QB3 N–QB4	17 P–KN4 P–Q5	21 N–B3 N×QP
5 0–0 B–K2	12 B–B2 B–B4	18 Q–K4 (*176*)	22 B–K3
6 P–Q4 P×P	13 B×B N×B	18 . . . N–QB4	Draw.
7 P–K5 N–K5			

THE LAZY ROOK

Black: B. Ivkov – Beverwijk 1963, International Tournament

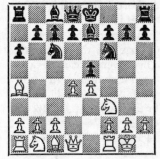

The old story: my hand does not want to move the white rook from KB1 to K1. And not even because often one has later to play the rook back to KB1 (there are many such games in this book), but simply because I am tired of the move R–K1, bored with it; in short, I don't want to play R–K1, and that's the only reason!

I don't want to, and yet I play it. What can I do? It is the strongest move. But sometimes, when I allow myself to think for just a moment about the point of it, I invariably play something different, either on move six or slightly earlier. It is more interesting that way.

Now, in this game I had wanted to try out a new idea: 9 Q–K2 N–B4 10 B×N QP×B 11 R–Q1!, but my shrewd opponent did not give me the chance. I was hoping to try and 'freeze' Black's QB to the spot by a veiled manoeuvre (Q–K2–K4–Q5), but this venture too was foiled.

'What you are saying is interesting, but is the game itself worth anything?' the reader might ask me.

Of course it is not worth much, but all the same I advise you to remember the idea of freezing the bishop.

If the position after Black's seventh move ever occurs in one of your games, try to get an attack going on the black king by using the sharp gambit move P–QB3. Who knows, after 6 P–Q4 P×P 7 P–K5 N–K5 8 P–B3 P×P 9 B–B2 P×P 10 B×P your opponent might not be able to find the best defence, might lose the game and thereby inspire you to look for gambit lines in other outwardly perfectly respectable opening variations!

1 P–K4 P–K4	6 ... P×P	12 Q–Q5 P–QB3	18 Q×Q QR×Q
2 N–KB3 N–QB3	7 P–K5 N–K5	13 Q–B3 P–Q4	19 B×B N×B
3 B–N5 P–QR3	8 N×P 0–0	14 P×Pep B×P	20 QR–Q1
4 B–R4 N–B3	9 Q–K2 N×N	15 B–KB4 B×B	20 ... KR–Q1
5 0–0 B–K2	10 Q×N N–K3	16 Q×B B–K3	Draw agreed.
6 P–Q4 (177)	11 B–N3 N–B4	17 N–B3 Q–N1	

CHAMPION OF MOSCOW

Black: A. Liliental – Moscow 1946, Moscow Championship

The open variation of the Ruy Lopez is the most logical system!

If the pawn has not been defended, why not take it? Nonetheless, it is only a rare bold spirit who includes the defence 5 ... N ×P in his regular opening repertoire. Why?

The essence of the question can be expressed succinctly: an ocean of possibilities.

That would be fine, were it not for the fact that it is an ocean of possibilities for White; all Black is ever left with is a few shallow streams.

As far as the game on this page is concerned, Black could have chosen any risky variation: the fact was that I was a point ahead of Simagin, who had been close on my heels right through the tournament, and only half a point separated me from acquiring the title of 'Champion of Moscow' for the first time in my life. So that Liliental was only threatened with losing half a point, no more.

That year I replaced as champion of Moscow grandmaster Smyslov, who before that had won the title in three consecutive championships. It is hard to believe it, but Smyslov has not played in the Moscow championship for twenty-two years. Was he offended, or grieved? I do not know.

I have had occasion both to win the Moscow championship and to lose it, but still I take part in it from time to time just as before. And last year (1968) I was particularly lucky: I shared first place with world champion Petrosian and sat side by side with him on the throne of Moscow for a whole year.

1 P–K4 P–K4	8 P×P B–K3	14 ... N×N	21 R×R R×R
2 N–KB3 N–QB3	9 P–B3 B–QB4	15 N×N Q–Q2	22 B–B2 N–K1
3 B–N5 P–QR3	10 QN–Q2 0–0	16 P–QR4 B–N5	23 R–K1 N–Q3
4 B–R4 N–B3	11 B–B2 P–B4	17 P–B3 B–KB4	24 P–KN3 R–K1
5 0–0 N×P	12 P×Pep	18 B×B Q×B	25 R×R+ Q×R
6 P–Q4 (*178*)	12 ... N×P/KB3	19 B–K3 Q–Q2	26 Q–Q3
6 ... P–QN4	13 N–N3 B–N3	20 P×P P×P	Draw agreed.
7 B–N3 P–Q4	14 N/N3–Q4		

A USEFUL LESSON

Black: S. Flohr – Moscow 1944, USSR Championship

Having obtained a huge advantage comparatively easily, I suddenly stopped any attacking I was doing and started waiting for the Black pieces to give themselves up.

Whilst I sat there dreaming about this, Flohr rebuilt his ranks and by an energetic attack forced my king to surrender.

However, the symptoms of White's light-headedness appeared as early as the opening, when I missed 18 P–KR4. And the traces of this policy could be seen in the middlegame in the move 23 Q–K3?, instead of 23 Q–Q7!

When the game was over, my opponent said that he had spent a whole month working with Liliental (veterans, too, were theoreticians) preparing for this tournament the variation where the Black bishop goes to KR4, but that 15 B–N5 had escaped him.

The subtlety of 15 B–N5 is hidden in the variation 15 ... Q–Q2 16 B–K3 N–K3 17 B×P+ K×B 18 N–N5+ N×N 19 Q×B+ K–N1 20 B×N, retaining an extra pawn with the better piece position. A mating attack is threatened: R–K3–KR3 and Q–R8+.

The intricate bishop manoeuvre, ... B–K3–N5–KR4 is not at all bad, but ... B–R4 should be delayed more.

In the Fischer-Larsen game from the Santa Monica tournament (1966) 14 ... R–K1 was tried, and in a complex tussle Black won.

My loss to Flohr served as a lesson to me for the future, and since then I now never wait for my opponent to show the white flag himself, of his own free will.

1 P–K4 P–K4	11 B–B2 B–B4	20 P–KN3 P–KB4	28 P–KR3 P–R3
2 N–KB3 N–QB3	12 N–N3 B–KN5	21 Q–K6+ K–R1	29 R–Q1 Q–K7
3 B–N5 P–QR3	13 N×B N×N	22 QR–Q1 R–B3	30 P–N5 R–K3
4 B–R4 N–B3	14 R–K1 B–R4	23 Q–K3 P–B5	31 Q×Q P×Q
5 0–0 N×P	15 B–N5 (*179*)	24 Q–K4	32 R–K1 N–B5
6 P–Q4 P–QN4	15 ... B×N	24 ... R/1–KB1	33 R–R4 P–KR4
7 B–N3 P–Q4	16 Q×B Q×B	25 R–Q5 Q–R3	34 P–N6 R–K4
8 P×P B–K3	17 Q×QP N–Q2	26 P–KN4 P–B6	35 P–B3 R–N4+
9 P–B3 B–QB4	18 Q×N/6 N×P	27 R–R5 Q–Q7	White resigns.
10 QN–Q2 0–0	19 Q–K4 N–N3		

THE BASE OF THE PAWN CHAIN

Black: V. Makogonov – Moscow 1944, USSR Championship

180B

It is annoying that the rules of chess do not allow a pawn to take either horizontally or backwards, but only forwards. . . .

This psychological tuning is ideal for attacking purposes, but what about for defence?

The natural result is that when pawns are drawing up in ranks they always have a quiet look around to see if there is any piece support; and they feel most comfortable when they can be deployed in a long chain, so that each pawn is defended from behind.

Each? But who defends the last one? As a rule, no one defends it, although the fate of not one, but two pawns usually rests on its shoulders. Look, for example, at the black pawn on QB3.

There is some excuse for this: usually the pawn which is given the role of being the base is right in the rear and will not be threatened in the middlegame.

This may be, but there are pieces which delight in making deep raids around the back of the opponent's position, and was not 22 R–R6 made with one aim in mind, to capture Black's QBP?

It is easily said, but not so easily done! White had first to loosen Black's pawn on KN3, and then work a combination with the quiet move B–K3 and the intriguing R–KR3.

1 P–K4 P–K4	13 N–B1 R–Q1	25 B–Q3 Q–Q2	36 R×B R–R8+
2 N–KB3 N–QB3	14 N–K3 B–R4	26 R/6–R1 R–R1	37 K–R2 N–B5
3 B–N5 P–QR3	15 N–B5 N–K3	27 Q–B3 P–QB3	38 Q–R6+
4 B–R4 N–B3	16 P–QR4 B–B4	28 P–R4 R–R2	38 . . . Q–KR2
5 0–0 N×P	17 P–QN4 B–QN3	29 P–R5 R/1–R1	39 R–R3 *(180)*
6 P–Q4 P–QN4	18 P×P P×P	30 R×R R×R	39 . . . Q×Q
7 B–N3 P–Q4	19 Q–Q3 B×N	31 Q–N4 Q–K2	40 R×Q+ K–N2
8 P×P B–K3	20 Q×B N–K2	32 P×P RP×P	41 R×P P–Q5
9 P–B3 B–K2	21 N×N Q×N	33 B×KNP P×B	42 P×P R–QN8
10 QN–Q2 N–B4	22 R–R6 0–0	34 Q×P+ K–R1	43 P–N3 N–Q6
11 B–B2 B–N5	23 Q–R3 P–N3	35 B–K3 B×B	Draw agreed.
12 R–K1 Q–Q2	24 B–R6 KR–K1		

EIGHT IS HALF OF SIXTEEN

Black: V. Alatortsev – Leningrad 1947, USSR Championship

181B

'Ration each piece to one move in the opening!'

We all know this commandment and try to bring all our pieces into play as quickly as possible.

But the candidate of pedagogy, Alatortsev, made eight of the first sixteen moves with the black cavalry.

How can that be? Are the general laws of strategy really not compulsory for everyone?

As soon as the opportunity presented itself, I rushed forward: I sacrificed a pawn and built up a rapid attack against Black's king which had got bogged down in the centre.

Following my preliminary calculations, Black, in what was a fortunate variation for him, was nonetheless left a piece down. What more could I have wished for?

Alas, I failed to win the ending with my extra piece.

I now recall with sadness those far-off days and think: today I would probably win that position, but on the other hand perhaps I am no longer capable of conducting such a sharp attack. . . .

And anyway, was I right to sacrifice a pawn and infiltrate with my queen to K5? Did I not rush things?

I leave it to my readers to answer this question.

1 P–K4 P–K4	13 P×P P×P	25 N–R4 (181)	36 N–K6 P–N5
2 N–KB3 N–QB3	14 Q–Q3 P–QB3	25 . . . Q–N1	37 K–B1 K–B7
3 B–N5 P–QR3	15 N–Q4 N×N	26 Q×Q R×Q	38 K–K2 K×P
4 B–R4 N–B3	16 P×N N–B5	27 R×B R–QR1	39 N–B5 K–N8
5 0–0 N×P	17 R×R Q×R	28 N–N6+ K×R	40 P–B4 P×Pep+
6 P–Q4 P–QN4	18 N–B3 P–N3	29 N×R K–B4	41 P×P B–B3
7 B–N3 P–Q4	19 Q–N3 Q–B1	30 B–R6 P–N4	42 K–K3 P–B6
8 P×P B–K3	20 B–Q3 B–N5	31 P–R4 P–B3	43 K–Q3 P–B7
9 P–B3 N–B4	21 B×N NP×B	32 P×P P×P	44 N–N3 K–N7
10 B–B2 B–N5	22 P–K6 B×P	33 B–N7 K–K5	45 N–B1 B–K2
11 R–K1 N–K3	23 Q–K5 K–Q2	34 N–B7 K–Q6	46 N–K2 B–N5
12 P–QR4 N–R4	24 B–B4 R–K1	35 B–R6 B–K2	Draw agreed.

THE MEXICAN NIKITIN

Black: A. Nikitin – Tiflis 1959, USSR Championship

The Mexican, Carlos Torre, played at the 1925 Moscow Tournament that immortal game where he sacrificed his queen against Dr. Emanuel Lasker.

The Moscow master, Nikitin, had a less well-known opponent, but the Mexican's achievement would not give him any peace.

In itself the combination called 'the mill' is one of the most dangerous, and it is not so much difficult to fight against it, as simply useless. But Nikitin's problem was that there was no 'mill'!

I remember that Nikitin thought for a long time over 28 ... R–KN1, and I thought for a long time over my reply.

But as soon as the white knight took the QP, the young master could not contain himself and in a flash executed the 'mill' à la Carlos Torre. But, as the reader already knows, it was non-existent.

Having thought for one or two seconds I took the black queen with my knight. Nikitin shuddered, looked at the board, realised everything himself and held out his hand to congratulate me on my victory.

Black's idea was absolutely right, but only the idea! Here is the main variation: 28 ... R–KN1 29 N×QP B–K5 30 N×Q R×P+ 31 K–R1 R×BP+ 32 K–N1 R–N7++ 33 K–R1 R–N8 mate!

Unfortunately the light-squared bishop did not have time to go into hiding on QR1, and with 32 N×B White liquidates the most dangerous piece.

It is a pity. Even though I won the game thanks to this mistake, it is a pity! It is always a pity if some tiny detail destroys the fruits of work that a lot of time has gone into....

1 P–K4 P–K4	10 Q–K2 N–B4	18 B–N5 R–Q2	25 ... K–R1
2 N–KB3 N–QB3	11 N–Q4 N×N	19 QR–B1 B–Q5	26 P–N4 Q–KB3
3 B–N5 P–QR3	12 P×N N×B	20 Q–N3 B–KB4	27 R–Q2 B–KB4
4 B–R4 N–B3	13 P×N 0–0	21 B–B6 B–N3	28 Q–Q1 R–KN1
5 0–0 N×P	14 N–B3 P–QB4	22 Q–N4 P×B	29 N×QP B–K5
6 P–Q4 P–QN4	15 P×P B×P	23 Q×R R–Q1	(182)
7 B–N3 P–Q4	16 B–B4 Q–N3	24 Q–N4 P×P	30 N×Q
8 P×P B–K3	17 Q–Q3 QR–Q1	25 R/B1–Q1	Black resigns.
9 P–B3 B–K2			

THE CHESS ART OF INDIA

Black: G. Katragadda – Liverpool 1952, International Studen Tournament

Just as chess itself is infinite, so are the number of legends about its origins.

Only one detail always remains un-changed and is passed on from mouth to mouth. That is the fact that the country where in ancient times this wise game of the East grew up is always said to be India.

At the first International Student Tourna-ment, in 1952, I was lucky enough to make the acquaintance of a talented and fascin-ating youth from India.

Unfortunately I have not once come across his name in chess magazine: since then.

Does he no longer like chess, or has he found a greater passion?

I hope this book will fall into his hands and that he will then respond to the call. I cannot for the world believe that love for chess can go cold

There appeared abroad not so long ago a monograph on the life and work of the great Indian player, and four-times English champion grandmaster Sultan-Khan, who scored successes against Flohr, Menchik, Capablanca, Euwe and Tartakover.

I have not yet seen the book and I do not know who the author is. But could it be Katragadda, the Indian student who was my opponent long ago?

1 P–K4 P–K4	11 RP×N B–K2	20 R/1–Q1 R×R	30 Q×R Q–K3
2 N–KB3 N–QB3	12 P–B4 NP×P	21 R×R Q–K1	31 N–K3 Q–QB3
3 B–N5 P–QR3	13 P×P P–Q5	22 Q–Q2 P–R3	32 P–B5 Q–N4
4 B–R4 N–B3	14 B–K3 B–QB4	23 P–R3 Q–K2	33 K–B2 Q–R4
5 0–0 N×P	(183)	24 P–B4 P–QR4	34 P–KB6 B–K3
6 P–Q4 P–QN4	15 N–B3 Q–B1	25 P–QB5 P–R5	35 K–B3 P–R6
7 B–N3 P–Q4	16 N×P B×N	26 Q–N4 B–N6	36 Q–Q8+ K–R2
8 P×P B–K3	17 B×B N×B	27 N–N3 R–Q1	37 Q–KB8 NP×P
9 Q–K2 N–B4	18 R×N 0–0	28 N–B5 Q–K1	38 KP×P
10 R–Q1 N×B	19 N–K4 R–Q1	29 Q–Q2 R×R	Black resigns.

A REHEARSAL IN THE INTERVAL

White: P. Keres – Moscow 1946, Training Game

184B

This was my first encounter with this celebrated player and I was very excited on that
autumn evening of long ago.

The national team had gathered for the
opening of the international match between
the USSR and the USA, but our guests had
been held up somewhere on the way and it
was decided to have a training session. It
fell to me to play Black against Paul Petro-
vich Keres.

That could only mean, of course, 1 ...
P–K4!, when my opponent would reply with the King's Gambit. For if
play was sharp I had no fear even of grandmasters in those days.

When Keres chose the Ruy Lopez, I decided to play the Open Variation
and the system of the Englishman, Dilworth. On my work desk there lay
an article ready for printing in *Shakhmaty v SSSR* (*Chess in the USSR*)
about this very variation, and I was armed to the teeth with all the moves,
both my own and my opponent's.

But I did not have the chance to play this variation either: Keres used
his own attacking line – 9 Q–K2!, 10 P–B4.

I remembered most of all the manoeuvre ... Q–Q4–K4–KR1–KR6.
I noted this idea and subsequently used it in a game with the Uzbek
master Mukhin.

I should add finally that the day before the start of my match with
Botvinnik I played another training game with Keres and I was completely routed in a very efficient manner.

1 P–K4 P–K4	11 B–R4 B–Q2	21 Q–R5 + (*184*)	30 N–K4 B–R5
2 N–KB3 N–QB3	12 P–K6 P×P	21 ... R–N3	31 R/2–B1 P–Q6
3 B–N5 P–QR3	13 B×N B×B	22 Q×P N×P	32 Q–Q2 R–N5
4 B–R4 N–B3	14 N–K5 B–N2	23 B×N R×P+	33 R–B2 B×R
5 0–0 N×P	15 Q–R5 + P–N3	24 K×R Q×B	34 Q×B Q×BP+
6 P–Q4 P–QN4	16 N×NP N–B3	25 Q–N6 + K–Q2	35 Q×Q B×N
7 B–N3 P–Q4	17 Q–R3 R–KN1	26 N–Q2 Q–R1	36 Q×B R×Q
8 P×P B–K3	18 N–K5 P–Q5	27 K–R1 R–KN1	37 R–Q1 R–K7
9 Q–K2 B–K2	19 P–B3 Q–Q4	28 Q–B2 Q–R6	White resigns.
10 P–B4 NP×P	20 B–B4 N–Q2	29 R–B2 B–Q4	

VARIATIONS UNDER A CLOUD

Black: V. Korchnoi – Leningrad 1962, USSR Team Championship

Usually White's QN in the Ruy Lopez goes to Q2 and then immediately to its best position, so as not to hinder the development of the QB. But if you have noticed, this is not altogether the case in the open variation.

The knight, once it is at Q2, waits for a certain time. But its fate is well-known: N–Q2–QN3, and then N–Q4. Why so much fuss then?

Only so that it can be exchanged for Black's knight on QB3 or his bishop on K3? If that is the case, can we not save a move?

The KN, which has been standing at KB3 since the second move of the game, is placed much closer to the square Q4. Can we not revise our plan and entrust the QN's role to the KN? That is, let each knight do what it is easier for it to do.

This was probably the origin of the idea of this opening variation where White delays the development of his QN and at the first opportunity transfers his KN to Q4. The moves B–B2 and Q–K2 suit this aim perfectly too: White waits to see how the opposition will react and then chooses a more concrete and positive plan.

White wants to find out what his opponent will try and do, in particular with his knight on K5. Will he defend the knight directly by . . . P–KB4, or . . . B–KB4, or indirectly by . . . B–KN5, also bringing pressure to bear from Black's QN on the white KP? Or perhaps the knight will just leave the centre?

It will depend on Black's actions what decision White takes. Whether to bring the KR to Q1 and centre his fire on the unattached black QP, or whether to realize the basic threat already referred to: N–Q4, making the threat of the pawn advance P–KB4–5–6! quite real.

I remember in my time having spent much energy on researching all the attacking possibilities of B–B2 combined with an early Q–K2. And no matter how much I studied this variation, I could not come to any categorical conclusions.

There are probably some curious people amongst the readers who would like to see an interesting variation.

Well, perhaps the most hectic variation arises after 11 . . . P–B4. If then 12 P × Pep, Black can take the pawn with his rook: 12 . . . R × P, and in answer to 13 N–N5 play, not 13 . . . B–KB4 (which would lose a pawn without the slightest compensation after 14 N × N: 14 . . . P × N 15 N–Q2 P–K6 16 B–N3 +) but the more subtle 13 . . . B–QB4, with extremely interesting complications.

The main variation is as follows: 14 N×N P×N 15 B×P B–B5
16 Q–R5 B×R 17 B×P+ K–B1 18 Q×B+ N–K2 19 B–N5 Q–Q8
20 N–Q2 Q×R 21 N×B.

The position after 21 N×B is difficult to assess; it needs a lot of thought.
White has a clear advantage: two strong bishops against the two passive
black rooks! In addition White has two extra pawns on the K-side,
whilst the black king is exposed and short of defenders.

But would any reader undertake to predict the fate of this game, given
that the players are of equal strength?

What is Black's best reply on move 11? One has to consult books on
opening theory in such cases. Of recent encounters one might cite Tal-
Keres, where Black replied 11 . . . Q–Q2!.

The fashion of 1967–70 has been 11 . . . Q–Q2.

Will the fashion last long? Like any fashion, until the next innovation.

When the reader finishes analysing this game and turns to the next page,
the question may interest him as to which of these two similar games was
played earlier: both were in 1962, both in Leningrad, and, I can also add,
both in the same week. In fact, first Korchnoi played 11 . . . N–B4, and
literally a day later it was 11 . . . P–B4. A direct result of home preparation.

I might also add that at one time theoreticians took a great interest in
the variation 10 P–QR4 P–N5 11 N–Q4 N×KP 12 P–KB4 B–N5
13 Q–B2 P–QB4! (13 . . . N–N3? 14 P–B5 N–K4 15 B–KB4!) 14 P×N
P×N with complex play. Also worth considering is 11 . . . N×N!
12 P×N P–QB4 13 P–B3 N–N4 14 P–B4 P–B5!

1 P–K4 P–K4	8 P×P B–K3	14 P×N N–N2	20 Q×P B×B
2 N–KB3 N–QB3	9 P–B3 B–K2	15 N–B3 B–KB4	21 Q×N QR–B1
3 B–N5 P–QR3	10 B–B2 0–0	16 B–N5 B/2×B	22 Q–Q4 R–B5
4 B–R4 N–B3	11 Q–K2 (185)	17 N×B P–B4	23 Q–Q2 B–B4
5 0–0 N×P	11 . . . N–B4	18 P–B4 P×P	24 P–QN3
6 P–Q4 P–QN4	12 N–Q4 Q–Q2	19 Q–Q2 N–B4	Draw agreed.
7 B–N3 P–Q4	13 N–Q2 N×N		

A CUNNING CHECK

Black: K. Abrabdkhmanov – Vilnyus 1961, 'Dinamo' Championship

One of those rare games where not only was *I* not very afraid of *my* opponent, but where my opponent was not at all afraid of me either!

I would go even further, for from the 20th move onwards I had to withstand a flurry of attacks. First the black bishop went to K5 and threatened my knight on KB3; then when the knight moved away, the black queen suddenly popped up, as if out of the ground, on KN4, training its sights on my KNP. When I had, with difficulty, repelled this threat and tried to go onto the offensive with P–K6, my talented adversary offered me a rook sacrifice!

But when the white rook, completely true to Nimzowitsch, observed the principle of centralization and ensconced itself on Q1, Black devised an extremely subtle combination involving the sacrifice of his queen.

If I took the queen with my rook, after 27 ... R–R8 + 28 R–Q1 R × R + White would be mated; but if I left my rook where it was, Black could take it with his queen and the result again would not be in White's favour. And moving the rook would be bad, because the QNP would fall. Very finely set up threats!

These feats by the Black pieces would have sufficed even for two games. But ... the prosaic 27 N–B5 + destroyed all Black's plans. And yet my opponent deserves praise. Bravo!

1 P–K4 P–K4	14 B–N5 B–K2	25 R–Q1 Q–K6 +	37 P–R4 K–Q3
2 N–KB3 N–QB3	15 B × B N × B	26 K–R1 Q–Q7	38 R–B5 B–Q4
3 B–N5 P–QR3	16 Q–K3 K–N2	27 N–B5 + B × N	39 P–N4 K–K3
4 B–R4 N–B3	17 P–QR4 N–B4	28 R × Q R–R8 +	40 R–B1 B–B5
5 0–0 N × P	18 B × N B × B	29 Q–N1 R × Q +	41 P × P P × P
6 P–Q4 P–QN4	19 P × P P × P	30 K × R B × P	42 R–KN1 P–B3
7 B–N3 P–Q4	20 Q–B5 R × R	31 P–QN4 K–B3	43 R–N7 K–B4
8 P × P B–K3	21 R × R B–K5	32 K–B2 P–R4	44 R–KR7 K–N3
9 P–B3 B–K2	22 N–Q4 Q–N4	33 K–K3 K–K4	45 R–QB7 B–Q4
10 B–B2 0–0	23 P–B3 Q–Q6	34 R–R2 P–Q5 +	46 K–B4 K–R3
11 Q–K2 B–QB4	24 P–K6 R–QR1	35 P × P + K–Q4	47 R–Q7
12 QN–Q2 N × N	*(186)*	36 R–QB2 P–QB3	Black resigns.
13 B × N P–N3			

A SABRE-DANCE

Black: V. Korchnoi – Leningrad 1962, Moscow v Leningrad

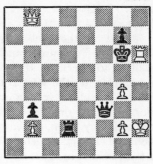

The concluding ten half-moves, five by White and five by Black, did the rounds in almost all the world's chess press. Nonetheless, the main content of the game was not in those moves!

The opening was played at lightning speed; in particular Korchnoi played his 12th move, which was the direct result of home preparation, quickly. Though even today I cannot say why this move so fascinated the Leningrader. 13 . . . B–B4 was also played without hesitation.

In any event, I am satisfied with my strategy.

First White reduced the number of fighting units, and then in the major-piece ending he began worrying his opponent on the Q-side, in an attempt to create a pawn weakness which might distract him there.

Such an object of attack emerged in the form of Black's isolated pawn on QN6, which Black had continually to keep within his field of vision. This allowed me to prepare a breakthrough with the major pieces.

34 P–N4 fully secured White against any counter-checks and he was ready to launch the decisive offensive. The finale requires no elucidating. The variation most to my liking is 39 . . . K × R   40 Q–KR8 + K–N3   41 Q–R5 + K–B3   42 P–N5 + !

1 P–K4 P–K4	11 Q–K2 P–B4	21 N × N R × N	31 Q–N5 R–Q2
2 N–KB3 N–QB3	12 P × Pep B × P	22 KR–K1 R–Q4	32 P–B3 P–R3
3 B–N5 P–QR3	13 QN–Q2 B–B4	23 QR–Q1 P–B4	33 Q–K3 R–Q1
4 B–R4 N–B3	14 N × N B × N	24 P–R4 R–Q1	34 P–N4 K–R1
5 0–0 N × P	15 B × B P × B	25 R × R Q × R	35 Q–N6 R–Q7
6 P–Q4 P–QN4	16 Q × KP Q–Q2	26 P × P P × P	36 Q–N8 + K–R2
7 B–N3 P–Q4	17 B–B4 QR–K1	27 Q–K2 P–N5	37 R–K8 Q × P
8 P × P B–K3	18 Q–B2 B–R5	28 P × P P × P	38 R–R8 + K–N3
9 P–B3 B–K2	19 B–N3 B × B	29 Q–N4 P–N6	39 R × P + (187)
10 B–B2 0–0	20 RP × B N–K4	30 K–R2 Q–B2	Black resigns.

A QUEEN? OR A KNIGHT WITH CHECK?

White: A. Cherepkov – Moscow 1961, USSR Championship

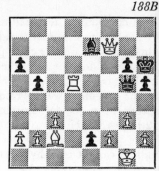

188B

29 ... P–K6 took a whole fifteen minutes for me to think out!

The idea of the combination with the rook sacrifice had matured much earlier, but I wanted to check all the details one more time. This, by the way, is the basic reason for my constantly getting into time-trouble. For although double checking never did anybody any harm, one must be reasonable about it. How many delightful combinations I have ruined in my many years of tournament practice only because of the fact that I noticed a counter-combination for my opponent, a combination which my opponent was not even thinking about and (which was more often the case) which just was not there at all, either on the board, or in his thoughts. The excesses of fantasy.

Precisely one such incident occurred in my game with Cherepkov.

I fancied that my opponent was enticing the black KP on to queen, so I ... promoted the pawn to a knight. But there was no need: the queen is a stronger piece and, as a rule, more useful. Why then did I do that? Time-trouble? Yes, but really I deceived myself.

Just as I was ready to say out loud 'P–K8, queen, check!', I suddenly noticed a most cunning trap: 34 ... P–K8 = Q+ 35 K–N2 Q–B3 36 R×RP+ P×R 37 Q–R7+ K–N4 38 P–KR4+ K–N5 39 Q–N8+. Black could not play his queen to N5 (35 ... Q–N5) because of the simple 36 P–KR3! and the queen is lost since she cannot leave her KN3 unprotected.

The queen, of course, is lost, but not for nothing: after 36 ... Q×RP+!! 37 K×Q Q–KR8+ the king is nicely mated.

Does this mean this is what Black failed to see? We cannot know, since no-one writes down the players' thoughts during the game. But afterwards. ... What is there we do not say afterwards! But the reader must believe the author on the odd occasion.

So I shall rely on your trust in me and continue the story.

The variation 35 ... Q–N5! 36 P–KR3? Q×RP+! I saw quite clearly, but what was I to do if White did not play 36 P–KR3 and chose a move directly attacking the black king? What then? And where was I to get the time for an accurate assessment of 36 R–Q8? Is there a defence against perpetual check: 36 ... B×R 37 Q–B8+ K–R2 38 Q–B7+?

There is no defence, but I overlooked the variation 36 ... Q–R6+ 37 K×Q Q–KB8 mate!

This is why time-trouble is terrible for the chess-player! Not for those bad moves, which he makes willy-nilly, but for the good ones that he does not have time to find.

And how much more annoying a mistake is when subsequent analysis reveals not one, but several, paths to victory, and when you satisfy yourself again that you were almost on the right path, but only almost!

The idea of promoting the pawn to a knight was not a bad one, but nothing would have come of realising the idea immediately: on 35 ... P–K8=N+ there is the reply 36 K–R3.

If we allow that it was impossible for White to save the game after the shock ... P–K7, then the decisive mistake must be reckoned to be the white rook move: 30 R–Q5; but which of you will believe this even now? ...

But am I being fair towards the author of the book? I have criticized all his decisions and torn them to shreds, but he did go on and win the game!

That, however, was not any of his doing, but Cherepkov's. The Leningrad master also failed to see the variations with the queen sacrifice on KR6 and was confident of victory. And since his flag too was fluttering over the last millimetres, he had only one thought in his mind: however things develop to sacrifice the rook on KR5, when the black king would be exposed and a mating variation would appear of its own accord.

When I promoted the pawn to a knight, Cherepkov was unabashed and in a flash executed his intended mating blow 39 R×RP+ K×R 40 Q–R7+ K–N5 41 Q×P+ K–B6 42 Q–B5 mate! And only when the moment came to give check with the queen on KN6 did my opponent notice with surprise that, firstly, the black king could hide on KN7, and secondly, Black himself can give check by ... B–N4.

It would be interesting to know if the reader believes me.

1 P–K4 P–K4	13 N×N P×N	24 Q–B7 R–K1	34 ... Q–B8+
2 N–KB3 N–QB3	14 B–KB4 Q–B3	25 R–Q7 B–B3	35 K–N2 Q–B8+
3 B–N5 P–QR3	15 QR–Q1 0–0	26 B–Q4 Q–R3	36 K–B3
4 B–R4 N–B3	16 B×QBP	27 B–K3 Q–B3	36 ... P–K8=N+
5 0–0 N×P	16 ... QR–K1	28 B–N5 Q×B	37 K–K3 N×B+
6 P–Q4 P–QN4	17 B–KB4 B–K2	29 Q×B P–K6	38 K–Q2 N–N5
7 B–N3 P–Q4	18 B–K3 R–Q1	30 R–Q5 P–K7	39 R×RP+
8 N×P N×N	19 R–Q4 R×R	31 Q×R+ K–R2	39 ... K×R
9 P×N B–N2	20 B×R Q–N4	32 B–B2+ P–N3	40 Q–R7+ K–N5
10 P–QB3 B–B4	21 Q–Q7 B–R1	33 Q×BP+	41 P×N B×P+
11 Q–N4 Q–K2	22 B–K3 Q–B3	33 ... K–R3	White resigns.
12 N–Q2 Q×P	23 R–Q1 P–KR4	34 P–KN3 (*188*)	

THE PASSED PAWN

Black: M. Tal – Moscow 1966, the Club of 'Izvestia'

189B

The ex-world champion Tal not only loves chess but, what is no less important, loves the chess spectator. Therefore he is prepared to take part in any contest which might give the slightest pleasure to his fans.

I once had the idea of playing a game where the players spoke their thoughts out loud – I invited Tal, and there he was! On another occasion I agreed to a proposal from our chess federation to play an experimental match on a Hungarian electronic board – then, lo and behold, my opponent is Tal, who has appeared out of the blue. Then when the lightning championship of Moscow was on, the Rigan, Tal, flew in for the tournament at lightning speed – it did not even enter his head that he might not be allowed to play.

It goes without saying that when the sports editor of *Izvestia* suggested I play a two-day match of four games with one of the grandmasters, I named Tal without hesitation. And he agreed immediately.

At the end of each game we commented on it briefly for the public. The first three games ended in draws, the fourth was won by my Rigan guest.

In the position here where a draw was agreed on, White might have hoped for a win: he would only have to exchange queens and then promote a passed pawn. But firstly, Black would not allow the exchange of queens, and secondly, it is not quite that easy to set up a passed pawn, Black does still have the two bishops.

1 P–K4 P–K4	8 N–B1 N–Q2	15 R–K1 B–N2	21 ... B×P
2 N–KB3 N–QB3	9 N–N3 N–N4	16 P–QR4 P–QN4	22 B×N R×R+
3 B–N5 P–QR3	10 B–B2 P–Q4	17 P×P P×P	23 N×R P×B
4 B–R4 N–B3	11 P×P Q×P	18 R×R R×R	24 N–K4 B–R4
5 P–Q3 P–Q3	12 P–N4 N–K3	19 Q–B2 R–R8	25 Q×NP B–N3
6 P–B3 B–K2	13 B–N3 Q–Q2	20 B–R2 N–B5	26 N–B3
7 QN–Q2 0–0	14 0–0 P–QN3	21 Q–N3 (*189*)	Draw.

FOR ENDGAME LOVERS

Black: G. Ravinsky – Moscow 1947, Moscow Championship

190W

The magical QN3–KB7 diagonal would not allow the white bishop to pass by the bewitching QN3 square! And that at a time when the black king was successfully castled and the formerly weak KBP had migrated to the ranks of the strong!

Can B–N3 therefore be considered a mistake? To some extent, yes, but mistakes of that sort rarely in themselves lead to defeat; they have a different peculiarity: by the law of chain reaction they call other minor mistakes to life.

For instance, why did I have to spend three moves on the manoeuvre P–KR3, N–KR2 and P–KB4? Surely not merely for the sake of reviving in my soul memories of the King's Gambit I did not play? Or did this inoffensive plan serve as a justification for the manoeuvre B–N3?

My opponent defended extremely skilfully and if it had not been for the eternal Q4 square being available to the white knight, he would have had quite good chances of invading White's camp via the Q-file.

1 P–K4 P–K4	19 B–N5 Q–K3	34 ... N/N4–B2	51 P–B5 R–KB2
2 N–KB3 N–QB3	20 Q–B3 N–Q2	35 Q–N3 K–R2	(190)
3 B–N5 P–QR3	21 QR–Q1 P–B3	36 P–R4 P×P	52 K–R2 R–B8
4 B–R4 N–B3	22 B–B4 N–B3	37 B×P R/1–Q1	53 Q–K2 Q×Q
5 P–Q3 P–Q3	23 Q–K3 N/3–K4	38 B–B2 N–Q6	54 R×Q R–B5
6 P–B3 P–KN3	24 N–K2 Q–K2	39 B×N P×B	55 R–QB2 R×NP
7 QN–Q2 B–N2	25 P–QN4	40 Q×QP B×P	56 P–B6 R–N1
8 N–B1 0–0	25 ... KR–K1	41 Q–N3 N–K4	57 K–N3 K–N2
9 N–N3 P–QN4	26 R–Q4 N–B1	42 R–K2 B–B3	58 K–B3 K–B3
10 B–N3 N–QR4	27 B–R6 B×B	43 N/2–B3 B×N	59 K–N4 K–K3
11 B–B2 P–B4	28 Q×B N–K3	44 N×B R–Q8	60 P–B7 R–QB1
12 0–0 Q–B2	29 R–Q2 N–N4	45 R/2–K1 R×R	61 R–B6+ K–Q2
13 P–KR3 P–Q4	30 Q–R4 QR–Q1	46 R×R R–K1	62 R×RP R×P
14 N–R2 P×P	31 N–Q4 K–N2	47 N×N P×N	63 K–Q5 P–K5
15 P×P P–B5	32 R/2–B2 R–Q3	48 R–K4 Q–Q3	64 R–Q6+ K–K1
16 P–B4 P×P	33 Q–B4 P–KR4	49 Q–K1 R–K2	65 K×P
17 B×P Q–N3+	34 P–KR4	50 P–B4 Q–Q6	Draw agreed.
18 K–R1 B–N2			

THE BOOMERANG TRAP

Black: L. Morgulis – Kiev 1938, Tournament of Adults and Schoolboys

191W

Black's attack grew stronger with every move.

The critical moment came after 26 ... P–N5! As the variation 27 P×P P×P 28 N×P R×P 29 N×P R×QNP 30 R–Q4 B–B5 31 N–Q3 B×N 32 R/1×B R/4–B7 33 R–KN4 R–B8+ was not to my liking, I was forced to go 27 N–R4.

Here Black could have retreated his rook to B2, retaining the better chances: 27 ... R–B2 28 P–B3 P×BP 29 N×P R–N2, but with both of us in severe time-trouble, he was tempted by the deceptive sacrifice of the rook for the knight and overlooked 32 R–Q4.

The preliminaries to all these events were as follows:

I read in some ancient manual that 5 ... P–QN4 and 6 ... P–Q4 was not good for Black, and I immediately decided to 'trap' my friend Morgulis in this variation.

And to be sure, my opponent pondered for a long time; but there was nothing he could do: he had to reconcile himself to the loss of his KNP.

And then the author of this whole enterprise began to 'creep into time-trouble'. What could I do?

Surely I could not take the KNP with my queen and open the KN-file for my opponent to attack along!

And so the end result was that I was the one who was caught in the net. A boomerang trap!

1 P–K4 N–QB3	13 Q–K4 R–Q1	25 P–QR3 P–QR4	37 K–Q3 K–Q3
2 N–KB3 P–K4	14 N–B3 P–QB3	26 P–B3 P–N5	38 K–B3 P–R4
3 B–N5 P–QR3	15 B×N P×B	27 N–R4 R–B3	39 K–N4 P–R5
4 B–R4 N–B3	16 Q–KB4 0–0	28 P–B3 P×RP	40 R–B3 B–B3
5 P–Q3 P–QN4	17 Q×Q B×Q	29 P–QN3 R×N	41 K–R5 P–N4
6 B–N3 P–Q4	18 B–N5 R–B1	30 P×R R–B5	42 K–N6 B–Q2
7 P×P N×P	19 QR–Q1	31 R–R1 R×RP	43 R–B7 P–B3
8 0–0 B–K2	19 ... B–QN5	32 R–Q4 R×R	44 R–R7 B–K1
9 R–K1 Q–Q3	20 R–Q3 R–B5	33 P×R B–Q2	45 R–R8 B–Q2
10 P–Q4 P×P	21 R/1–Q1 P–R3	34 R×P P–R5	46 R–Q8 K–K2
11 N×P N×N	22 B–K3 R/1–B1	35 K–B2 K–B1	47 K–B7
12 Q×N B–K3	23 B–Q4 B–QB4	36 K–K3 K–K2	Black resigns.
(191)	24 B×B R/1×B		

RED-HEADED HANAN

Black: H. Muchnik – Kiev 1938, Tournament of Adults and Schoolboys

192B

The Doctor of Technical Sciences, Master of Sport, H. L. Muchnik, was in that distant year quite simply a pupil in one of the schools of Kiev, and at our chess club he was called even more simply: red-headed Hanan.

But this competitively-minded player was not to be trifled with! He had a keen eye and a vigilant and penetrating brain.

Who, tell me, has not suffered from his mating attacks at the chess board and his weighty punches when it came to settling relationships outside the classroom!

So to calculate on his blundering away his queen would have been extremely naive, and I did not do so. But my secret plan was justified: having spotted the threat 24 N×B+ and 25 Q×Q, Muchnik considered his role in defence as over and no longer pondered over the undercurrent running through White's moves.

Hence his blunder 28 ... P–N4? can to some extent be considered my psychological victory ... possibly the first of my life.

What kind of tournament was it? Six of the strongest Kiev candidate masters played each of six schoolboy champions. I was fortunate enough to win, whilst at the same time I exceeded the norm for the first category by two points.

1 P–K4 P–K4	12 N×N P×N	23 Q–N2 (*192*)	32 P–KR4
2 N–KB3 N–QB3	13 N–K2 N–R4	23 ... K–N2	32 ... B–K6+
3 B–N5 P–QR3	14 0–0 0–0	24 QR–B1 QR–B1	33 K–N2 R–KB3
4 B–R4 N–B3	15 P–B4 P–KB4	25 P–N3 P–QN4	34 K–R3 P–QR4
5 P–Q3 P–Q3	16 P×P Q×P	26 R–QB2 B–K2	35 R–KN2 R–R3
6 P–B4 B–Q2	17 P–KR3 Q–Q2	27 Q–B3 R–QB3	36 P–N5 P×P
7 N–B3 P–KN3	18 P–KN4 N–B3	28 P–B5 P–N4	37 P×P P–R5
8 B–KN5 B–N2	19 B×N B×B	29 N×NP Q×Q	38 P–B6+ K–B1
9 Q–Q2 P–R3	20 N–N3 P–Q4	30 N×Q B–N4	39 P–N6
10 B–R4 N–Q5	21 P×P Q×QP	31 N–K5 R–QB2	Black resigns.
11 B×B+ Q×B	22 N–K4 P–B4		

THE DUEL OF VETERANS

Black: A. Bannik – Kiev 1938, Tournament of Adults and School-boys

I first took part in a serious chess competition one year before the game given on this page was played. What's more, it was the final of the mass schoolboys' tournament in which several second category players were taking part and even two first category players!

Even now I cannot explain how I managed to win a game with Black from the veteran second-category player Anatoly Bannik. By sharing 7th–9th places with him and Mark Usachy (nowadays a master), I was accepted into the clan of players of the third category, which absolutely delighted me.

I might be so bold, then, as to call this second encounter with Bannik the duel of veterans. I ought not to have taken the rook (26 B ×R): after 26 QR–Q1 White has the better endgame. But at that time the author's thoughts were guided by completely different evaluative criteria, and neither I nor you should blame him for that. In the endgame the black knight demonstrated its superiority over the bishop.

1 P–K4 P–K4	16 R–B1 B–B3	29 B ×P R–N1	44 K–Q2 N–Q2
2 N–KB3 N–QB3	17 Q–Q2 B–N5	30 B–N5 N–B6	45 P–N3 R–R6
3 B–N5 P–QR3	18 B–K2 N–K3	31 B–R4 N ×P+	46 P ×P R–R7+
4 B–R4 N–B3	19 N–Q5 B ×N	32 K–K2 P–N4	47 K–B3 R ×P
5 P–Q3 P–Q3	20 B ×B N/B3–Q5	33 R–B1 K–N2	48 P–N5 N–N3
6 P–B4 B–Q2	21 B–N4 (193)	34 R–B2 P–B4	49 R–K1 N–R5+
7 N–B3 B–K2	21 ... P–KN3	35 K–Q3 K–B3	50 K–Q4 N–B4
8 P–Q4 0–0	22 P–B4 P ×P	36 K–Q4 K–K3	51 P–N6 R–QN7
9 P–Q5 N–N1	23 N ×B+ Q ×N	37 R–R2 R–N5	52 P–N7 P–R4
10 B–B2 P–B4	24 B/3 ×N	38 R–N2 P–N5	53 R–K8 R–N6
11 P ×Pep N ×BP	24 ... Q ×B+	39 B–B6 N–B4	54 R–K3 R–N3
12 0–0 R–B1	25 Q ×Q N ×Q	40 B–Q5+ K–B3	55 R–K8 R–N6
13 B–Q3 B–K3	26 B ×R N–K7+	41 K–B3 R–N1	56 R–K3 R–N3
14 P–QN3 N–Q2	27 K–B2 N ×R	42 R–N1 R–K1	57 R–K8 R–N6
15 B–K3 N–B4	28 B ×P N ×RP	43 P–N4 R–K6+	Draw.

A DANGEROUS OPPONENT

Black: L. Szabo – Budapest 1955, USSR v Hungary

Black's exceptionally strong 10 ... P–N6 reversed the roles at a stroke: White began looking for ways of defending, Black for ways of breaking through the defence.

But I reconciled myself immediately to the duties of a defender: I had to spend most of my allotted time on the opening.

If one counts Black's pawns and White's, one can see at what price Black has earned the right to an attack: he has selflessly sacrificed two pawns!

I, too, felt the need to distinguish myself and I began studying the consequences of 12 Q–N4.

The queen move is a simultaneous attack on Black's knight on Q5 and his KNP. My opponent was not going to give away the knight, so the white queen would get the KNP. All the same, it would be interesting to know where the knight will go at this juncture.

Will it really go chasing White's rook on QR1? Will it choose the variation 12 ... N–B7 + 13 K–Q1 N × R? No, that would not be like Szabo at all! He would not think of sending his knight off into uncharted lands. Besides, after 14 Q × NP R–B1 15 R–K1! Black's king-position is indefensible.

So what was Black doing? Szabo cannot have blundered away a knight! And only then did I realize: 12 Q–N4 is parried by the quiet reply 12 ... 0–0, and if 13 Q × N, then 13 ... B–B3.

It cannot be denied: he is a dangerous and wily opponent!

1 P–K4 P–K4	(194)	22 N–N6 Q–Q1	33 P–KN3 N–Q6
2 N–KB3 N–QB3	12 N–Q2 B–N2	23 N × B R × P	34 R–N1 P–B5
3 B–N5 P–QR3	13 0–0 B × P	24 N × B Q × N	35 N–B3 Q–KB4
4 B–R4 N–B3	14 Q–N4 P–QB4	25 Q–QB4 Q–Q3	36 Q–K2 K–R2
5 P–Q3 P–QN4	15 N–K4 0–0	26 KR–K1 R–Q5	37 R–B3 Q–K3
6 B–N3 B–K2	16 B–R6 N–K3	27 Q–B3 Q–Q4	38 Q–K3 N–K4
7 P–QR4 P–N5	17 N–N3 R–N5	28 N–K2 R–Q7	39 R–B4 R–Q6
8 B–Q5 N × B	18 N–B4 K–R1	29 N–N3 R–QN1	40 Q–K4+ K–N1
9 P × N N–Q5	19 B–Q2 R × NP	30 N–K4 R–Q5	41 K–N2 P–Q4
10 N × P P–N6	20 B–R5 Q–R1	31 Q–B2 P–KR4	White resigns.
11 P × P R–QN1	21 B–B3 R × B	32 R–K3 N–B5	

A REPETITION OF THE PAST

Black: P. Dely – Moscow 1962, International Tournament

I am proud of this game.

Possibly White's play will also appeal to the readers. Externally everything is simple, but in reality it is very complex.

Were it not for my innate modesty, I might have commended myself for my neat work, light touch and high level of technique.

I was taught to win logical games of a complex nature in this economic way by none other than the world champion of many years and legendary chess philosopher, Wilhelm Steinitz.

One of the most brilliant masterpieces is his victory in a match game against Chigorin in 1892.

Could Dely have organized a defence? It is difficult to answer that in one word.

Nevertheless, once Black had allowed White to play P–KR5 and replied ... P–KN4, he ought not to have removed his knight from K2 to QN3.

The white knight hoisted itself onto the unattended black KB4 square, whilst the black knight on QN3, after making its protracted raid, could only observe the downfall of the black pieces from a distance.

The black king's tragedy lay also in the fact that the knight that had penetrated to Q6 could neither be taken – 32 ... Q ×N 33 Q ×P+, nor be driven away – White answers the preparatory 32 ... P–B3 with 33 Q–B5+ Q ×Q 34 P ×Q, and after 34 ... B–K2 the knight will not return to its own camp, but will take Black's QNP.

1 P–K4 P–K4	10 N–B1 N–K2	19 R–Q1 N–N3	28 P–N3 (195)
2 N–KB3 N–QB3	11 B–QN3 P–B3	20 N–R2 QR–Q1	28 ... B ×N
3 B–N5 P–QR3	12 N–K3 Q–B2	21 Q–K2 K–N2	29 Q ×B/4 Q–Q2
4 B–R4 N–B3	13 Q–B2 0–0	22 Q–B3 B–B1	30 Q–B3 B–Q1
5 P–Q3 P–Q3	14 P–Q4 KR–K1	23 0–0 R ×R	31 N–B5+ K–R2
6 P–B3 P–KN3	15 P ×P P ×P	24 R ×R R–Q1	32 N–Q6 K–N2
7 B–KN5 P–R3	16 B ×N B ×B	25 R ×R Q ×R	33 N ×BP
8 B–R4 B–N2	17 P–KR4 N–B1	26 N/2–N4 P–R4	Black resigns.
9 QN–Q2 B–Q2	18 P–R5 P–KN4	27 P–R4 Q–Q3	

THE BISHOP'S BITTER LOT

Black: L. Lengyel – Miskolc 1963, Asztalos Memorial Tournament

196W

What was the most instructive thing in this long game?

Perhaps it was the bitter lot of the bishop, shut in by its own pawns? Or White's sharp thrust P–QN6, made from fear that the position would end up too blocked? Or the move N–QR3, made with the intention of executing the complicated raid N–N5–B7 K6? Or was it yet the double-rook endgame?

Personally what sticks in my memory is the move 50 ... K–N2, which totally upset the combination planned by me: 50 ... R ×RP? 51 P–B5! P ×P 52 R–N8+ K–B2 53 R/1–N7+ K–K3 54 R–K8 mate! Black was not forced to lose after that, but I am not the only one time-trouble is fond of.

Probably 18 ... Q–K3 should not have been played so quickly. Black's KBP lost any mobility, besides which all the black pieces were forced, because of the hasty queen move, to conduct a long defence in the endgame with poor prospects. In Black's place I would also not have played .. P–KR4.

P–K4 P–K4	18 P–QR4 Q–K3	35 QR–N1 N–B4	53 R–R2 R–Q2
N–KB3 N–QB3	19 Q ×Q P ×Q	36 N ×N R ×N	54 R–R1 R–Q3
B–N5 P–QR3	20 K–K2 R–B5	37 R–B2 R–Q2	55 R–KR3 R–Q2
B–R4 N–B3	21 N–Q2 P–R4	38 B–B1 B–B1	56 R ×BP R ×RP
P–Q3 P–Q3	22 P–N5 N–N1	39 B–N2 B–K2	57 R ×P R–R7+
P–B3 B–Q2	23 P–N6 P–B4	40 P–R4 R–B3	58 K–K3 R–KN7
QN–Q2 P–KN3	24 N/3–B4 N–B1	41 P–B4 P ×P	59 P–B5 R–QB7
N–B1 P–R3	(196)	42 B ×P B–B4	60 R/3–B6 R ×BP
P–KR3 B–N2	25 N–R3 R–R3	43 B–K5 P–B6+	61 R ×P+ K–R2
0 P–KN4 Q–K2	26 N–N5 P–Q4	44 K–Q2 N–Q3	62 R/KN6–Q6
1 N–K3 N–Q1	27 B–R3 R ×NP	45 B ×N B ×B	62 ... R ×R
2 B ×B+ Q ×B	28 B ×P R–QB3	46 N ×B R/3 ×N	63 R ×R P–R5
3 Q–B2 N–B3	29 B–K3 R–KB2	47 R–B3 P–K4	64 K–B3 R–B6
4 P–N4 P–KR4	30 N–N3 P–N3	48 K–K3 R–KB2	65 K–N4 P–R6
5 P–KN5	31 P–B3 N–R3	49 K–B2 R–B5	66 R–KR6+
5 ... N–KN1	32 KR–QB1 N–B2	50 R/3–N3 K–N2	66 ... K–N2
6 B–N2 KN–K2	33 P–QB4 P–Q5	51 R–KR1 R–Q2	67 R ×P
7 Q–N3 0–0	34 B–Q2 N–R3	52 R–KR3 R–Q3	Black resigns.

A LITTLE HOUSE OUT OF PAWN-BRICKS

Black: I. Sydor – Debrecen 1967, International Tournament

For some reason we very rarely mention the fact that, apart from the four knights (the two white ones and the two black ones), not one of the other pieces is able to jump over pawns.

And if that is so, why not take advantage of this discovery and create draw after draw by the very simple technological plan of quickly exchanging off the four knights and building a little house with the remaining pieces, the walls and roof of which would be constructed of bricks made with pawns?

Pawns are excellent building material; you can create what you lik with them.

I do not know whether this is how my opponent, the Polish maste Sydor, reasoned or not, but his actions bore a markedly deliberat character: when only the major pieces were left on the board, the sensibl idea occurred to him of sitting back behind his wall.

A cunning opponent! If I had guessed his plan earlier, then instead o the modest 15 P–KN4 I would have played the somewhat more forcefu 15 B×N!. I would have been left with both my knights – and jumpin over walls is an elementary matter for them.

All would have been well, but Sydor forgot the most trifling detail even the castles of knights of old had gates, which is nothing compare with the houses of today. . . .

1 P–K4 P–K4	13 P–R4 B–N2	24 B×B P×B
2 N–KB3 N–QB3	14 P–R5 P–KN4	25 N×B K×N
3 B–N5 P–QR3	15 P–KN4 P–N4	26 Q–B2 P–B3
4 B–R4 N–B3	16 B–B2 N–Q1	27 P–Q4 Q–KB2
5 P–Q3 P–Q3	17 N–Q2 N–K3	28 0–0–0 R–R2
6 P–B3 B–Q2	18 N/2–B1 N–B5	29 KR–K1
7 QN–Q2 P–KN3	19 N–N3 B–K3	29 . . . R–QB1
8 N–B1 B–N2	20 B–N3 Q–N1	30 P–B3 R/2–B2
9 B–KN5 P–R3	21 N/N3–B5	31 K–N1 (197)
10 B–R4 0–0	21 . . . Q–N2	31 . . . R–N2
11 N–K3 Q–K1	22 N–Q5 KR–K1	32 P–B4 P×P
12 B×KN B×B	23 N×N KP×N	33 Q×P R–N4

34 R–K2 Q–K1	
35 R–QB2	
35 . . . R/1–N1	
36 Q–B3 K–N1	
37 Q–R3 Q–K2	
38 Q×RP	
38 . . . R/4–N3	
39 Q–Q3 Q–QN2	
40 P–N3 Q–KB2	
41 R/1–QB1 P–K	
42 K–R1	
Black resigns.	

FILE FOR A BISHOP

Black: G. Abrahams – London 1947, USSR v Great Britain

ust on adjournment time I overlooked an lementary win: 44 K–K4? dragged out the ruggle, whilst 44 R×P K–N3 45 B–Q5 ould have forced an immediate capitu- ation.

But every cloud has a silver lining: there merged the variation 46 ... R–K6+ 47 –Q5 P–B6 48 R–B7 R–K7 49 B–R6 P–K5 0 P–B5 R–Q7+ 51 K–B6 R–QB7 52 –B5 P–K6 53 K–N6 P–K7 54 R–B4+!, 5 R×P+, 56 B×P, and the pawn queens.

There was probably no necessity for White to cause all the commotion f a complicated endgame: the quiet 22 P–N3 N/5–N3 23 N–B5+ would ave assured him of a steady attack.

This game is also characteristic in that it reveals yet again the strength f the light-squared Lopez bishop. By comparison with it the knight ems like a little insect....

But did you notice that, in order to guarantee the bishop freedom of iovement and to widen its influence over the opponent's territory, White oes not as a rule play P–Q5, but opens up the Q-file. A file and not a iagonal? It's strange, isn't it? A file for a bishop!

P–K4 P–K4	17 P×Q N–K2	30 ... K–N4	44 K–K4 R–R6
N–KB3 N–QB3	18 P–Q4 QR–Q1	31 B–B7 K×P	45 P–B4+ K–N5
B–N5 P–QR3	19 B–N3 K–N2	32 R–R5+ K–K5	46 R×P P–B6
B–R4 N–B3	20 R–Q2 P–KB3	33 B–N6+ K–Q4	47 B–Q5 P–B7
P–Q3 P–Q3	21 K–R2 P–KN4	34 B–B5 R–KN1	48 R–B7 R–R8
P–B3 B–K2	22 N–B5+ N×N	35 R–R6 P–N6	49 R×P R–K8+
QN–Q2 0–0	23 KP×N (*198*)	36 R×P P×P+	50 K–Q3 K–B4
0–0 B–N5	23 ... P–KR4	37 K×P R–KR1	51 R–K2 R–Q8+
R–K1 N–KR4	24 P–N3 RP×P	38 K–B3 R–R7	52 K–B2 R–KB8
P–KR3 B×N	25 P×N NP×P	39 P–N3 R×P	53 R×P K–Q5
Q×B P–KN3	26 R–KN1	40 B–K4+ K–B4	54 R–R5 R–KN8
N–B1 B–N4	26 ... R–KR1+	41 B×P R–R6	55 B–B7 R–N2
B–K3 B×B	27 K–N2 K–R3	42 R×RP R×P	56 R–KB5 K–K5
N×B N–B5	28 P×P QP×P	43 R–QB6+	57 R–B1
QR–Q1 Q–N4	29 R×R R×R	43 ... K–N4	Black resigns.
Q–N4 Q×Q	30 R–KR1+		

ANCIENT TRADITIONS OF HOSPITALITY

Black: R. Teschner – Hastings 1953–4, International Tournamen

Hastings' international tournaments!

Which grandmaster does not dream of taking part in this competition, which will celebrate its centenary in 1995!

But I would like to have played in the Hastings tournament of 1895. What a tournament that was! The tournament of tournaments.

Of course, in later years too the Christmas Hastings Congresses attracted famous names: Capablanca, Alekhine, Botvinnik, Smyslov, Euwe, Spassky, Larsen; but that tournament was the best.

One year before the tournament Emanuel Lasker beat the vetera Steinitz in a match, and then, after beating off the ex-champion's attac in the return match of 1896, he established himself firmly on the che throne. We know now that it was firmly, but then. . . .

Then the chess world was in ferment, passions ran as high as could b and organizers worked feverishly.

Moreover, only shortly before then the German grandmaster Tarrasc had arrogantly refused to play a match with Lasker, and the latter ha gone straight to Steinitz, gone straight to him and beaten him!

Also dissatisfied, of course, was the famous Chigorin, who had playe two matches with Steinitz for the world crown and could feel perfect justified in considering himself the uncrowned world vice-champio There were also quite a few other stars, both amongst the young playe and the veterans.

So this was the tense atmosphere in which the English decided to arrang a test for the new champion.

'An excellent idea', thought Lasker's enemies and enviers. Howeve even they could not have foreseen the result.

The hitherto unknown American youth Harry Pillsbury in a ver stubborn struggle left all the leading figures behind and took first priz And, what is far more important, he demonstrated a whole wealth fresh chess ideas.

I seem to have been carried away, but these thoughts were with n when I flew in for the tournament.

And what shall I say about the game with Teschner?

A cautious opening, an adventurous middlegame and . . . no, no, w never actually reached a genuine quiet endgame. The encounter too place in the exceptionally nervous setting of the last round, and th cunning Caissa had prepared a nasty experience for our delegation: i the very first hour of play, A. Tolush, trying to help me, spoilt his chanc as White with two ordinary mistakes and gave a point away without any struggle to C. H. O'D Alexander, who drew up level with me. I had to go 'full-steam ahead'. When Teschner resigned the game a minute before midnight the first to congratulate me was Alexander, who had been the most attentive spectator for the whole of the resumption. The second person after him was, of course, Tolush.

I could give the following purely chess commentary: in the opening stages my pieces already felt a definite nervousness and failed outright to find a common tongue for combined operations.

The white QP first went to Q3 and then, as if correcting its mistake, moved on to Q4.

White's queen came out to K2, although the pawn was already supported perfectly reliably, and she also, quite irrelevantly and inopportunely, moved forward into an open position on Q3. She did not really intend giving mate on KR7, surely?

The white rook, whose place is on KB1, and whose assignment is to support the advance P–KB4, swung its sails and set off for the thoroughly blocked Q-file.

That is to say nothing of the QN, which spent two tempi on the route from QN1–Q2–KB1, to return immediately to Q2.

Whilst these amazing manoeuvrings were going on in White's camp, Black was not idling.

1 P–K4 P–K4	19 Q–Q3 B–K2	36 R × R N–N5	54 N–N6+ K–R2
2 N–KB3 N–QB3	20 P–QR4 P × P	37 Q–B4 N/N5 × P	55 Q–N1 P–Q4
3 B–N5 P–QR3	21 P × P P–QR4	38 N–K4 P–R3	56 Q–N6 N–N4
4 B–R4 N–B3	22 P–B4 P–KB4	39 P–N3 N × B	57 N–B8+ K–N1
5 P–Q3 P–Q3	23 P–B5 QP × P	40 BP × N N–N3	58 N–N6 R–KN5
6 P–B3 B–K2	24 Q–B3 K–R1	41 R–KB1 Q–Q2	59 Q–R7 R × P+
7 0–0 0–0	25 B × P B–Q3	42 K–R2 P–R5	(199)
8 Q–K2 N–Q2	26 B–K3 P × P	43 P–R4 R–QN1	60 K–R2 R–R6+
9 P–Q4 B–B3	27 B × P N × RP	44 P–R5 R–N7+	61 K–N2 Q–K1
10 B–K3 P–QN4	28 Q–B2 R–N7	45 N/3–Q2 N–B1	62 R–QN1 N–B2
11 B–B2 N–N3	29 Q–B1 N–B5	46 K–N1 N–K3	63 R–N8 N–Q1
12 QN–Q2 B–N5	30 R–K1 R–N5	47 N–KB3 R–N5	64 K × R Q–K3+
13 P–Q5 N–K2	31 N–B4 B–N4	48 Q–Q5 R–N4	65 K–N3 Q–Q3
14 KR–Q1 N–N3	32 N/4–Q2 N–N7	49 Q–R8+ Q–Q1	66 Q–K7 Q × Q
15 P–KR3 B–Q2	33 Q–B2 B–Q6	50 Q × P R–N5	67 N × Q+ K–B2
16 N–B1 N–KR5	34 B × B N/7 × B	51 Q–B2 Q–R1	68 R × N
17 N/1–Q2 R–N1	35 KR–N1	52 N × B P × N	Black resigns.
18 P–QN3 N–N3	35 ... R × R+	53 N–R4 R–K5	

THE BISHOP ENSNARED BY PAWNS

Black: N. Kopylov – Moscow 1949, USSR Championship

Capablanca's stratagem of shutting out the enemy bishop has been known for a long time. Here we shall see it executed in a different way.

Although Black's bishop on KN5 is usually driven back by the KRP and KNP, in my game with Kopylov the role of harrier was entrusted to the QN. And it was only after the manoeuvre QN–Q2–B1–N3 that the KN entered the fray: N–B3–R4–B5 –R6+!

The pawns at the same time were not sitting idle. The rook's foot-soldier made a very successful march from KR2 to KR6, and after the first 40 moves had elapsed the KNP too cast its vote. Both made their own small contributions to the general victory.

The most decisive move of the game, however, was made by the QN. I am referring to N–KB5! This piece went to its certain death, but it was also the end for the whole of Black's army.

The dozen moves of Black's that followed were nothing more than agony . . . or was it curiosity? Surely chess pieces too are not wooden; they have their own nervous system. They, too, do not like to lose – just the same as us.

1 P–K4 P–K4	12 Q–K2 B–Q3	23 P–KR4 (*200*)	33 R×N R×R
2 N–KB3 N–QB3	13 R–Q1 N–R4	23 ... P–B5	34 R×R Q×R
3 B–N5 P–QR3	14 B–B2 Q–B1	24 B–B2 N–Q2	35 Q×R+ B–K1
4 B–R4 N–B3	15 N–B1 R–K1	25 N/6–B5 P–B3	36 B×N P×B
5 0–0 B–K2	16 N–N3 B–N3	26 P–R5 B–B2	37 Q×P Q–K2
6 P–Q3 P–QN4	17 N–R4 N–N2	27 P–R6 P–N3	38 Q–K6+ K–B1
7 B–N3 0–0	18 Q–B3 N–B4	28 N–Q6 B×N	39 Q×Q+ K×Q
8 P–B3 P–Q4	19 N/4–B5 B–B1	29 R×B K–N1	40 B–K4 K–Q3
9 QN–Q2 P×P	20 B–K3 N–K3	30 R/1–Q1 R–K2	41 P–KN4 P×Pep
10 P×P B–KN5	21 N–R6+ K–R1	31 N–B5 P×N	42 P×P K–K4
11 P–KR3 B–R4	22 B–N3 P–B4	32 P×P N–B5	43 B–B2 B–Q2,

and Black simultaneously resigned.

THE VISIONARY PAWN

Black: A. Liliental – Moscow 1945, USSR Championship

Liliental could have exploited White's early castling by a manoeuvre rare in its beauty: 10 ... R×R   11 P×R Q–B1   12 P–R7 B×N   13 P×B Q–R6   14 P–R8 = Q + K–Q2   15 B–R4 +   K–K3   16 Q×R N×KBP +   17 K–R1 Q×P mate.

Has the reader recognized the hand at work here? No? Or does he not want to admit it?

Fine. Then I shall own up. It is my hand. Oh, how I love such groundless variations! You let your imagination run away with you and you dream things up – then you look, and sometimes you can even use it!

Who knows, possibly those few seconds thought over the 'forced variation' given above did in fact help me to find, eleven years later, an elegant win in my game with grandmaster Szabo.

But returning to the real game we played, I will say only that White was wrong to treat the manoeuvre . . . N–QB3–Q5 so lightly.

After allowing Black's QN onto my important Q4 square and the black bishop to pin my knight from KN4, I did indeed begin to fear for the fate of my KB3. And where KB3 is, there is KR2.

So that my fantastical variations are based on the firm ground of chess experience.

And in conclusion I want to answer the question, why did White give back so easily, by 19 B–Q2, the pawn he had won?

I could have gone 19 P–QN3, but then the variation 19 ... K–B2 20 R–Q1 R–QN1 21 R–Q3 B×P 22 P×B R–N8 23 R–B3 B–R6 also led to equality.

1 P–K4 P–K4	7 B–N3 P–Q3	11 P×B R×R	16 Q×N P–KB3
2 N–KB3 N–QB3	8 P–QR4 B–N5	12 P×R Q–R1	17 Q–B4 Q×Q
3 B–N5 P–QR3	9 P×P N–Q5	13 P–Q4 Q×RP	18 P×Q B–K3
4 B–R4 N–B3	10 R×P (201)	14 P×P P×P	19 B–Q2
5 0–0 B–K2	10 ... N×B	15 N–Q5 N×N	Draw agreed.
6 N–B3 P–QN4			

IN SOMEONE ELSE'S SHOES

Black: O. Ulvestad – Moscow 1946, USSR v USA

I was 22 then and the youngest in the team. When, on the eve of the match, the strategical battle plan was being decided upon, the first to speak was the elder, M. M. Botvinnik.

Looking steadily at me, he pronounced in a clear and imposing tone: 'I hope that everyone understands the crucial nature of this match and that no one will play the reckless King's Gambit.'

That the ex-world champion was right in his assessment of the moves 1 P–K4 P–K4 2 P–KB4, I did not realize straight away, but much later, when he convincingly refuted my opening construction in our personal encounter. But at that time, in 1946, I loved the King's Gambit with all my heart and never lost with this opening.

But the word of an older man is law. And I chose the solid Ruy Lopez. Already in the opening my game was not coming on well; then I missed my opponent's strong manoeuvre . . . Q–B3–B5! and lost, one might say, rather wretchedly.

No, it is no mere coincidence that people say you should choose your opening according to your nature.

For those interested in looking at the move 5 Q–K2 in more detail, I will say a few more words: it is not a bad move. I can pass on only one last recommendation: do not play 12 P–K5?, but boldly take Black's QP: 12 P×P N–N5 13 P–KR3, and Black is faced with the difficult problem of where to put his bishop.

1 P–K4 P–K4	12 P–K5 N–K5	23 B–R3 KR–K1	33 Q–K2 Q–B3
2 N–KB3 N–QB3	13 N–B3 N×N	24 B×N B×B	34 Q–K4 P–K4
3 B–N5 P–QR3	14 P×N Q–Q2	25 Q–Q2 B–R2	35 K–R2 R–B5
4 B–R4 N–B3	15 P–KR3 B–R4	26 N–N2 Q–KR5	36 Q–Q5+ K–R2
5 Q–K2 P–QN4	16 B–B2 B–N3	27 B×B RP×B	37 R–Q2 B–B6
6 B–N3 B–K2	17 N–K1 N–Q1	28 N–Q3 P–Q5	38 R–Q1 P–K5
7 P–B3 0–0	18 N–Q3 N–K3	29 QR–B1 QR–B1	39 N–B1 B×P
8 0–0 P–Q3	19 P–QR4 Q–B3	30 P×P B×P	40 K–N1 B–N3
9 P–Q4 B–N5	20 B–N2 Q–B5	31 R×R R×R	41 K–R1 Q×P
10 R–Q1 P×P	21 P–R5 P–QB4	32 P–K6 (*202*)	42 Q–K6,
11 P×P P–Q4	22 P×P N×P	32 . . . P×P	

and simultaneously White resigned.

White: A. Chistyakov – Moscow 1947, Moscow Championship

203B

The early queen attack, 5 Q–K2, is one of the strongest methods of combatting enemy fortifications around K5.

If the black KP survives in other variations, with the 5 Q–K2 attack it can almost always be forced to exchange itself for White's QP.

If we open any book on theory we learn that in answer to the white queen's thrust one should play quietly, and not try and fish in troubled waters with variations like 5 ... B–K2 6 0–0 P–QN4 7 B–N3 0–0 8 P–B3 P–Q4 9 P×P P–K5 etc., and not because such a way of playing it is bad, but because it is minutely documented.

For a long time theoreticians also supposed that the continuation 9 P–Q3 P–Q5 etc. was safe for Black, but the brilliant analysis of Paul Keres, who is a master of the Ruy Lopez, revealed the falseness of this general assessment: the logical variation, 10 P×P B–KN5 11 P×P N–Q5 12 Q–K3 B×N 13 P×N B×BP 14 P×B B–N4 15 Q×N Q×Q 16 B×B, leads to a considerable activation of the white minor pieces, whereas the lonely black queen does not have a secure haven anywhere.

Wishing to avoid all these elaborations I too did not risk playing 8 ... P–Q4. This decision could be explained by the motto, new times require new fighting methods.

1 P–K4 P–K4	9 P–QR4 P–N5	18 R–K1 R–K1	27 Q×NP R–N4
2 N–KB3 N–QB3	10 P–R5 B–K3	19 B–Q2 B–Q1	28 Q–N3 N–B2
3 B–N5 P–QR3	11 B×P P×B	20 Q–Q3 N/3–K2	29 P–R4 K–R1
4 B–R4 N–B3	12 P–Q4 KP×P	21 P×P P×P	30 R–QB1 R–Q4
5 Q–K2 B–K2	13 P×QP Q–Q2	22 R–K2 N–QB3	31 R/2- B2 N–N4
6 0–0 P–QN4	14 R–Q1 KR–N1	23 N–N5 B×N	32 B–K3 P–QR4
7 B–N3 0–0	15 QN–Q2 R–N4	24 B×B P–N6	33 Q–N4 R–KB1
8 P–B3 (*203*)	16 N–B4 R–KB1	25 R–Q1 N×RP	Draw agreed.
8 ... P–Q3	17 P–K5 N–Q4	26 N×N R×N	

SEVEN KILOMETRES INTO THE DEPTHS OF THE EARTH

Black: L. Winiwarter – Krems 1967, International Tournament

204W

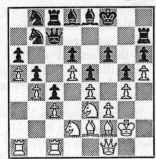

The international tournament at the Austrian town of Krems coincided with an international congress of correspondence chess-players also taking place there.

The day of my encounter with Dr. Winiwarter was a free day for the congress and the correspondence-players hurried across to the tournament. For them a game where more than one move a day is played is a wonder. As is for a mathematician-programmer friend of mine 'the crocodile pear' (a perfectly edible fruit, something like a coconut which grows in some region of South America) which he read about somewhere and now secretly dreams of. . . .

Sometimes I would tear myself away from the play and, contrary to normal competition rules, would go into the rows set out for the public to get to know the correspondence grandmasters' opinions. We, the practical players, calculate to a considerable degree on swiftness of reaction and the opponent's fear, whilst everything with them is based on a scientific assessment of the position. The controller did not object.

And then when I played P–Q5 our vice-president of the Institute of Geological Research, Yakov Stanislavovich Eventov asked shyly:

'Are you sure you won't want Q5 for a piece?'

I did not have time to reply as I had to go back to my board. I came back again and he then asked me, this time anxiously:

'Why did you play P–QR5? Are you really counting only on breaking through on the K-side?'

'How do you mean, Yakov Stanislavovich? I don't want to break through on the K-side at all! Oh, excuse me, it's my move.'

I went away, played P–KR5, and came back again to the vice-president – I felt I had not answered all his questions yet. And I was not mistaken.

'I can't understand. What, have you decided to play for a draw as White?!'

'Why for a draw? I'm beginning to win now . . .'

'Would you kindly stop pulling my leg?' said Professor Eventov angrily and he was about to walk off.

'Forgive me, but you, I remember, have said that you have already looked seven kilometres below the earth's surface and you can see everything there?'

'Yes, I can, but what are you looking for in this blocked position?'

'I am not looking for anything! It is there to be seen. Listen now.

I played P–QR5 to take QN3 away from the black knight, and then P–KR5 so that this same knight should not leap onto KN3.

That means its fate is clear: to travel the route from KB1–KR2–KB1 –Q2 and back again, just like an express taxi.

But since I have played P–Q5 even earlier, life is not too easy for Black's second knight either: his destiny is the walk from QN2–Q1–KB2 and back to QN2. The pawn on Q5 keeps both knights in.'

'Interesting!' said the Professor in a conciliatory tone. 'But what then?'

'Then? If Black has two knights out of action, White has only to open up the position a little bit, and . . .'

'You're not going to sacrifice, surely; besides, your opponent won't allow you to. He's probably already guessed what you're planning.'

'Therein lies the secret of the plan with P–QR5, P–Q5 and P–KR5, that my opponent is incapable of preventing the breakthrough I'm preparing! I shall sacrifice on QB4, and I have rather more means of breaking through than Black has of defending this pawn.

But besides that . . . are you quite sure my opponent has guessed my plan?

Look how serenely his bishops are shuffling about. He is clearly waiting for the beginning of negotiations for a draw!'

When the game was over, Yakov Stanislavovich looked with pride at the chain of White pawns, associating them, obviously, with some geological deposits of various mysterious rocks – and finally he brought himself to offer a word of praise:

'If you, grandmaster, were working in my Institute, I would entrust the exploration of the riches of the mountains to you. I think in chess you can see deeper than seven kilometres down!'

'Thank you, but I do not deserve this myself: knowledge helped me, and previous games. . . . For how many times have I sacrificed in exactly the same way and lost!'

1 P–K4 P–K4	12 B–B2 P–B4	23 K–N2 P–R3	34 B–K2 R–B1
2 N–KB3 N–QB3	13 R–K1 N–Q2	24 R–R1 R–R1	35 N–K3 N–N1
3 B–N5 P–QR3	14 P–KN4 B–N3	25 P–R5 P–N4	(204)
4 B–R4 N–B3	15 N–B1 P–B3	26 N–B5+ K–B1	36 N/2×P P×N
5 0–0 B–K2	16 N–K3 B–B2	27 B–K3 R–KR2	37 N×P B–N4
6 Q–K2 P–QN4	17 P–Q4 R–K1	28 N–Q2 B–N1	38 N–N6 B×B
7 B–N3 P–Q3	18 P–Q5 P–B5	29 P–B3 B–Q1	39 Q×B B–K2
8 P–B3 B–N5	19 P–N4 N–N2	30 B–B2 B–K2	40 N×R Q×N
9 P–KR3 B–R4	20 P–QR4 Q–B2	31 KR–QB1 B–Q1	41 B–R7 N–Q2
10 P–Q3 0–0	21 P–R5 P–N3	32 Q–B1 B–B2	42 Q×P
11 QN–Q2 N–R4	22 P–R4 K–N2	33 B–Q1 B–K1	Black resigns

DOUBLED BLACK PAWNS

Black: V. Smyslov – Zurich 1953, Candidates' Tournament

The exchange variation of the Ruy Lopez is the enigma of chess theory. Appearing and disappearing, each time it provokes a multitude of the most contradictory opinions and evaluations.

Nevertheless, one thing is clear: there is no special, superhuman force behind the move B×N. Black has quite a number of promising methods of defence.

The numerous failures by White in this variation are the best proof of this and I give quite a number of examples of these in this book.

Personally speaking, the move holds only bitter memories for me: sometimes a draw, due to various circumstances surrounding a tournament, to poor health, to having lost any chances of winning the competition, and so on; sometimes even a loss, for the same reasons but adding up to a whole negative charge, when I did not even have the strength to scrape a draw!

I would not have included these games at all were there not amongst them one pearl, my pride, a pinnacle of psychological work and the synthesis of hundreds and thousands of combinative variations.

By way of an exception I shall be giving this game with more extensive notes, and, again by way of an exception, I shall be annotating it 'on various levels'.

Which game am I referring to? To my game with Gligoric from the 1967 Moscow International Tournament (see p. 234–5).

And just in case some critic might start thinking that it is possible to win like that every day, I have also included practically all my failures in the Exchange Variation. My score with B×N in play is a negative one; but if it comes off only once, the game will undoubtedly be worth something.

Since our journey is nearing its end, it is time for me to reveal a little secret. All my thoughts on the Exchange Variation can be applied at equal length to the previous sections of the book, the good and the bad put together. The reader will then see what a difficult task it is when one has to decide upon the future of each individual piece or pawn.

And in conclusion, a few words about the grandmasters whose names are closely connected, in my view, with the principal subtleties of Lopez strategy in the B×N variation.

It is no secret that, in giving up bishop for knight of his own free will, White counts on more than compensating for this deficit by having the better pawn formation.

224 Ruy Lopez's Opening

Who, then, first thought of this variation?

Chess variations, like people, have complicated fortunes, far from straightforward and full of every kind of surprise.

As an example – could anyone have predicted that such different players as Emanuel Lasker and Robert Fischer, coming from different chess eras, would meet on the same page of theory? Nonetheless, this unlikely event has taken place.

At first, owing to his youthfulness, Fischer was unable to fathom Lasker's style and refused to accord him a place in the top ten immortals. But later, taking the baton from Lasker, he himself began crushing opponents with 4 B×N. One after the other, he completely destroyed them!

The explanation for this lies in Fischer's limpid style of play, his polished endgame technique and his great will to win. In fact, almost like the great Lasker.

However, there is one important qualification: whereas Fischer is the Professor of openings research, the world champion of many years, Lasker, stubbornly, and as if to tease the whole world, refused to waste his energy on swotting up opening variations.

'Variations are transient; the important thing in chess is method, and that can always be employed', Lasker liked to say.

So wherein lies the strength of Lasker's and Fischer's common weapon, 4 B×N!?

The last thing I would want to do is to surprise the reader, but there is only one reply, and it belongs to Philidor: 'Pawns are the soul of chess!' And the Frenchman was on this earth even before Lasker.

To whom, then, do wise chess moves belong?

1 P-K4 P-K4	6 P-Q4 P×P	12 N-N3 B-QN5	17 R-Q1 R×R+
2 N-KB3 N-QB3	7 Q×P Q×Q	13 N-K2 KR-K1	18 K×R N-K4
3 B-N5 P-QR3	8 N×Q B-Q2	14 P-R3 B-B1	19 B-B5 B-Q3
4 B×N QP×B	9 B-K3 0-0-0	15 N-B3 B-K3	20 B×B P×B
(205)	10 0-0-0 N-K2	16 R×R+ R×R	Draw.
5 N-B3 P-B3	11 P-KR3 N-N3		

DOES THE READER KNOW?

White: B. Goldenov – Moscow 1952, USSR Championship

206W

Which pawns are better? Those that are doubled, or . . . However, if you look at the diagram all the questions no longer arise: in this game there are three pairs of doubled pawns; other types can hardly be seen.

Not quite: White's pawn chain KR3 –KN2–KB3–K4 has no doubled groups. All white pawns, all right pawns. They are supported by both wings of that tender cherub, the KNP.

But can it not be attacked from the rear and taken by force? No, there is no way of stealing up on the KNP!

But Black could not be persuaded; he would not believe it. He played 20 . . . B–N4, offering White an all round exchange of the major pieces. Who would defend KB1 after the exchange of rooks?

Therefore White declined to exchange off the second pair. And no matter how much Black tried to cross the defensive lines, a draw was inevitable.

It might have been that the variation 21 R×R+ R×R 22 R×R+ K×R 23 N–Q2 B–K7 would be obligatory for White. Then to all intents and purposes White's knight would not be able to move, because of . . . B–B8, nor the bishop, because of . . . N–B5 or . . . N–R5. What might seem an overwhelming advantage.

But I hope you have not forgotten the question: which pawns are better?

The strongest pawn is White's on K4! How can the black king get past this guard-post?

I do not know the answer. . . .

1 P–K4 P–K4	11 Q×Q RP×Q	(206)	30 P–R4 K–Q1
2 N–KB3 N–QB3	12 B–B4 B–QN5	21 R×R+ R×R	31 R×P K–K1
3 B–N5 P–QR3	13 0–0–0 N–K2	22 N–Q2 P–R4	32 N–B1 B–B1
4 B×N QP×B	14 P–B3 P–B3	23 P–QB4 B–R3	33 N–K3 P–B3
5 N–B3 Q–Q3	15 P–R3 B×N	24 R–K1 R–K1	34 R–N1 B–K3
6 P–Q4 P×P	16 P×B P–KN4	25 K–N2 P–R5	35 N–N2 P–B4
7 N×P Q–N3	17 B–N3 N–N3	26 K–B3 N–B5	36 P–K5 R–Q2
8 Q–B3 B–KN5	18 R–Q2 P–QB4	27 B×N P×B	37 R–N1 R–Q5
9 Q–N3 0–0–0	19 N–N3 P–N3	28 P–N3 P×P	38 R×P R×BP+
10 P–KR3 B–Q2	20 R/1–Q1 B–N4	29 R–KN1 R–K2	Draw agreed.

RECORD TIME-TROUBLE

Black: E. Geller – Tiflis 1967, USSR Championship

The start of the championship turned out successfully for me: three wins and two draws. It seemed very reasonable to count on getting a place in the Interzonal.

But in the middle of the tournament I declined the offer of a draw from Krogius without justification and lost. At the same time a whole group of players was already ahead of me. It was in these conditions that my duel with Geller took place.

I was ready for 1 ... P–K4 and had prepared a harmonious attacking system. But after seven moves for no reason I refrained from the prepared 8 B–K3 and chose QN–Q2, so that by move 18 I had got into terrible time-trouble.

Geller deployed his pieces superbly and was able to be the first onto the offensive. Especially beautiful was his manoeuvre ... N(KN1)–R3–B2 –R1!

1 P–K4 P–K4	21 B–R3 B×B	43 R–B5 R–K4	61 R–R7 P–B4
2 N–KB3 N–QB3	22 R×B R/7–K2	44 R–Q2 R×P/6	62 K–B4 R–QR8
3 B–N5 P–QR3	23 N–K3 R–Q2	45 N×P N×N	63 R–QB7 R–R6
4 B×N QP×B	24 R–R4 N–B2	46 R×N R×R+	64 R–R7 R–R5+
5 0–0 P–B3	25 R–N4 N–Q3	47 P×R R–B6+	65 K–N3 R–R8
6 P–Q4 B–KN5	26 R–Q1 Q–B2	48 K–Q2 R×P	66 R–QB7 R–QB8
7 P–B3 B–Q3	27 K–B1 R/1–Q1	49 R–Q7+ K–N1	67 R–R7 P–B5
8 QN–Q2 Q–K2	28 Q–B2 N–N4	50 R×QNP	68 K–B4 R–B8+
9 P–QR4 N–R3	29 Q–B5 Q–B1	50 ... R×RP	69 K–K3 R–KN8
10 P–R5 N–B2	30 Q×Q+ K×Q	51 K–K3 K–R2	70 K–B4 P–B6
11 Q–B2 0–0	31 N–B2 P–B4	52 K–B4 R–R8	71 R–QB7 R–QB8
12 P–R3 B–Q2	32 R–B4 P×P	53 R–QB7 K–R3	72 R–B8 P–N3
13 P–QN3	33 R–Q3 K–B2	54 K–N3 R–QB8	73 K–K3 P×P
13 ... QR–K1	34 P–QN4 P–B3	55 K–R4	74 P×P K–N4
14 B–N2 N–R1	35 P–N4 P–R4	55 ... R–KR8+	75 R–B5 R–K8+
15 N–R4 Q–B2	36 K–K2 R–Q4	56 K–N3 R–QB8	76 K–Q3 R–K4
16 N–B4 P×P	37 K–Q2 R/1–Q2	57 K–R4 P–R4	77 R×BP K×P
17 P×P Q–R4	38 P–B3 R–Q1	58 R–R7	78 R–R3 K–N5
18 N–B5 B×N	39 N–K1 P×P	58 ... R–KR8+	79 K–Q4 R–K8
19 P×B R–K7	40 RP×P R–KR1	59 K–N3 R–R8	80 R×P P–B4
(*207*)	41 N–B2 R–R7+	60 R–QB7 R–QB8	White resigns.
20 Q–Q3 R/1–K1	42 K–B1 R–B7		

KORCHNOI AT HIS BEST

White: V. Korchnoi – Kiev 1965, USSR Championship

208W

In this game three positions deserve attention.

The first is after 3 ... N–B3. Korchnoi pondered for a full thirty minutes. What was he thinking about? How can one know? ... About everything.

The second position is after 15 ... P–B4. It would be worthwhile checking all the details of Black's idea: 16 P×P P–K5 17 QR–K1 Q–B2 18 N–N5 P×P 19 N–K6 P–Q7, but I have a terrible dislike of going back in my thoughts to lost games.

The third position is before the move 39 ... Q–Q3. I fancied that with this cunning manoeuvre I might be able to float to the surface, but the confident check, 41 Q–N5 +, dispelled my deceptive hopes.

Black got quite a strong position from the opening, although play was extremely complex, in the style of Korchnoi, and so I had to avoid resting content with what I had achieved. I kept this in mind and perhaps even tried too hard. ...

I ought probably to have exchanged queens and accepted the endgame as it was, and not busied myself with endless manoeuvring.

Black was afraid of the pawn breakthrough by P–QB3 and P–Q4–Q5, but what is fated cannot be escaped. When White managed to carry out his plan, the presence of the queens only strengthened his attack.

But this is all very general talk: Black's final mistake was his king-march from KN1 to K2.

1 P–K4 P–K4	13 0–0 0–0	24 Q–K2 Q–B6	35 P×P P×P
2 N–KB3 N–QB3	14 P–N3 KR–K1	25 R–KB1	36 K–N1 Q–B3
3 B–N5 N–B3	15 K–R1 P–B4	25 ... R/3–K2	37 P–B4 P×P
4 B×N QP×B	16 N–Q2 P×P	26 R–R2 Q–N5	38 Q–N4 P×P
5 P–Q3 B–Q3	17 N×P N×N	27 Q–K1 Q–B4	(208)
6 QN–Q2 B–K3	18 Q×N Q–Q3	28 R–B2 R–K3	39 R–K5 Q–Q3
7 P–QN3 N–Q2	19 K–N2 R–K3	29 R–K2 K–B2	40 R–Q5 K–K2
8 N–B4 B–QN5 +	20 P–QR4 P–QR4	30 R–K4 Q–Q3	41 Q–N5 + K–Q2
9 B–Q2 B×B +	21 KR–K1	31 R–R1 K–K2	42 R×R R×R
10 Q×B B×N	21 ... R/1–K1	32 Q–K2 K–Q2	43 Q×P/3
11 NP×B N–B4	22 P–R4 P–QN3	33 R–K1 P–B4	Black resigns.
12 Q–K3 Q–K2	23 P–KB3 Q–N5	34 P–R5 P–N3	

THE PANEL TOOK FRIGHT

Black: A. Bykhovsky – Moscow 1967, Moscow Team Championship

209W

The reader has probably noticed that I am not very fond of going into the detail of concrete variations. One can argue about tastes, but I am not alone in this.

For example, Bykhovsky also does not like sharp variations, so I decided to go along with him. Following protracted manoeuvres play transposed into a won endgame for White, but here I stumbled twice.

Firstly, I wrongly rejected the exchange of queens on the 40th move, although I had been hoping for this all evening. When putting my mistake right I transposed to a rook ending; I was quite wrong in not playing the natural 45 P–R5!; I lost an important tempo and let the win slip once and for all. According to the conditions laid down for the competition, games were not played on, but adjudicated. I was afraid of the strict panel – would they not assess the endgame in Black's favour?

But I had no need to worry! Judges themselves like to sacrifice!

And yet the drawn outcome of the game must be acknowledged as completely fair. White attacked, Black defended: what could come of that? Black must defend, and attack only if he is given a lucky break. Here he did not have one.

1 P–K4 P–K4	13 B–B3 QR–K1	25 R–B3 R/1–KB1	36 R–B5 P–B4
2 N–KB3 N–QB3	14 0–0 P–B4	26 K–N2 R–Q1	37 P–R4 Q–K3
3 B–N5 N–B3	15 Q–N5 P–KB3	27 Q–N3	38 Q–B4 Q–Q2
4 B×N QP×B	16 Q–Q2 P–QN3	27 ... R/1–KB1	39 R–Q5 Q–B2
5 P–Q3 B–KN5	17 R–B5 R–B2	28 R–B5 N–K2	(209)
6 P–KR3 B×N	18 R/1–KB1 N–B3	29 R–R5 N–B3	40 Q–B3 R–K1
7 Q×B B–N5+	19 Q–B2 Q–K3	30 R/5–B5 N–K2	41 P–N5 BP×P
8 N–Q2 B×N+	20 P–QN3 N–K2	31 R/5–B2 N–B3	42 Q×R+ Q×Q
9 B×B Q–Q3	21 R–B3 N–B3	32 P–KR4 Q–Q3	43 R×Q K×R
10 Q–B5 0–0	22 P–KN4 P–KR3	33 R–B4 N–Q5	44 P×P P×P
11 P–KB4 N–Q2	23 R–B5 N–K2	34 Q–B2 Q–Q2	45 R×NP R–K3
12 P×P N×P	24 R–B4 N–N3	35 B×N P×B	46 R–Q5

The game was stopped for adjudication. The verdict of the panel, M. Tal and L. Polugayevsky, was a draw.

MY TELEPHONE BEGAN RINGING

White: A. Lein – Kiev 1965, USSR Championship

'Who's speaking?'

'Lein. Grandmaster, you wouldn't have any objections, would you, to moving into the second row tomorrow? You know, I play terribly badly when I am right next to the public. The noise, sighs, gasps, even suggestions. So you agree then?'

'I'll willingly agree to that. I myself can't stand too much bustle.'

'Thank you. I'll tell the controller right away about our arrangement.'

And if I felt rather afraid of Lein's positional style before this telephone call, I now felt more cheerful: he himself, after all, had asked for the second row. He must want to play a lively, sharp game.

In answer to 1 P–K4 I blithely played 1 ... P–K4. A Ruy Lopez, fair enough. And suddenly what do I see? The bishop takes my knight on QB3. In an instant I felt demoralized, a deep yearning came over me. What can I say here? The move B×N is not bad, not bad at all, but was it worth all the commotion of moving us to the quiet second row for such a game? Hardly.

White has no difficulty in getting a draw here, even to the sound of the Niagara Falls!

Grudgingly I went over to defence. Such positions are quite difficult to play, mainly because they have no prospects.

But is the author right to condemn Lein's B×N? Is it really a move played for a draw? No, of course not. In the hands of Korchnoi even this position is a spring-board to victory – but for this you need to be Korchnoi, and there is only one Korchnoi in the world.

1 P–K4 P–K4	(210)	12 N–K3 N–K3	18 QR–B1 Q–N4
2 N–KB3 N–QB3	7 N–B3 B–KN5	13 N–B5 P–B3	19 Q–B2 0–0
3 B–N5 P–QR3	8 Q–K2 N–Q2	14 B–K3 Q–Q2	20 N–B5 KR–K1
4 B–R4 N–B3	9 P–Q3 B–Q3	15 P–B3 P–B4	21 P–QN3 B–N3
5 0–0 B–K2	10 P–KR3 B–R4	16 KR–Q1 Q–B3	22 N/5–R4
6 B×N QP×B	11 N–Q1 N–B4	17 N–N3 B–B2	

Draw by mutual agreement.

A SACRIFICIAL WATERFALL

Black: I. Prameshuber – Krems 1967, International Tournament

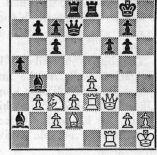

It all started from something trivial.

The precipitate (for the *n*th time!) P–KB4 led to an appreciable activation of forces . . . Black's; but at the same time White's position seemed to me to give improved prospects. Therefore when my opponent made his surprising 20th move, I took it for a joke and was punished. It served me right.

I should have played 23 Q–K2 with the obvious continuation 23 . . . B×N 24 B×B P–R5 25 R–N3 P×P 26 R×NP, but I was reluctant to pass by the chance of Q–B2–R4–R8+.

And then – I would not say in a flash, no, after pretty good thought – I finally chose the variation which seemed to me obligatory here: 23 Q–B2 B×N 24 B×B P–R5 25 P–R4 P×P 26 P–R5 P–KN4 27 P–R6 – my aim is achieved, the backbone of Black's pawns on KN2, KN4 and KB3 no longer exists. . . .

These sweet dreams were completely blotted out by a whirlwind of blows from the unchecked black pieces: the bishop, and then the queen too, as if mocking White's plans, used the pawns on the Q-side and in the centre to the full!

It was a good thing that I managed to retain a drop of humour in my soul and, whilst secretly cursing my tireless imagination, that I could make a sober assessment of the real course of events.

1 P–K4 P–K4	12 B×P N–K4	22 R–K3 P–R4	32 R–QB2 P–QN4
2 N–KB3 N–QB3	13 N–K3 N–N3	*(211)*	33 B×P P×N
3 B–N5 P–QR3	14 N×N P×N	23 Q–B2 B×P	34 P×P R–Q5
4 B–R4 N–B3	15 K–R1 B–K3	24 P×B B–B4	35 R×P R×RP
5 0–0 B–K2	16 Q–B3 R–QB1	25 R/1–K1 Q×P	36 B×P B×B
6 B×N QP×B	17 QR–K1 B–QB4	26 R×Q B×Q	37 R×B R×P
7 P–Q3 N–Q2	18 N–Q1 Q–Q2	27 R×R R×R	38 P–R4 R–K7
8 QN–Q2 0–0	19 N–B3 B–QN5	28 R–K2 B–Q5	39 K–N1 K–B1
9 N–B4 P–B3	20 B–Q2 B×P	29 P–N3 B–K4	40 K–B1 R–K2
10 N–R4 R–K1	21 P–QN3	30 N–R4 P–N3	41 R–B8+
11 P–B4 P×P	21 . . . R/B1–Q1	31 B–B3 R–Q6	

Drawn on move 50.

THE TRAVELLING BISHOP

Black: M. Udovcic – Leningrad 1957, USSR v Yugoslavia

212l

After the white bishop had left the battle-field of its own free will, his opposite number became sole master of 32 squares of the board.

The bishop assimilated his rights and obligations well. At the first rays of the spring sun it set off on a long journey from QB1–K3–N5–K7–N5, in which it had time to visit the K7 square twice. And what is more, it was even able to give check to the white king.

If the QB had not occupied so much of Black's time, he would not perhaps have got into time-trouble and would not have lost – so not every journey is a useful one.

What aims is White pursuing by choosing such a delayed exchange variation? And is it not better to take the knight on QB6 without losing time on the preliminary B–R4? Is the black KN really worse placed on KB3 than KN1?

My mood usually decides this. If I feel pity for the bishop, I play B–R4. Whereas when I feel hurt at the thought that the black pawns will start chasing it from square to square, then I play B×N.

But I will almost never take on QB6 on the fourth move! I can also answer two other questions. The black knight on KB3 takes that square away from the KBP. It is because of this that White captures so late on QB6, so as to force Black to defend his KP with a piece instead of with a pawn.

1 P–K4 P–K4	11 N–B4 P–B4	20 P×P Q×P	29 Q–K1 Q–B1
2 N–KB3 N–QB3	12 P–QR4 R–N1	21 B–N4 Q–B3	30 P–R4 B–N5
3 B–N5 P–QR3	13 P–R5 P–QN4	22 N–Q2 B–K3	31 N–Q2 B–K7
4 B–R4 N–B3	14 P×Pep P×P	23 N–K3 N–B5	32 R–R1 B–N5
5 0–0 B–K2	15 P–R3 P–QN4	24 K–R2 R–R1	33 N/2–B4 R–R3
6 B×N QP×B	16 N–K3 N–B1	25 B–R5 B×B	34 R×P R–R3
7 P–Q3 N–Q2	17 B–B3 Q–Q3	26 R×B Q–B6	35 K–N1 N–K7+
8 QN–Q2 0–0	18 N–Q5 N–N3	27 R–QR1	36 K–B1 N–Q5
9 P–QN3 B–B3	19 P–QN4 (*212*)	27 ... P–QR4	37 N×P B–K7+
10 B–N2 R–K1	19 ... B–Q1	28 N–B3 P–N5	38 K–N1 Q–B2

Black overstepped the time limit.

'LOOK OUT, BORA!'

Black: B. Ivkov – Sochi 1968, USSR v Yugoslavia

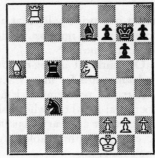

'Look up, Bora!' – this appeal was printed in huge letters in one of the Yugoslav newspapers in 1954 during the Belgrade international tournament.

At the start of that tournament Ivkov, in a winning position and with plenty of time to spare, forgot about his clock, and only came to his senses when the hall began humming like a beehive. The flag on his clock fell and the judges were forced to mark down a loss for the Yugoslav grandmaster. Bora Ivkov was extremely upset about it, which goes to explain the appeal in the newspaper.

I was also playing in that tournament and I remember the incident well.

Since then our own particular tradition has been established: whenever we meet at a tournament I cannot help saying: 'Look up, Bora!' And in reply I hear: 'You still remember?'

This was also how we greeted each other at the famous resort of Sochi. A warm sun and the gentle sea did not dull the Yugoslav grandmaster's usual extreme vigilance, and he displayed this very quality when he cooled White's attacking ardour with the moves 15 . . . P–B5 and 16 . . . N–B4. The game lost its sharpness and dead calm gradually spread over the board.

In such chess weather a draw is the most likely outcome, and I did not, with 29 B–N4, even try to hold on to the accidentally won pawn.

Ivkov willingly accepted the variation proposed by White and we honourably played out the game to a forced draw with the help of a three-fold repetition of moves.

1 P–K4 P–K4	10 P–R5 P–QN4	19 QR×Q R×P	28 R–QN8 N–R5
2 N–KB3 N–QB3	11 P×Pep P×P	20 KR–K1 N–B4	29 N–B3 N×P
3 B–N5 P–QR3	12 N–Q6 P–QR4	21 P–B3 R–K1	30 N–K5 R–B4
4 B–R4 N–B3	13 N×B R×N	22 B–B7 R×R+	31 B–N4 R–B2
5 B×N QP×B	14 B–Q2 P–QB4	23 N×R N–Q6	32 B–R5 R–B4
6 P–Q3 N–Q2	15 0–0 P–B5	24 B×P N×NP	(*213*)
7 QN–Q2 P–KN3	16 B–B3 N–B4	25 R–Q8+ B–B1	33 B–N4 R–B2
8 P–QR4 B–N2	17 P×P N×P	26 B×P K–N2	34 B–R5 R–B4
9 N–B4 0–0	18 B×KP Q×Q	27 K–B1 B–K2	Draw agreed.

THE ART OF IMPROVISATION

Black: S. Gligoric – Moscow 1967, International Grandmaster Tournament

What is it principally that attracts to chess creativity the millions of devotees of this ancient game?

Of course, it is not craftmanship in the endgame: it is far more interesting to solve studies and problems. It is not the study of openings: for those who wish to memorize things, there are marvellous lines of verse ... or even logarithm tables. Whichever is to one's taste.

People come to the sanctuary of Chess Art with a sole aim: to delight in the beauty of combinations. And it is not terribly important whether you yourself create these intricate, artful designs of pieces and pawns, or whether you admire the ornaments created by other, more skilful followers of Caïssa.

A beautiful, succulent combination containing numerous variations is my ideal.

In order, however, to create an original combination, one has to work extremely hard and it is essential to study the work of one's colleagues and the masterpieces of players of years gone by.

And it can quite easily happen that a lazy player, with no bent for improvisation, during a long life will simply not produce a single perfect combination.

Once I was lucky; I created my own pearl, and now I want to boast about it to you.

If one were to show the diagrammed position to several players of different strengths and ask them to give their assessment of White's chances – and at the moment it is White to move – then it is quite likely that one would get the following results.

The beginner's assessment:

'It's a pity one can't check-mate by Q ×NP!'

The assessment of players of the 4th category:

'It would be good to get KR5 for the white queen and at a convenient moment penetrate with a check on K8!'

The 3rd category player's assessment:

'Oh, if only one could invade Black's weakened back rank with the rooks!'

The 2nd category player's assessment:

'It wouldn't be a bad idea to organize a breakthrough into the enemy's camp along the 7th rank – after all, Black's P–KB3 has exposed his KN2 to attack along the rank.'

The 1st category player's assessment:

'It's impossible to squeeze anything out of this position! As soon as a rook gets to the 7th, Black will immediately protect his KN2. You won't be able to get anywhere without some clever bluff, but it's worth trying!'

The candidate master's assessment:

'A combination always requires a sacrifice, so what can we sacrifice here? Not the knight on Q4, it's the pride of White's position!'

The master's assessment:

'The pride of White's position, you say? That's all very well, but even after the knight sacrifice the rook would not be able to penetrate down the Q-file because of Black's rook on Q4. There is only one way to break through: along the QB-file, but even here the black knight won't let us through. We must, then, find some bait for the knight. Excellent; a rook will be the bait – but which rook? We'll have to think about this; it's a difficult one.'

The assessment of the master of international class:

'A rook? Of course, a rook! One must bring a rook to bear more closely on QB5, then the knight won't be able to hold out; it will beat a hasty retreat. Just like the crow with the cheese, whilst the rook, like the fox, will slip through with lightning speed down the QB-file. Where to? To QB8, of course!'

The assessment of an objective observer:

'There are a lot of pretty ideas there, my friends; only, could they all be combined? Still, heart-felt thanks for the visionary plans. But it would be even better if one of you were personally to show us what should be played.'

From the educational point of view moves 29–40 can be divided into three independent parts:

1) The trap: 29 R–Q2 Q–Q2 30 R–B1 P–N5 31 P–KR3 N–K5 32 R/2–B2 R ×N 33 R–B7 Q–Q4 34 B ×R Q ×B

2) The combination: 35 R ×P + B ×R 36 R–B8 +

3) The forced continuation: 36 ... K–B2 37 Q–R5 + K–K2 38 Q–K8 + K–Q3 39 R–B6 + K–Q4 40 Q–Q7 + N–Q3 41 R ×N + K–K5 42 R ×Q mate!

1 P–K4 P–K4	12 P ×B R–K1	23 B–K3 P–QN4	32 R/2–B2 R ×N
2 N–KB3 N–QB3	13 P–QN3 Q–Q4	24 N–Q2 R–Q4	33 R–B7 Q–Q4
3 B–N5 P–QR3	14 B–N2 P–K5	25 P–QB4 R/4–Q1	34 B ×R Q ×B
4 B–R4 N–B3	15 N–K3 Q–B2	26 P ×P BP ×P	35 R ×P + B ×R
5 0–0 B–K2	16 P–Q4 N–Q2	27 N–B3 R–Q4	36 R–B8 + K–B2
6 B ×N QP ×B	17 Q–N4 P–B4	28 N–Q4 R/1–K4	37 Q–R5 + K–K2
7 P–Q3 N–Q2	18 Q ×KP P ×P	(214)	38 Q–K8 + K–Q3
8 QN–Q2 0–0	19 B ×P P–B3	29 R–Q2 Q–Q2	39 R–B6 + K–Q4
9 N–B4 P–B3	20 QR–Q1 N–N4	30 R–B1 P–N5	40 Q–Q7 +
10 N–R4 N–B4	21 Q–N4 B–B1	31 P–KR3 N–K5	Black resigns.
11 N–B5 B ×N	22 N–B4 QR–Q1		

20 Alapin's Opening

MY ENCOUNTER WITH MR QUEENABBER

White: B. S. Queenabber – Kiev 1938, Friendly Game

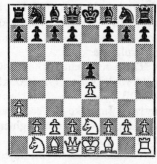

215B

An editor always has a part to play in the creation of a book: his task is to ensure harmony, order and fine proportions, as well as to review the manuscript with a critical eye.

When I had submitted the manuscript of this book my editor condemned me for lack of self-criticism ('there were too few lost games') and incompleteness ('there was no Alapin's opening'). Moreover, I had promised 200 games, and there were only 199. But the most serious failing was that there was no mention of grand-master B. S. Queenabber. 'Although,' he added, 'I am absolutely convinced that this personage is fictitious – no one has ever seen him face to face.'

'That's an excellent idea!' I exlaimed. 'But I must disappoint you: not only have I heard of Queenabber, I have even played against him.'

And I told the editor of how, in the spring of 1938 in Kiev, when I was only 14, I came across my chess teacher, A. M. Konstantinopolsky, talking to a tall gentleman outside the conservatory where the next round of the semi-finals of the national championship was due to be played.

'I have to go now and play', said Konstantinopolsky to the stranger, 'but you have a game with this little chappy here,' and he pointed to me.

My opponent took White, removed his QR from the board and put his QRP on QR3.

'I never play young fellows without giving odds,' he said.

1 P–K4 P–K4 2 N–K2 215

'What's this?' I asked. 'I wanted to get into a Ruy Lopez.'

'You'll have your wish some time, but not now,' the stranger answered. 'Anyone who wants to nab the other person's queen (here he was, Queenabber himself, talking about 'nabbing queens'!) mustn't move his queen before the middle of the game; so I am playing Alapin's opening.'

2 . . . N–KB3 3 P–Q4 N × P 4 N–N3 N × N 5 RP × N N–B3

Having been brought up in the strict positional-logical style, I was perfectly content with my game. I had one piece developed, my opponent had none.

6 N–B3 P × P 7 N–Q5 B–K2

'In such positions Alapin used to shout "Allora!" – which means "Forward!",' said my opponent and played **8 Q–N4!**

A terrible thought flashed through my mind. If Alapin used to bring his queen out in the middle of the game, then how many moves would the whole game last.

So before moving again I asked:

'Did you, er, know Alapin?'

'I even knew B. Lapin. He wrote stylized oriental verse: 'Where now is the glory of Darya, Rustam? Who remembers the name of Steinitz Wilhelm?'

'I remember the name of Steinitz Wilhelm,' I replied.

8 . . . P–KN3 9 B–QB4 P–B4 10 R × P P × Q

'Queenabber!' I shouted. I wanted the mysterious stranger to realize that his secret was well known to me.

11 N × P + Q × N 12 B–B7 + K–Q1 13 R × R + B–B1 14 B–N5 + N–K2 15 R × B mate

'In the present circumstances, it is not Queenabber but Kingnabber,' said the stranger. . . .

'This incident took place more than thirty years ago in Kiev,' I said to the editor as I came to the end of my story. 'Since that time Queenabber and I have become friends. Could I put this tale about him in the book?'

'Oh, okay,' muttered the editor with a sigh, though thinking to himself that it was all sheer hyperbole.

But having thought a little more, he added:

'Now the book has 200 games, there is a solid dose of losses, we have Alapin's opening, and we have B. S. Queenabber.'

Index of Opponents